LAW & RHETORIC

LAW &

RHETORIC

A PRIMER

Delia B. Conti

Linda L. Berger

Michael J. Cedrone

Mark A. Hannah

Melissa E. Love Koenig

Julie A. Oseid

CAROLINA ACADEMIC PRESS
Durham, North Carolina

LIBRARY OF CONGRESS

CATALOGING-IN-PUBLICATION DATA

Names: Conti, Delia B., 1961- author.
Title: Law and rhetoric : a primer / Delia B. Conti, Linda L. Berger, Michael J. Cedrone, Mark A. Hannah, Melissa E. Love Koenig, and Julie A. Oseid.
Description: Durham, North Carolina : Carolina Academic Press, 2023. | Includes bibliographical references and index.
Identifiers: LCCN 2023031402 | ISBN 9781531019822 (paperback) | ISBN 9781531019839 (ebook)
Subjects: LCSH: Law--Language. | Law--Methodology. | Law--United States--Language. | English language--United States--Rhetoric.
Classification: LCC K213 .C667 2023 | DDC 340/.1--dc23/eng/20230822
LC record available at https://lccn.loc.gov/2023031402

CAROLINA ACADEMIC PRESS
700 Kent Street
Durham, North Carolina 27701
(919) 489-7486
WWW.CAP-PRESS.COM

Printed in the United States of America

To my family.

D.B.C.

To the legal imagination.

L.L.B.

Familiae meae.

M.J.C.

To C, E, and D.

M.A.H.

To Jonathan and Olivia, and my parents George and Edith, whose constant love and support lift me up.

M.E.L.K.

To Legal Storytellers.

J.A.O.

Contents

PART ONE

PART TWO

Authors' Biographies & Acknowledgments

Linda L. Berger is a Professor of Law Emerita at the William S. Boyd School of Law at the University of Nevada, Las Vegas. I am grateful for research assistance provided by the UNLV Law Library, Professor James Rich, and law student Austin Dykstra.

Michael J. Cedrone is a Professor of Law, Legal Practice at Georgetown University Law Center in Washington, DC. I am very grateful for the assistance of Professor Mark Hannah, the Georgetown Law Library, Suzanne Miller, Jennifer Lane, Fiona O'Brien, Harrison Voss, and Luci Cedrone.

Delia B. Conti is an Associate Professor of Communication Arts and Sciences at Penn State Fayette. I would like to thank my family for their lasting support on this project, from my attendance at Duquesne Law School through the over twenty-year journey completing this book.

Mark A. Hannah is an Associate Professor of English and Director of Writing, Rhetorics, and Literacies at Arizona State University. I am grateful for the review assistance provided by Professor Christina Saidy and freelance editor Sheila Sybrant.

Melissa E. Love Koenig is a Professor of Legal Writing at Marquette University Law School. I am very grateful for the assistance of Linda Berger, Michael Cedrone, Andrew Depkon, Olivia Greipp, Michael Kiener, Jonathan Koenig, Mary Paul, and Sheila Sybrant.

Julie A. Oseid is a Professor of Law and the Morrison Family Director of Lawyering Skills at the University of St. Thomas School of Law in Minneapolis, Minnesota. Thank you to Luke Paschka and Sheila Sybrant for their excellent help with proofreading and cite checking.

Preface

DELIA B. CONTI

Law and rhetoric have an intimate connection in subject matter and in practice. Rhetorical theory is concerned with all matters of persuasion and law at its core focuses on persuasion. Many law students have a background in debate and individuals who like to argue are often encouraged to attend law school. I came to the field of law after many years of teaching rhetoric at the university level and studying political communication. This text originated when I attended law school and began to realize the contributions that rhetorical theory could make to the field of law for both practitioners and scholars. The fields of law and rhetoric are both fundamentally concerned with persuasion. For example, in law school we learned about the theory of the case and about the persuasiveness of stories. Yet there was no explicit connection to the rhetorical theory of narrative that illuminates how stories are fundamental to all persuasion. In law school we talked about the importance of credibility and legal reasoning. Aristotle's conception of ethos, pathos, and logos and Toulmin, Weaver, and Perelman all provide theoretical frameworks for understanding these persuasive elements typically considered a component of rational thinking.

The genesis of this book thus began many years ago. I wrote a draft in the years following my graduation from law school. Originally accepted for publication with revisions suggested, I was waylaid as I took a detour through administration for many years. Upon my return to faculty, I also returned to this text. Fortunately, I met a wonderful group of collaborators through participation in conferences focusing on legal writing. Each co-author was able to revise their chapter based on their experience, knowledge, teaching, research, and practice of law.

This text is truly a collaborative endeavor. Over the course of several conferences and several years, the co-authors have worked together discussing the interrelation between law and rhetoric. Each co-author has assumed primary authorship on the chapter to which their name is attached. We have benefitted immensely from our critiques, comments, and discussions, and the text has profited immensely from this extended dialogue.

Kenneth Burke wrote of the ongoing discussion that we join and then leave, and this truly reflects the development of this work:

> Imagine that you enter a parlor. You come late. When you arrive, others have long preceded you, and they are engaged in a heated discussion, a discussion too heated for them to pause and tell you exactly what it is about. In fact, the discussion had already begun long before any of them got there, so that no one present is qualified to retrace for you all the steps that had gone before. You listen for a while, until you decide that you have caught the tenor of the argument; then you put in your oar. Someone answers; you answer him; another comes to your defense; another aligns himself against you, to either the embarrassment or gratification of your opponent, depending upon the quality of your ally's assistance. However, the discussion is interminable. The hour grows late, you must depart. And you do depart, with the discussion still vigorously in progress.[1]

We welcome you to this discussion. Our hope is that through reading this brief book you will become more effective lawyers through your understanding of rhetorical theory. Law students will benefit from learning about persuasion in the development and practice of law. Legal academics can explore the theoretical connections between the fields and discover new avenues for research. Legal practitioners can become more effective advocates. We have included bibliographies to provide you with the opportunity to delve into these rhetorical concepts in greater detail. The fields of law and rhetoric are fascinating, interconnected, and are fundamental to our society's success through collaborative efforts. The law grows and changes reflecting civilization's evolution. Rhetoric's fundamental underpinnings in the establishment of human interactions and productive communication provide a gateway to better understanding the study and the practice of the law.

---

1. Kenneth Burke, The Philosophy of Literary Form 110–111 (Berkeley: University of California Press, 3d ed. 1974).

PART ONE

PART ONE

Introduction

Understanding Language

The Principles of Rhetoric & Persuasion in the Law

DELIA B. CONTI

The study of law is immersed in the study of language, and law's foundations are rooted in rhetoric. The goal of this primer is to introduce the field of rhetoric to the field of law. Rhetorical theories, from classical rhetoric to modern concepts, provide invaluable insights for the practice of persuasion in all permutations of law.

Law involves the close textual analysis of words. This is fundamentally the province of rhetoric. Justice Oliver Wendell Holmes recognized the power of language: "Language is the gate of perception, and its masters therefore see farther than the rest of us."[1] A complete understanding of rhetoric, including its concern with substance in addition to style, the critical role of emotions, and the essential nature of character in persuasion, is a necessary step in understanding and practicing law.

First, the negative connotations of rhetoric undermine its perceived usefulness. Defining rhetoric as ornament, as mere fluff, or as excessive style often meant to detract from substance is a common misconception that is fundamentally flawed. Rhetoric is not merely style gone bad: "In this sense, plainly, the man who speaks most persuasively uses the most, or certainly the best, rhetoric; and the man whom we censure for inflation of style and strained effects is suffering not from too much rhetoric, but from a lack of it."[2]

1. Richard A. Posner, ed. The Essential Holmes xxxiii (University of Chicago Press, 1992).

2. Hoyt H. Hudson (1923) *The field of rhetoric*, Quarterly Journal of Speech, 9:2, 167–180, DOI: 10.1080/00335632309379424.

Second, misconstruing the relation between reason and emotion in persuasion unnecessarily limits the practice of persuasion in the law. This error involves granting reason and rationality an undeserved privilege over emotion and desire. This disconnection of reason and emotion, fatally severing the very essence of humans as symbol-using creatures, misses the essential reason why language is persuasive and ultimately capable of uniting and dividing. Effective persuasion addresses the whole person. While appealing to emotions without a sound basis in reason is the essence of demagogic appeals, appealing to reason without appealing to emotions is the essence of ineffective rhetoric.

Third, identifying the importance of character adds a critical element to effective persuasion. Law implicitly recognizes the importance of character to both jurists and to trial participants, with testimony emphasized as a means of judging trustworthiness as well as culpability. If the listener does not trust the speaker, all else fails.

It is quite fascinating to parse the connections between law and rhetoric and discover how specific rhetorical theories illuminate legal thought and practice. The origins of the law, democracy, and rhetoric are one and the same: ancient Greece and the scholarly tomes of Aristotle, Plato, and Socrates. Law has the Socratic method, and rhetoric has Aristotelian analysis. The popularization of rhetoric, its application to the masses, began with the Sophists' teaching of persuasion to citizens who were tasked with defending themselves in trials before audiences of their fellow citizens. These Sophists engaged in a lucrative practice, yet were not held in high esteem by pure theorists, paralleling the continuing division between the practice of law and academic pursuits. The core critique is ultimately an ethical issue carrying the charge of selling one's soul to the highest bidder regardless of the merits of a case.

As we will see in our early chapters, the fields of law and rhetoric diverged through the centuries. The study of rhetoric was relegated to undergraduate training in English and in Communications. The practice of rhetoric did not respect this artificial division. Rhetorical analysis of the law abounds, from journalism including analyses of Supreme Court opinions to law school discussions including specific cases and comparative legal theory. Yet the rhetorical analysis of law is often presented in partialities, relegated to one area. For example, the field of Conflicts, focusing on differences of opinions among distinct jurisdictions, highlights issue analysis and argumentation. Literary theory has assumed a preeminence in applying textual analysis to legal works. The focus on interpretation is valuable. Literary criticism is distinguished by concern for permanence through timeless language and universal values. Rhetorical analysis brings an immediacy, a focus on audience and situation, to the table. Rhetorical criticism is more temporal and more concerned with effect.[3]

Thus we turn to the purpose of this short volume. This work will provide you with a comprehensive, albeit brief, introduction to the field of rhetoric as it relates to the field of law. The first section of the book focuses on the classical elements of rhetoric. Chapter 1 provides an introduction to the fields of rhetoric and law: their common origins, their distinct development, and the tremendous benefit to be gained by reintegrating the two disciplines. This first chapter is especially important for introducing rhetorical theory to the legal field. The definition of rhetoric, the confluence of reason and emotion, the entwining of politics and history, and the features of legal and rhetorical patterns of thought are essential elements laying the foundation for understanding the evolution of rhetorical theory, the interpretation of language, and the resultant implications for law. Examining existing scholarship on the relationship between rhetoric and law grounds us in important principles while revealing what remains to be explored.

The second chapter in this section asks us to consider the classical roots of rhetoric and the law. In examining the rhetorical theories of Plato, Aristotle, and the Sophists, we embrace legal and rhetorical theories and the essence of persuasion with the components of ethos, pathos, and logos. Herein are the roots of the Socratic method, so fundamental to law school education. As we progress to the theories of Cicero and Quintilian, we examine both the practical benefits of speaking well and contributing to the polity and the ethical requirements of sound discourse.

In sum, classical rhetorical theory grounded the fields of rhetoric and law and remains critical to effective persuasion and the sound practice of law. An introduction to these fundamental theories both enhances our understanding of the law and provides the foundation for understanding modern rhetorical theories and their relation to the law.

---

3. For a detailed discussion of the distinction between literary criticism and rhetorical criticism, see Herbert Wilchelns, *The Literary Criticism of Oratory*, *in* THE RHETORICAL IDIOM: ESSAYS IN RHETORIC, ORATORY, LANGUAGE, AND DRAMA (Donald C. Bryant ed., Ithaca, NY: Cornell University Press, 1958).

Chapter One

Law, Rhetoric & the Fundamentals of Language

MARK A. HANNAH

---

1. Introduction

Concerned with persuasion in all of its permutations, rhetoric simultaneously focuses on the development and deployment of messages for specified audiences, the examination of ideas, and the discovery of truth. Taking language as its object, rhetoric offers a vocabulary and critical framework for evaluating language use and anticipating its effects on individual and/or group decision-making and action.

In the contemporary practice of law, rhetoric plays this very role and increasingly has been identified as an indispensable component of lawyers' training, yet this positive disciplinary relationship has not always been a given. Rather, it has experienced periods of both closeness and growth and neglect and separation. Demarcating the contours of this relationship are important historical, social, and political influences that give shape to the law-and-rhetoric interface. By understanding how these influences permit law and rhetoric to interact, we can understand the context in which lawyers work and the communicative conditions in the legal community.

This chapter details and unpacks these influences—specifically, situating law and rhetoric historically, describing conceptions of rhetoric that develop from this history, and explicating the shared yet distinct parameters of legal and rhetorical patterns of thought that emerge. Equipping readers with this knowledge is essential to fostering the conversational imperative between law and rhetoric that this book asserts is needed to imbue the practice of law with the rhetorical sophistication necessary for effective practice and advocacy.

2. The evolving relationship between law and rhetoric

Law and rhetoric have had an on-again, off-again relationship over the years, evolving into its current, on-again status.

2.1. A marriage made in (Grecian) heaven

Law and rhetoric began as intimately connected "partners": their shared disciplinary roots can be traced directly to their common origins in Greek society stemming from a practical need to prepare citizens for participation in civic life.[1] Trained to be generalists, free citizens in Athens spoke for themselves and "were expected to join in [public] Assembly debates on topics ranging from war and peace, to finance, legislation, national defense, and commerce."[2]

1. Mark A. Hannah & Susie Salmon, *Against the Grain: The Secret Role of Dissents in Integrating Rhetoric Across the Curriculum*, 20 Nev. L.J. 935, 935 (2020); *see also* Malthon Anapol, *Rhetoric and Law: An Overview*, 18 Today's Speech 12, 12 (1970); Linda Levine & Kurt M. Saunders, *Thinking like a Rhetor*, 43 J. Legal Educ. 108, 109 (1993).

2. James L. Golden, Goodwin F. Berquist & William E. Coleman, The Rhetoric of Western Thought 37 (3d ed. 1976); *see also* Peter Goodrich, Read-

Additionally, legal suits were an everyday occurrence in ancient Greece; and because there were no lawyers, citizens were required to represent themselves.[3] In this social and political context, speaking well was considered to be the most important skill for success in public life.[4] Recognizing the need to cultivate this skill in the citizenry, rhetoricians of classical Greece developed handbooks on rhetoric that combined theory and practice to train citizens for public service.[5]

Gorgias, the most famous of the Sophists, recognized the close relationship between rhetoric and law when he explained that "rhetoric was the art of persuading the people about matters of justice and injustice in the public places of the state."[6] Importantly, Gorgias believed the acquisition of knowledge and the expression of knowledge were inseparable.[7] Though not welcomed by all classical orators,[8] this attitude toward knowledge tightened the relationship between law and rhetoric over time.

ING THE LAW: A CRITICAL INTRODUCTION TO LEGAL METHOD AND TECHNIQUES 169 (1986).

3. *See* Anapol, *supra* note 1, at 12–13; Levine & Saunders, *supra* note 1, at 109; GOLDEN, BERQUIST & COLEMAN, *supra* note 2, at 38–39; GEORGE A. KENNEDY, CLASSICAL RHETORIC AND ITS CHRISTIAN AND SECULAR TRADITION FROM ANCIENT TO MODERN TIMES 20 (2d ed. 1999) ("Men involved in litigation or accused of a crime were normally expected to speak on their own behalf. Women were represented in court by a male relative.").

4. *See* GOLDEN, BERQUIST & COLEMAN, *supra* note 2, at 38; GOODRICH, *supra* note 2, at 169.

5. Kristen K. Tiscione, *How the Disappearance of Classical Rhetoric and the Decision to Teach Law as a Science Severed Theory from Practice in Legal Education*, 51 WAKE FOREST L. REV. 385, 387 (2016); *see* GOODRICH, *supra* note 2, at 169.

6. Linda L. Berger, *Studying and Teaching Law as Rhetoric: A Place to Stand*, 16 LEGAL WRITING 3, 13 (2010) (quoting James Boyd White, *Law as Rhetoric, Rhetoric as Law: The Arts of Cultural and Communal Life*, 52 UNIV. CHI. L. REV. 684, 684 (1985) (quoting Plato's *Gorgias*)).

7. *See* Tiscione, *supra* note 5, at 400.

8. When discussing the dialectic method, for example, Plato elevated the acquisition of knowledge through philosophical inquiry over the expression of knowledge. *See* PATRICIA BIZZELL, BRUCE HERZBERG & ROBIN REAMES, THE RHETORICAL TRADITION: READINGS FROM CLASSICAL TIMES TO THE PRESENT 97–102 (3d ed. 2020); GOLDEN, BERQUIST & COLEMAN, *supra* note 2, at 45–53.

2.2. A falling-out

Eventually, forces like religion began replacing rhetoric as the preferred practice and/or pathway to the acquisition and expression of knowledge.[9] Importantly, however, although religion's ascendance often is credited with prompting a decoupling of the law-and-rhetoric relationship, the beginnings of this separation in fact arose from the professional class of lawyers in the Roman Empire. In particular, forensic oratory, the rhetoric specific to law, declined as speakers were interested more in legal procedure than in the development and delivery of oral speeches.[10] In this context, epideictic, or praise-or-blame, rhetoric became more relevant as less attention was paid to the development of argument.[11] Through this transformation, rhetoric "became a form of entertainment and escape for Roman citizens" rather than a knowledge-building practice intimately connected to everyday life in a democratic society.[12]

With the eventual decline of democracy during the Roman Empire, rhetoric's transition away from the concerns of argument and content became complete as political decisions were taken out of citizens' hands. Driving this decline of rhetoric's value in political and social contexts was the Church Fathers' general distrust of the pagan rhetoric of Greece and Rome.[13]

Yet, despite this distrust, interest in rhetoric was not extinguished. In fact, the rise of Christianity spurred new interest in how rhetoric could be used to support the Christian cause.[14] In particular, opportunities for rehabilitating rhetoric emerged through the work of classical rhetoricians like Saint Augustine, who developed a Christian rhetoric that emphasized scriptural interpretation and the delivery of sermons.[15] For example, Augustine's articulation of the Christian orator's three functions—to conciliate those who

---

9. *See* Hannah & Salmon, supra note 1, at 935–36; Tiscione, *supra* note 5, at 392.

10. *See* Golden, Berquist & Coleman, *supra* note 2, at 39 ("Legal speaking in the law courts was referred to as forensic discourse."); Kennedy, *supra* note 3, at 7; Bizzell, Herzberg & Reames, *supra* note 8, at 3.

11. *See* Golden, Berquist & Coleman, *supra* note 2, at 94.

12. *Id.* at 95.

13. *See* Golden, Berquist & Coleman, *supra* note 2, at 94–98.

14. *See id.* at 94–97; Tiscione, *supra* note 5, at 392; Kristen K. Robbins-Tiscione, *A Call to Combine Rhetorical Theory and Practice in the Legal Writing Classroom*, 50 Washburn L.J. 319, 336 (2011).

15. Mark A. Hannah, *St. Augustine: The Place of Rhetoric in the Law and Religion Interface, in* Classical Rhetoric and Contemporary Law: A Critical Reader (Francis J. Mootz III, Kirsten K. Davis, Brian N. Larson & Kristen K. Tiscione, eds., forthcoming 2024).

are opposed, arouse those who are remiss, and teach those who are ignorant[16]—crafted a discursive space for rhetoric's application.

However, the parallel neglect of forensic rhetoric at that time plainly amplified the severing of the relationship between law and rhetoric, thus completing rhetoric's transition from a practical art intimately connected with legal and political issues to a truncated art of style and delivery divorced from the civic affairs of the Roman Empire.[17]

2.3. Separate ways

Despite the decline of law and rhetoric's relationship, interest in classical rhetoric persisted beyond the Middle Ages as universities continued to provide instruction in rhetoric along with logic and grammar.[18] Also, "the Renaissance revived the classical interest in writing, painting, sculpting, architecture, and science"; and for approximately two centuries, the study and practice of rhetoric was again valued, as evidenced by the increasing popularity of the works of Aristotle, Cicero, and Quintilian.[19]

In the context of this revival, though, rhetoric and law as intellectual disciplines "tended to develop in isolation from each other."[20] For example, teachers of rhetoric more explicitly shifted their attention from content to expression—that is, style.[21] Much of this new interest in style was attributable to the work of Peter Ramus, a sixteenth-century French logician and philosopher who argued that the invention and arrangement of ideas in argumentation belonged more properly to the study of dialectic than to the study of rhetoric.[22] This truncation of rhetoric, specifically Ramus's assertion that style and the expression of knowledge, rather than the creation of knowledge, was a function of rhetoric, cast rhetoric as an "aesthetically oriented art of ingratiation" devoid of substance that was relevant only to teaching expression.[23]

---

16. St. Augustine, On Christian Doctrine 117–18 (R.P.H. Green trans., 1997).
17. *See* Anapol, *supra* note 1, at 15–16.
18. Tiscione, *supra* note 5, at 392.
19. *Id.*; *see* Kennedy, *supra* note 3, at 226–30.
20. Anapol, *supra* note 1, at 16.
21. *See* Tiscione, *supra* note 5, at 392–93.
22. *Id.*; *see* Levine & Saunders, *supra* note 1, at 110.
23. Golden, Berquist & Coleman, *supra* note 2, at 99 (citing Douglas Ehninger, *On Rhetoric and Rhetorics*, 31 W. Speech 244 (1967)); *see* Tiscione, *supra* note 5, at 393; Anapol, *supra* note 1, at 16.

Compounding Ramus's severing of rhetoric from the creation of knowledge was the continuing inattention to the practice of forensic rhetoric and its interest in "the determination of the justice or legality of a past action," a trend carried over from the Middle Ages.[24] Any attention paid to legal practice in England occurred in the study of jurisprudence, namely, the work of philosophers like Immanuel Kant, Thomas Hobbes, and Jeremy Bentham, thus further sustaining law and rhetoric's segregated relationship.[25]

2.4. A new knowledge interest

In the seventeenth century, a significant epistemological shift occurred regarding how knowledge was acquired. In particular, Francis Bacon claimed that new knowledge acquisition could only be achieved by the "systematic method of careful observation that leads from particular observations to more general conclusions about the nature of things."[26] Through this assertion, Bacon rejected Aristotelian deduction in favor of induction and thus replaced logic as the source of knowledge with science and its emphasis on method.[27]

The rise of science significantly affected legal education at the turn of the nineteenth century.[28] Though rhetorical theory was acknowledged at that time as playing an important role in legal education, rhetoric became less relevant when Christopher Langdell introduced the case study method in the 1870s.[29] Langdell insisted that law ought to be taught as a science, urging the discovery of legal principles in appellate opinions that "could be applied to legal disputes in a logical and systematic way."[30] As a systematized approach to legal training, the Langdellian "scientific" method disclaimed a rhetorical approach to developing knowledge and understanding about legal issues.

This method contrasted sharply with rhetoric's "focus on persuasion and probability," which was "viewed as nonrational—a 'failed science'—and anti-

---

24. KENNEDY, *supra* note 3, at 7; *see also supra* note 10 and accompanying text.

25. *See* Anapol, *supra* note 1, at 17.

26. Tiscione, *supra* note 5, at 393; *see also* BIZZELL, HERZBERG & REAMES, *supra* note 8, at 817–21; GOLDEN, BERQUIST & COLEMAN, *supra* note 2, at 127–31.

27. *See* Tiscione, *supra* note 5, at 400.

28. *Id.* at 394.

29. *See* Levine & Saunders, *supra* note 1, at 111.

30. Tiscione, *supra* note 5, at 395; *see also* Ralph Michael Stein, *The Path of Legal Education from Edward I to Langdell: A History of Insular Reaction*, 57 CHI-KENT L. REV. 429, 449 (1981); Robbins-Tiscione, *supra* note 14, at 320.

thetical to the goals of the [case study] method."[31] Through this pedagogical shift, the liberal arts, which included rhetoric, were purged from law school classrooms and estranged from legal education.[32] Consequently, wide-ranging investigations of questions beyond the law of the case were discouraged, and the study of law became depersonalized and devoid of its classical rhetorical influences.[33]

2.5. A renewed commitment

Over the next fifty years, the case study method entrenched itself as the predominant pedagogical approach in law school classrooms; but around the 1920s and 1930s, the rise of the legal realism movement created momentum for pushing back and questioning the soundness of the case study approach.[34] For instance, individuals like Professor Karl Llewellyn and Judge Jerome Frank expressed concern over what they perceived as failures of law schools to prepare students to look beyond the general legal principles discovered in textbooks to extralegal factors such as values, attitudes, and politics that influence legal decision-making.[35] In encouraging investigations of the extralegal, legal realists created conditions for rehabilitating and reaffirming rhetoric and law's close association, which the case study method had disrupted. Complementing legal realists' calls for studying rhetoric as part of legal training, noted legal professionals like the English jurist Lord Macmillan added their voices to the chorus of calls for more attention to the conscious and systematic study of the correct use of language.[36] Continuing this renewed interest in the role of rhetoric and language in legal decision-making was Chaïm Perelman, who asserted that rhetoric leads to the discovery of knowledge and ultimately helps legal scholars and practitioners "convince their audience of what the law is, requires, or ought to be."[37] Taken together, these calls laid the groundwork for bringing rhetorical theory and legal practice together again.

---

31. Hannah & Salmon, *supra* note 1, at 938.
32. *See* Stein, *supra* note 30, at 453.
33. *See id.* at 454.
34. *See* Anapol, *supra* note 1, at 17.
35. *Id.*
36. Lord Macmillan, *Law and Language, in* Voices in Court 106 (William H. Davenport ed., 1958).
37. Tiscione, *supra* note 5, at 401; *see also* Melissa Love Koenig, *infra* chapter 3.

Building off this groundswell of support for reunifying rhetoric and law, contemporary scholars and legal practitioners sought to broaden understandings of rhetoric as a productive art that is an essential component of legal training and practice. James Boyd White, for example, emphasized rhetoric's constitutive capacity, setting it in sharp contrast to traditional understandings of law as a mechanistic system of rules. He wrote:

> [L]aw is most usefully seen not, as it normally is by academics and philosophers, as a system of rules, but as a branch of rhetoric; and that rhetoric, of which law is a species, is most usefully seen not, as it normally is, either as a failed science or as the art of persuasion, but as the central art by which community and culture are established, maintained, and transformed.[38]

Establishing law as a constitutive, rhetorical activity in this instance, White encouraged readers to think about law as a way of talking about events and people, a way of telling stories with legal meaning and effect.[39] Additionally, framing law as constitutive establishes that lawyering occurs in specified, unique situations that include individuals; groups (legal and nonlegal); and their respective purposes, values, and constraints.[40] Working from White's description of law as rhetorical activity, legal educators revived and implemented explicit instruction in rhetorical theory and practice, most notably in legal research and writing classrooms.[41]

Highlighting law and rhetoric's close relationship has had many benefits for law students. Importantly, classical rhetoric provides a vocabulary and natural framework for teaching legal analysis and argument.[42] Armed with

---

38. James Boyd White, *Rhetoric and Law: The Arts of Cultural and Communal Life*, *in* The Rhetoric of the Human Sciences: Language and Argument in Scholarship and Public Affairs 298, 298 (John S. Nelson, Allan Megill & Donald N. McCloskey eds., 1987); White, *supra* note 6, at 684.

39. *See* White, *supra* note 38, at 302, 305, 308–09, White, *supra* note 6, at 688, 690–91; James Boyd White, The Legal Imagination, at xiii (1985).

40. *See* White, *supra* note 38, at 308–09; *see also* Hannah & Salmon, *supra* note 1; Mark A. Hannah & Michael J. Cedrone, *infra* chapter 6.

41. *See* Linda Berger, *Applying New Rhetoric to Legal Discourse: The Ebb and Flow of Reader and Writer, Text and Context*, 49 J. Legal Educ. 155, 167–68 (1999); *see also* Berger, *supra* note 6; Michael Frost, *Introduction to Classical Legal Rhetoric: A Lost Heritage*, 8 S. Cal. Interdisc. L.J. 613 (1998); Tiscione, *supra* note 5; Robbins-Tiscione, *supra* note 14; Hannah & Salmon, *supra* note 1; Levine & Saunders, *supra* note 1.

42. *See* Robbins-Tiscione, *supra* note 14, at 324–25; Levine & Saunders, *supra* note 1, at 109.

these analytic tools, students begin to see their writing not only as a means to communicate information but also as a mode for creating knowledge and for deepening their own understanding beyond fixed notions of blackletter law.[43] As an additional benefit, contemporary rhetoric is invaluable in training students to develop persuasive skills in argumentation,[44] narrative,[45] and the use of metaphor and analogy.[46] More recently, legal writing and rhetoric scholars have deepened law and rhetoric's close connection in legal education in areas including applications of ethos[47] and kairos,[48] considerations of ethics[49] and identity formation,[50] and speaking publicly both in times of crisis[51] and in new digital formats.[52]

All told, such work has captured and reinvigorated the spirit of law and rhetoric's close relationship that was propagated in classical Greek society; and, in doing so, it has created the grounds for accepting, rather than denying,[53] the centrality of rhetoric to contemporary legal practice.

3. Conceptions of rhetoric

Though generally understood as the art of persuasion, rhetoric has been associated with a rich array of definitions and conceptualizations throughout its history. Influenced by the various historical, political, and social conditions described in the previous section, rhetoric "experienced very fluctuating fortunes [and] numerous deaths and revivals" as its perceived value and use changed

---

43. *See* Berger, *supra* note 41, at 155–56; Hannah & Salmon, *supra* note 1, at 940.

44. *See* Koenig, *infra* chapter 3.

45. *See* Julie Oseid, *infra* chapter 4.

46. *See* Linda Berger, *infra* chapter 5.

47. Melissa H. Weresh, *Ethos at the Intersection: Classical Insights for Contemporary Application*, 20 Nev. L.J. 877 (2020).

48. Clarke Rountree, *Kairos and American Legal Praxis*, 20 Nev. L.J. 855 (2020).

49. Lori D. Johnson & Melissa Love Koenig, *Walk the Line: Aristotle and the Ethics of Narrative*, 20 Nev. L.J. 1037 (2020).

50. Laura A. Webb, *Speaking the Truth: Supporting Professional Advocacy with Professional Identity Formation*, 20 Nev. L.J. 1079 (2020).

51. Michael J. Cedrone, *Cicero and Barack Obama: How to Unite the Republic Without Losing Your Head*, 20 Nev. L.J. 1177 (2020).

52. Kirsten K. Davis, *[Classical] Lawyers as [Digital] Public Speakers: Classical Rhetoric and Lawyer Digital Public Commentary*, 20 Nev. L.J. 1137 (2020).

53. Gerald Wetlaufer, *Rhetoric and Its Denial in Legal Discourse*, 76 Va. L. Rev. 1545, 1550–51, 1555 (1990).

within and across the different religious, legal, and political institutions in which it played a significant role.[54]

At the time of this writing, rhetoric arguably still is in a period of ascendance initiated in the post-1920s revival and has become, according to some, "something of a fashion again as the 'new rhetoric.'"[55] Thinking back to its origins in ancient Greece, the most classic definition of *rhetoric* that the "new rhetoric" embraces is that offered by Aristotle, namely, the discovery in any given situation of all of the available means of persuasion.[56]

3.1. Ancient Greeks' perspective

Operating in the context of this definition in ancient Greece, the ancients developed a system of concepts for defining, understanding, and explaining rhetoric.[57] In particular, they "taught the rules of effective speech, of language as action tied to the . . . religious, legal and political activities and decisions of the assembly."[58]

To organize these rules conceptually, the ancient Greeks perceived rhetoric as operating through speech situations made up of three elements: speaker, speech, and audience;[59] and they articulated rhetoric as a five-step process of invention, arrangement, style, memory, and delivery—that is, an analytical framework that prompts speakers "to invent and arrange arguments, choose an appropriate speaking style, and deliver a convincing speech."[60] When participating in this process, the evaluation of audience is fundamental as effective decision-making is constrained by the needs, wants, and desires of individual readers or speakers and/or those of a group, such as judges or jury members in legal contexts.[61]

Attendant with considerations of audience is rhetoric's concern with the embeddedness of discourse, for its meaning does not emerge in a vacuum but instead is contingent on the factors of the situation in which it operates.

54. Goodrich, *supra* note 2, at 171.
55. *Id.*; *see also* Berger, *supra* note 41.
56. Aristotle, Rhetoric I.2.1, at 37 (George A. Kennedy trans., 2d ed. 2007).
57. *See* Michael Cedrone, *infra* chapter 2.
58. Goodrich, *supra* note 2, at 173.
59. *See id.* (citing Aristotle, Rhetoric I.3.1 (see Aristotle, *supra* note 56, at 47)).
60. Tiscione, *supra* note 5, at 390.
61. *See* Hannah & Cedrone, *infra* chapter 6.

Guiding speakers' consideration of audience and how speakers invent and deliver speech are various analytical concepts useful in classifying and anticipating an argument's impact. For example, Aristotle described three modes of persuasion—appeals to ethos (character), pathos (emotion), and logos (reason)—that speakers can craft when structuring an argument.[62] Aristotle characterized those arguments as forensic (judicial), epideictic (praise or blame), or deliberative (parliamentary/legislative); and he assigned each a corresponding time component—past, present, and future, respectively.[63] Threading each of these rhetorical concepts and the development of argument is rhetoric's orientation toward dealing with what is probably the case rather than what is known.[64] More specifically, eschewing the pursuit of transcendent, philosophical truth, rhetoric persuades and leads to "the best truth in human affairs—probable knowledge."[65]

3.2. Technical, sophistic, and philosophical approaches

Noted classical rhetoric scholar George Kennedy identified three approaches to rhetoric: technical, sophistic, and philosophical; and he characterized them according to how each privileges the three elements of Aristotle's speech situation (speech, speaker, and audience).[66] Technical, or handbook, rhetoric is pragmatic and privileges speech; it concerns itself with conveying "how to" present a subject effectively using rhetoric's guiding principles, and it often finds its home in public arenas such as law courts.[67] Rather than emphasizing speech itself, sophistic rhetoric emphasizes the speaker and the speaker's achievement of goals. Drawing on a speaker's character as ethos in ceremonial and cultural contexts, it typically is not oriented to decision-making and action in the moment.[68] Philosophical rhetoric, on the other hand, deemphasizes speakers and instead spotlights the soundness of decisions in furthering an audience's interests.[69]

62. *See* ARISTOTLE, *supra* note 56, at I.2.3–6, at 38–39.

63. *Id.* at I.3.3–4, at 48–49.

64. *See* White, *supra* note 38, at 301.

65. Tiscione, *supra* note 5, at 390; *see also* FRANCIS J. MOOTZ III, RHETORICAL KNOWLEDGE IN LEGAL PRACTICE AND CRITICAL LEGAL THEORY (2006); Cedrone, *infra* chapter 2 (discussing Plato's critique of probable knowledge).

66. *See* KENNEDY, *supra* note 3, at 13–14.

67. *Id.* at 14.

68. *Id.*

69. *Id.* at 14–15.

When these approaches are situated in the context of law, lawyers' relationship with rhetoric is clearly dynamic. Specifically, when legal rhetoric is described as involving the reading of legal texts as acts of communication—as discourses designed to influence, to persuade, and to induce action[70]—lawyers take on various roles as advocates and engage in nuanced thinking within and across the approaches. Thinking technically, a lawyer can ask, "What is the best way to arrange or organize this argument?" Thinking sophistically at the same time, a lawyer can ask, "What parts of my character and achievements suggest my fitness for this situation?" Thinking philosophically, too, a lawyer can ask, "What ethical effects and benefits for the audience can we anticipate from a decision?"

3.3. Mere rhetoric versus constitutive rhetoric

Working within this broad sense of rhetoric and its purposes and values, lawyers encounter two predominant, yet competing, accounts of rhetoric that shape perceptions of their work: mere and constitutive.

3.3.1. Mere rhetoric

Tracing its roots back to the Sophists up through the rise of ornamental rhetoric and Ramus's separation of invention and style, mere rhetoric casts a long shadow over the rhetorical tradition as a rhetoric that privileges form over substance and winning at the expense of truth. Defined pejoratively, mere rhetoric is criticized as "the ignoble art of persuasion, . . . a second rate way of dealing with facts" that cannot be known, and as trying to manipulate people to get them to do what a speaker wants.[71] Relying on "amplification, elaborate conceits, and stylistic refinement" to persuade an audience,[72] mere rhetoric lacks any substantive interest in producing knowledge and, at times, leads to the obfuscation of truth.[73]

Regrettably, lawyers often labor under the "mere" label, which is refined and perpetuated through popular media representations like *Law & Order* episodes, plaintiff's attorneys' advertisements promising big returns in personal injury cases, and the exhibition of NTGUILTY vanity plates in popular

70. *See* Goodrich, *supra* note 2, at 171.
71. White, *supra* note 38, at 301.
72. Kennedy, *supra* note 3, at 14 (associating these strategies with sophistic rhetoric).
73. *See* Golden, Berquist & Coleman, *supra* note 2, at 39.

fiction crime writing.[74] Arguably unethical manipulations of language that put a gloss on speakers' words unite these representations. Rhetoric here is not reality, reason, or logic; rather, it is fabrication, emotions, and word tricks all the way down.[75]

3.3.2. Constitutive rhetoric

Counter to claims that rhetoric is a deceitful, ornamental practice ill-suited to the search for truth, rhetoric more recently has been articulated as a productive art for thinking about language use and how it fashions the conditions of everyday life and decision-making. As previously noted in this chapter, rhetoric is considered a constitutive art in that it influences how we see, how we think, and what we know.[76] It teaches us that "through our particular rhetorical conventions and commitments, we constitute ourselves, our communities, and perhaps, our world" whenever we use language.[77]

As applied to law, constitutive rhetoric aptly characterizes legal practice. White, for example, explained that as an art of persuasion, law "creates the objects of its persuasion, for it constitutes both the community and the culture it commends."[78] As a set of habits of mind and expectations, law features a culture of argument that grounds and constrains, in a milieu of discursive practices, a community of speakers who make and remake the law by crafting legal arguments in specified rhetorical situations.[79] To put it another way, law tells us what counts as argument. Take a typical contract formation dispute. Lawyers do not base their arguments out of any available facts in a particular case but rather only those relevant to the legal requirements of offer, acceptance, and consideration. To shape those facts in an argument, lawyers filter precedents to determine which are relevant and useful. When making their choices of facts and precedents from what the culture of law makes available, lawyers push against the boundaries of the culture of law and define, or rather redefine, what is "law." Most important, through their advocacy, lawyers evolve the grounds for future argument and decision-making in contract disputes.

---

74. *Law & Order* (Wolf Entertainment 1990–2010, 2022); Michael Connelly, The Lincoln Lawyer (2005).

75. *See* Berger, *supra* note 6, at 10.

76. *See supra* note 38 and accompanying text; Wetlaufer, *supra* note 52; at 1588 ("Rhetorics shape not just how we speak but also how we see, how we think, and what we know.").

77. Wetlaufer, *supra* note 52, at 1548; *see also* White, *supra* note 38, at 304.

78. White, *supra* note 38, at 304; White, *supra* note 6, at 691.

79. *See* White, *supra* note 39, at xiii; Wetlaufer, *supra* note 52, at 1558–59.

Ultimately, framed as constitutive, rhetoric and law are disciplines that fundamentally create and invent rather than merely adorn, thus reuniting the inventional dimensions of rhetoric set aside during the Renaissance with the stylistic dimensions of rhetoric that were retained during that period.[80]

4. Patterns of thought

Despite law and rhetoric's close relationship, legal and rhetorical patterns of thought can be distinguished because they are subject to different constraints.

4.1. Rhetorical pattern of thought

Wayne Booth's conception of rhetorical stance is a useful opening for articulating and understanding the rhetorical pattern of thought. Generally, *rhetorical stance* refers to a "position taken by the communicator with respect to the listener, the occasion, and the desired response."[81] It involves an attitude that the speaker assumes toward the relationships that exist among speaker, context, and audience.[82] The attitudinal, positional dimension of the rhetorical pattern of thought that Booth described operates in many respects like a first principle—in other words, it is what activates and initiates the processes of rhetorical thought in a specified occasion and context.[83] Once initiated, rhetorical thought is constrained by the conditions and features of situations. Put differently, and drawing from Booth, the critical work of rhetorical thought is shaped by the "'natural context of persons, events, objects, [and] relations' surrounding an 'exigence,'" that is, the "'imperfection [or defect] marked by urgency'" that calls for a response.[84]

Key among the different factors of rhetorical situations is their relationality—how they inform each other, conflict with each other, constitute each other:

80. *See supra* notes 21–22 and accompanying text.

81. Golden, Berquist & Coleman, *supra* note 2, at 303.

82. *Id.*

83. *See* White, *supra* note 38, at 308; White, *supra* note 6, at 695.

84. Berger, *supra* note 6, at 45 (quoting Lloyd F. Bitzer, *The Rhetorical Situation*, 1 Phil. & Rhetoric 1, 5 (1968)); *see also* Hannah & Cedrone, *infra* chapter 6 (discussing rhetorical situation).

> I am not just Joe. I am Joe walking down the street. I am Joe walking down the street without an umbrella. I am Joe walking down the street without an umbrella as it begins to rain. I am Joe arguing with a friend that he/she/they should give me his/her/their umbrella. I am Joe pushing, struggling, and ultimately injuring my friend as I gain control of the umbrella.

In this example, we see rhetorical thought evaluate a situation through increasing attention to detail at each step, a progression that could lead a person to conclude that Joe was being a jerk to his friend.[85]

Admittedly, this walk-through of situational elements is a bit crude, but it captures the conditions through which those elements exist in productive strife in rhetorical thought—how they intermingle and build on or mutually constitute each other once triggered by a rhetorical exigence.[86] As part of its relationality, too, rhetorical thought is constrained by the materials and other available means of persuasion (facts, texts, dialogue, attitudes, behaviors, values, etc.) in any given rhetorical situation: it is necessarily specific to and contingent upon the discursive potentiality that inheres in the materials that ultimately produce and/or shape knowledge.[87] Put simply, rhetorical thought does not invent out of nothing but instead out of a situated something.[88]

Within this situational understanding, rhetorical thought accepts meaning as socially contingent, namely, "the meaning of knowledge is contingent on social assumptions, conceptualizations, and construction."[89] Underlining this interest in contingency is rhetorical thought's acceptance of the radical uncertainty of everyday life, the uncertainty of the meaning of words and their effects on others, and even uncertainty as to a speaker's own motivations.[90] In seeing

85. Legal thought, in comparison, would attend to such details, but its attention to those details would be shaped by an impulse to force the progression of events in the rhetorical situation into a legal box, such as a tort: Joe's behavior in the situation was intentional and unreasonable (*see infra* Section 4.2 for a detailed discussion of legal thought).

86. Debra Hawhee locates the notion of "productive strife" in her discussion of agonism—specifically, the encounter between opposing sides in a gathering or assembly of people. DEBRA HAWHEE, BODILY ARTS: RHETORIC AND ATHLETICS IN ANCIENT GREECE 192–93 (2004); Debra Hawhee, *Agonism and Arete*, 35 PHIL. & RHETORIC 185, 185–86 (2002).

87. *See* White, *supra* note 38, at 308; White, *supra* note 6, at 695.

88. White, *supra* note 38, at 308; White, *supra* note 6, at 695.

89. Paul M. Dombrowski, *Challenger and the Social Contingency of Meaning: Two Lessons for the Technical Communication Classroom*, 1 TECH. COMMC'N Q. 73, 73 (1992).

90. *See* White, *supra* note 38, at 309; White, *supra* note 6, at 695.

meaning in this way, rhetorical thought believes that "communication is not the simple reflection of a pre-existent reality but the social, creative, interested" creation of reality that emerges from the interplay among context, audience, and place.[91] Rather than search for a universal truth in some preexistent reality, then, rhetorical thought's goal is the development of knowledge that emerges relationally and agonistically through the reader's, writer's, speaker's, and audience's contextual use of language.[92] Such knowledge is recognized as dynamic, as not reducible to rules, and as unable to achieve certitude.[93]

Ultimately, rhetorical thought refuses to privilege any conception of knowledge or adhere to any one set of values or any one conception of truth. Through contingently produced knowledge, rhetorical thought "seeks to induce cooperation between speaker and audience" to produce agreement and identification.[94] Such inducement is possible because of rhetorical thought's capacity to accommodate diversity and imagine change, its sensitivity to middle grounds and alternatives, and its strident opposition to all-or-nothing arguments.[95] Furthermore, rhetorical thought attends to "pluralistic and complicating forces including [individuals'] experiences, values, and senses of themselves."[96] It achieves this by thinking beyond the kinds of categories that foster adversarial, binary thinking trained on winning—the very hallmarks of legal thought.[97]

4.2. Legal pattern of thought

In comparison to rhetorical thought, legal thought, generally speaking, is involved in a process of translation—an internal, recursive process of work-

91. Dombrowski, *supra* note 89, at 74; *see also* Goodrich, *supra* note 2, at 179.

92. *See* Berger, *supra* note 6, at 11–12.

93. *See* White, *supra* note 38, at 309; White, *supra* note 6, at 695–96; *see also* Mootz, *supra* note 64.

94. Goodrich, *supra* note 2, at 176.

95. *See* Berger, *supra* note 6, at 12.

96. *Id.* at 10.

97. An example of a category in law is the concept of immediacy in self-defense criminal cases. *See infra* text at notes 104, 106 (discussing "legal intelligibility" and categorical boxes). To contextualize how a person acts in a self-defense situation, rhetorical thought looks beyond the temporal component of immediacy in the rhetorical situation and tries to account for things such as the person's general behavioral disposition, family history, history of experiencing and witnessing violence, and/or experience with weapons.

ing "from ordinary language to legal language and back again."[98] Believed to operate in a "closed linguistic system,"[99] the process of legal thought, contra rhetorical thought, is geared "to the closure of controversies... and to the one right (or best) answer to questions and the one true (or best) meaning of texts."[100] It is inherently adversarial and strives to pin down indeterminacy and contingency so that its final expression represented in the form of legal argument sounds closed. Consequently, legal thought is never neutral, but it sustains the appearance of neutrality through its rhetorical commitments of relevance and orderliness in discourse, objectivity, clarity and logic, binary judgment, hierarchy and authority, and the impersonal voice.[101]

Legal thought meets these rhetorical commitments by thinking simultaneously about both substantive and procedural issues.[102] Focusing on questions of how a legal issue should be understood, substantive thinking asks:

- Is there a legal issue to begin with?
- What is at stake with the issue?
- What area of law will govern its adjudication?

Constraining and guiding this substantive thinking is the coincident asking of procedural questions centered on how the identified issue of law should be answered, specifically, by whom, that is, which jurisdiction; under what authority, that is, which texts establish a legal rule and its standards; and by what procedures, that is, civil, criminal, or administrative.[103]

Guiding this simultaneity of legal thought is a quest for legal intelligibility,[104] i.e., the achievement of the translation of the nonlegal to the legal:

---

98. White, *supra* note 38, at 305; White, *supra* note 6, at 692. *See generally* ELIZABETH MERTZ, THE LANGUAGE OF LAW SCHOOL: LEARNING TO "THINK LIKE A LAWYER" (2007).

99. Elizabeth Mertz, *Inside the Law School Classroom: Toward a New Legal Realist Pedagogy*, 60 VAND. L. REV. 483, 504 (2010).

100. *See* Wetlaufer, *supra* note 52, at 1552.

101. *See* Wetlaufer, *supra* note 52, at 1552, 1589 ("The rhetoric of law serves three purposes—advocacy, closure, and the rule of law."). *See generally* EDWARD H. LEVI, AN INTRODUCTION TO LEGAL REASONING (2013).

102. *See* James Boyd White, *An Old-Fashioned View of the Nature of Law*, 12 THEORETICAL INQUIRIES IN L. 381, 394–95 (2011).

103. *See id.*

104. Mark A. Hannah, Kristen R. Moore, Nicole Lowman & Kehinde Alonge, *Legal Resource Mapping as a Methodology for Social Justice Research and Engagement*, *in* EQUIPPING

> I was not just scared in that situation when the man raised his voice. Rather, I was in an immediate fear of harm when he raised his fist while yelling my name.[105]

The crucial distinction in this self-defense example is the existence of the legally required category of time expressed in a statute. In other words, the rhetorical situation has been placed into the box of something recognized within the law. Mere fear of harm is nonlegal. Bounding one's fear in a situation with immediacy renders that fear intelligible and available for deployment in legal argumentation. To create the discursive space for legal intelligibility to emerge, legal thought draws on its rhetorical commitments to exclude considerations of extralegal factors like values, beliefs, and attitudes that rhetorical thought works so hard to include.[106] This constraining impulse away from extralegality ultimately enables legal thought to sustain itself in a pluralistic society where extralegal factors are in constant tension.

5. The unification of rhetorical thought and legal thought

Contrasting rhetorical thought and legal thought via their different constraining influences, while important as a descriptive matter, potentially muddies understandings about how law and rhetoric are united. Yes, rhetorical thought and legal thought both operate within boundaries, the former by the interests and features of rhetorical situations and the latter by rule-of-law principles and concerns of objectivity, neutrality, and rationality operating in legal rhetorical situations. Yet, the capacity of these bounding mechanisms to in fact bind and constrain is limited. That is, despite the best efforts of each thought pattern to constrain, seepage is inevitable. And it is inevitable for readers to ask:

Technical Communicators for Social Justice Work: Theories, Methodologies, and Pedagogies (Rebecca Walton & Godwin Y. Agboka eds., 2021).

105. The Model Penal Code defines *self-defense* in section 3.04(1) as "justifiable when the actor believes that such force is immediately necessary for the purpose of protecting himself against the use of unlawful force by such other person on the present occasion." Model Penal Code § 3.04(1).

106. *See supra* note 35 and accompanying text.

- What seeps through rhetoric's and law's constraints and influences legal argumentation and decision-making?
- What creates the conditions for seeping to occur? Is it negative public opinion about the issue under consideration? Is it a judge's personal experiences with the issue? Is it the emotions stemming from a controversial legislative initiative or an economic crisis?

Answering these questions brings us to considerations of rhetorical circulation. Generally speaking, rhetorical circulation is understood as the ways in which texts and discourse move through our everyday lives via their use, revision, co-option, and even abuse and bring various rhetorical situations together to collaborate and produce some change through discourse.[107] Stated another way in the context of law, discourse does not die after it is used in a specific situation: it retains a rhetorical energy that circulates forward in time for lawyers to use in framing new rhetorical situations.

Rhetorical circulation is described more fully in chapter 6, but, for present purposes, what is important to recognize is the constitutive power of the retained rhetorical energy, i.e., how that energy shapes the emergence and application of law. For example, at the time of this writing, the U.S. Supreme Court is facing intense public criticism from some audiences for its decisions in cases addressing issues ranging from voting rights and reproductive health to religious freedom and public health. Focusing less on who is winning or losing in these cases, what these examples reveal is the discursive force of language over time and place—that is, how language-use practices shaped by factors such as professional practice, disciplinary history, values, attitudes, and the like break through the constraints of rhetorical and legal thought to influence contemporary argumentation and decision-making.

Using reproductive rights—specifically, the right to terminate pregnancies in light of the legal standards established in the 1973 landmark case *Roe v. Wade*[108]—as an example to illustrate the work of rhetorical circulation, we can trace how legal language and texts are used and morph over time and place in response to legal and social developments and events such as antiabortion advocacy; the establishment of Planned Parenthood; violence and bombings at abortion clinics; and decisions in *Planned Parenthood of Southeastern Penn-*

---

107. *See* Hannah & Salmon, *supra* note 1, at 950–52; Hannah & Cedrone, *infra* chapter 6.

108. 410 U.S. 113 (1973).

sylvania v. Casey,[109] *Whole Woman's Health v. Hellerstedt*,[110] and, most recently, *Dobbs v. Jackson Women's Health Organization*.[111] Together, these developments and events are in conversation with each other, spur deliberation, and create conditions for present-day decision-making across state and federal courts. When judges and lawyers engage in legal readings of briefs and case law in cases like *Casey*, *Hellerstedt*, and *Dobbs*, they principally draw from the pattern of thought that was inculcated through their legal education and focus on form, authority, procedure, and the like; but, secondarily, they also will refer to elements involved in rhetorical situations such as history, culture, or a brief author's background or intentions. Central to this reading process for both judges and lawyers is the generation of alternatives to suss out what the language of law means and how such meaning(s) will shape the tenor and scope of the legal arguments developed in the case that ultimately influence judges' and lawyers' interpretive, translational work.[112] Each of these alternatives is to be understood as a probable argument not concerned "with a necessary or scientific logic, but with . . . evaluative reasoning and not with absolute certainty."[113]

Looking closely here at the transitional moment between certainty and probability, we can see the merging of legal thought and rhetorical thought. Specifically, the sussing out of alternatives generates a rhetorical force that disrupts the constraints of law's rhetorical commitments and generates new argumentative landscapes for considering how the legal and the extralegal intersect. Using reproductive health again as an example, we can ask:

- How do medical innovations refigure understandings of the legal concept of viability, and how do those understandings intersect with evolving standards of morality regarding what constitutes life?
- How do rule of law principles stand up in the context of courts operating with new justices who rely on competing legal, interpretive methodologies?

Answers to such questions are frustratingly elusive, but the challenge for lawyers in such scenarios is learning how to leverage and capture in their arguments the discursive resources made available through rhetorical circulation

109. 505 U.S. 833 (1992).
110. 579 U.S. 582 (2016).
111. 142 S. Ct. 2228 (2022), *on appeal from* 945 F.3d 265 (5th Cir. 2019).
112. *See* Berger, *supra* note 41, at 166.
113. GOODRICH, *supra* note 2, at 171.

that simultaneously merge and disrupt legal thought and rhetorical thought. It is the work of the remaining chapters of this book to fit readers with both the rhetorical knowledge and rhetorical practices for doing this very work.

Summing It Up

- Rhetoric is concerned with persuasion in all of its permutations and simultaneously focuses on the development and deployment of messages for specified audiences, the examination of ideas, and the discovery of truth.
- Law and rhetoric began as intimately connected "partners" whose shared disciplinary roots can be traced directly to their common origins in Greek society stemming from a practical need to prepare citizens for participation in civic life.
- The ascendancy of religion during the Middle Ages and the decline of democracy in the Roman Empire initiated the severing of law and rhetoric's close relationship as interest in forensic oratory, the rhetoric of the courts, waned.
- The classical interest in writing, painting, sculpting, architecture, and science revived the study of and interest in rhetoric during the Renaissance, yet in the context of this revival, rhetoric and law as intellectual disciplines developed in isolation from each other. Importantly, rhetoric then came to be understood as principally concerned with style and the expression of knowledge rather than the creation of knowledge.
- Influenced by the late seventeenth century epistemological shift towards science and its emphasis on method as the source of knowledge acquisition, Christopher Langdell introduced the case study method approach and insisted that law ought to be taught as a science. As a consequence, legal education came to focus on the discovery of legal principles in appellate opinions for later application in legal cases, a focus which contrasted sharply with rhetoric's concerns with persuasion and probability.
- The rise of the legal realism movement during the 1920s and 1930s created momentum for pushing back and questioning the soundness

of the case study approach. Calls for broader investigations of extralegal factors as well as increased attention to the study and use of language in legal practice laid the groundwork for reuniting rhetorical theory and legal practice.

- Contemporary scholars and legal practitioners have advocated for new understandings of rhetoric as a productive art that is an essential component of legal training and practice. Specifically, rather than a mechanistic system of rules, law is cast as a constitutive, rhetorical activity that encourages people to think about law as a way of talking about events and people, a way of telling stories with legal meaning and effect.
- Motivated by understandings of law as constitutive, rhetorical activity, legal educators in legal research and writing classrooms began implementing explicit instruction in rhetorical theory and practice, thus reinvigorating the spirit of law and rhetoric's relationship propagated in classical Greek society.
- Despite law and rhetoric's close relationship, their related patterns of thought are distinguishable because they are subject to different constraints. Rhetorical thought is constrained by the conditions of situation, namely the relationships that exist among speaker, context and audience, and it accepts meaning as socially contingent. Legal thought on the other hand is generally involved in a process of translation that is inherently adversarial and is constrained by procedural and substantive thinking as well as rhetorical commitments like objectivity, hierarchy, clarity, logic, authority, and a belief in one true or best meaning of texts.
- Legal thought and rhetorical thought merge in lawyers' reading processes when generating alternatives for legal argument that stem from the dual consideration of law's rhetorical commitments and extralegal factors such as history, culture, and values. Those alternatives have the potential to disrupt the constraints of law's rhetorical commitments and generate new landscapes for legal advocacy.

Suggestions for Further Reading

Janet Atwill, Rhetoric Reclaimed: Aristotle and the Liberal Arts Tradition (1998).

Edward P. J. Corbett & Robert J. Connors, Classical Rhetoric for the Modern Student (1998).

William A. Covino, The Art of Wondering: A Revisionist Return to the History of Rhetoric (1988).

Thomas B. Farrell, Norms of Rhetorical Culture (1993).

Cheryl Glenn, Rhetoric Retold: Regendering the Tradition from Antiquity Through the Renaissance (1997).

Richard A. Lanham, A Handlist of Rhetorical Terms (2012).

Thomas O. Sloane, On the Contrary: The Protocol of Traditional Rhetoric (1997).

Chapter Two

The Ancient Rhetoric of Law

MICHAEL J. CEDRONE

1. Introduction

In *The Colorado Kid*, one of Stephen King's characters employs the popular adage, "[s]ooner or later, everything old is new again" when talking about writing.[1] The sentiment applies with particular power to legal rhetoric. Many, if not all, of contemporary lawyers' rhetorical moves—even those that seem most innovative—find their origins in the rhetoric of Greece and Rome.

1. Stephen King, The Colorado Kid 45 (2005).

If it doesn't fit, you must acquit.

Rhetorical gesture, the strategy of deliberately using the body through movement or presentation as a means of persuasion, is one example of a seemingly modern practice with ancient roots.[2] Consider a famous failed rhetorical gesture at OJ Simpson's 1995 trial for the murder of his ex-wife, Nicole Brown Simpson, and her friend Ronald Goldman: during an in-court demonstration in front of the jury, the prosecution required Simpson to try on a bloody glove. Prosecutors aimed to show that the glove belonged to Simpson, fit him, and linked him to the murder. However, the demonstration was a spectacular failure. Simpson struggled to put on the glove, which appeared not to fit him at all.[3] During his closing argument, defense lawyer Johnnie Cochran pounced. He declared of the glove, "If it doesn't fit, you must acquit," arguing that just as the glove didn't fit Simpson, so the whole body of evidence "didn't fit" a verdict of guilt beyond a reasonable doubt.[4] Cochran's line is a rhetorical success: it is certainly memorable, and it is brief, symmetric, rhythmic, rhymed, and vivid. For the jury, Cochran's argument inextricably linked the scene of Simpson struggling to fit into bloody gloves to reasonable doubt about the prosecution's entire case. On the strength of the failed demonstration, Cochran's arguments, and other factors, the jury acquitted Simpson.

Today's lawyers are not the first to attempt legal persuasion based on gesture. The ancient Greek courtesan Phryne, one of the very few women remembered in connection with legal cases in the ancient world, was put on trial in the fourth century BCE for failing to honor the Athenian gods.[5] Though ancient Greeks typically argued their own cases in law courts, women were not allowed

---

2. For more on rhetorical gesture, *see* ADAM KENDON, GESTURE: VISIBLE ACTION AS UTTERANCE 17–42 (2004).

3. Various theories have been posited for the gloves' failure to fit: perhaps Simpson struggled to put them on because he was required to wear latex gloves underneath; perhaps the gloves themselves shrank due to various processes they had been subjected to; or perhaps Simpson stopped taking arthritis medication causing his hands to swell. The purpose of this speculation is not to suggest that the gloves should or should not have fit, but rather, to show that the courtroom demonstration was a risky and potentially unreliable way for the prosecution to support its case.

4. For the fascinating background as told by the member of the defense team who suggested the line to Cochran, *see* GERALD UELMEN, IF IT DOESN'T FIT: LESSONS FROM A LIFE IN THE LAW 3–16 (2016).

5. This episode is recounted and analyzed in Audrey Kali, *Phryne and the Rhetoric of Gesture*, *in* THE RHETORIC OF WESTERN THOUGHT 49–52 (James L. Golden et al., eds., 10th ed. 2011).

to do so. Phryne's gesture came as her advocate was arguing to the jury. As her advocate argued, Phryne famously revealed her breasts to the jury. Many of the surrounding circumstances of this episode are lost to history. However, where the prosecution's bloody glove demonstration at the 1995 OJ Simpson trial failed, Phryne's rhetorical gesture succeeded. Ancient sources tell us that upon seeing Phryne's bare breasts, members of the jury were moved by "fear" and "compassion" and could not bring themselves to put her to death.[6] The rhetorical strategy of gesture, which seems unique and innovative in courtrooms today, has its roots in the ancient world. Indeed, a bevy of ancient rhetorical strategies remain a vital part of contemporary law practice.

In considering the ancient foundations of today's legal practice, care must be taken to understand cultural differences between the United States and other modern countries on the one hand, and ancient Greece and Rome on the other. As we saw in Chapter 1, rhetoric is inextricably intertwined with culture.[7] Aristotle's definition tasks rhetoric with seeing all available means of persuasion in a given situation. The boundaries of available persuasion are set by culture: a given culture will recognize some arguments as persuasive and others as unpersuasive. Thus, culture shapes rhetoric, while rhetoric functions within a particular culture.

Ancient rhetoric—here referring specifically to the rhetoric of Greece and Rome—grew up in a context that required political, legal, and ceremonial speech by citizens. As Greek city-states embraced democracy, disputes could no longer be settled by councils of kings and elders. Further, disputes involving public policy or competing claims to property were often not amenable to claims of absolute truth arrived at through science and formal logic. Rather, these disputes required a rhetoric which recognized the contingent nature of the claims at issue. Technical rhetoricians created the earliest writing on rhetoric: handbooks designed to help citizens accomplish their goals in public fora.

Claims about who developed the "first rhetoric" are subject to dispute, but attention centers on Corax, a shadowy figure whose writings have not sur-

6. Athenaeus, The Deipnosophists 13.590–91 (Charles Burton Gulick trans. 1937), *quoted in* Kali, *supra* note 5, at 49.

7. *See, e.g.*, The Rhetoric of Western Thought 4 (James L. Golden et al., eds., 10th ed. 2011), "By understanding evolutionary developments in media [i.e., mode of communication] and society, we will be able to make sense of how, in various historical eras, a specific kind of discourse emerges in concert with the surrounding culture and politics."

vived.[8] Corax wrote at the Greek colony of Syracuse after 467 BCE, when the colony cast off its tyrant in favor of democratic rule. According to tradition, this change in government led to legal disputes about which property owners had superior claims to land. Property owners had to argue their own cases. Corax developed a system for making legal arguments and taught that system to others for pay.[9] The "for pay" aspect of the work of Corax and others leads to a critique of ancient origin: the technical rhetoricians and the Sophists were criticized as hired guns, willing to argue anything and insufficiently devoted to finding the philosophical truth of a given situation. Nonetheless, the systems of argument developed by Corax and others spread to Athens and larger city states and served the increasing need for citizens to settle legal disputes and resolve important public questions in an early democratic society.

Contemporary culture is, of course, quite different from the ancient world. Greek and Roman understandings of citizenship, inclusion, and equality differed greatly from our own. The purpose of this chapter is not to put the ancient world on an undeserved pedestal. Scholarship spanning the millennia has rightly emphasized the cruelties of ancient Greece and Rome—cruelties that sadly run parallel to many seen in the modern world. Ancient women faced exclusion from the franchise and from participation in most of public life; children possessed few rights; and ancient societies condoned slavery, sexual violence, gruesome warfare, and public executions.

Dismantling the influences of these ancient cruelties in our modern systems will require the sharpest tools available to today's lawyers. While new rhetorical techniques have emerged as culture has changed, many of modern rhetoric's most foundational elements find their roots in the ancient world. Classical rhetoric still offers a framework for exploring some of the most compelling dynamics of legal communication. This chapter will explore the continuing vitality of those ancient influences on modern legal rhetoric, even across vast cultural differences.

By looking so far into the past, we can better understand the role, commitments, skills, and struggles of today's lawyers. Ancient rhetoricians recognized

---

8. For background about Corax, *see* THE RHETORICAL TRADITION: READINGS FROM CLASSICAL TIMES TO THE PRESENT 20–21 (Patricia Bizzell et al., eds., 3d ed. 2020); THE RHETORIC OF WESTERN THOUGHT, *supra* note 7, at 36; GEORGE A. KENNEDY, CLASSICAL RHETORIC AND ITS CHRISTIAN AND SECULAR TRADITION FROM ANCIENT TO MODERN TIMES 21 (2d ed. 1999).

9. Some ancient accounts omit Corax's contribution to the area of forensic rhetoric, and instead focus on his contribution to political deliberation. THE RHETORICAL TRADITION, *supra* note 8, at 21.

that legal rhetoric deals with situations where absolute truth can be elusive. They evolved a system still in effect today that allows decision-makers to judge truth based on probability. Romans recognized the need for professional advocates—that is, for professional legal rhetoricians. Ancient methods of legal persuasion survive in adapted form today.

This chapter first examines the emergence of classical legal rhetoric, its relationship to philosophy and truth, and ancient conceptions of the nature of rhetoric, including the question whether rhetoric is an art in the ancient sense. Following that discussion, the chapter examines

- the species of ancient rhetoric, that is,
  - forensic, or judicial;
  - deliberative, or political; and
  - epideictic, or the rhetoric of praise and blame;
- approaches to time and occasion, that is, chronos and kairos;
- inartistic and artistic proof, including logos, ethos, and pathos;
- the parts of a formal oration; and
- the activities of an ancient orator.

For each of these topics, the chapter describes modern legal applications.

2. Rhetoric, law, and the quest for meaning in the classical and modern worlds

The legal system in ancient and modern times imbues human action with legal meanings; language creates and communicates these meanings. The study of legal rhetoric reveals how ancient and modern cultures understood themselves and ordered their public affairs.

Examining the human instinct to make meaning in the most extreme circumstances makes clear the important stakes involved. Austrian psychiatrist, philosopher, and Holocaust survivor Viktor Frankl (1905–1997) devoted his life's work to the idea that the human search for meaning is "the primary motivation in... life."[10] While imprisoned in a Nazi concentration camp, Frankl was called upon to speak words of encouragement to his fellow prisoners.[11]

10. Viktor Frankl, Man's Search for Meaning 105 (1984).
11. *Id.*, at 88–91.

His rhetoric endeavored "to find a full meaning in our life, then and there, in that hut, and in that practically hopeless situation."[12] Frankl recognized that he and his fellow prisoners still had a limited ability to make choices; they could resist the relentless mental indoctrination of the camps, and they could express this resistance by comforting the starving and dying. Through making interior mental choices, the prisoners "preserve[d] a vestige of spiritual freedom, of independence of mind, even in such terrible conditions of psychic and physical stress."[13] For Frankl and other victims of Nazi atrocities, making meaning of their lives and being able to author their own stories—even in an entirely interior way—could be a matter of their very survival.

The ancients had different ideas about the self, their communities, the meaning of citizenship, suffering, and the purposes of life than Viktor Frankl and other modern philosophers, but their speech and writing reveals that they nonetheless pursued meaning and self-understanding communally and individually. Like citizens of the twentieth and twenty-first centuries, the ancients lived at a time of rapid change and sometimes violent upheaval, a time that some historians note as the emergence of the "modern" world. This emergence saw the medium of communication transition from orality to literacy, as the oral tradition exemplified by the epic poets gave way to a written record of literature, philosophy, rhetoric, and other communication.[14] Within the context of this newly literate world, individuals came to live in cities and to forge economic relations in early market economies. To conduct public business, Greeks and Romans invented and developed systems of government and law. Over centuries, in both Greece and Rome, early forms of democracy emerged and were practiced.

The new institutions of government in the ancient world required rhetoric, and many of their accomplishments happened as a result of rhetorical speech. The Parthenon on the Acropolis at Athens, constructed in the fifth century BCE under orator and statesman Pericles, has been called "a living testimonial

---

12. *Id.* at 91.

13. *Id.* at 74.

14. On the transition from orality to literacy, *see generally* Walter J. Ong, Orality and Literacy: The Technologizing of the Word (1982). For more about rhetorical practices within oral culture in the Graeco-Roman, Egyptian, Confucian-era Chinese, and Aztec Mesoamerican worlds, *see* The Rhetoric of Western Thought, *supra* note 7, at 4–10.

to the power of the spoken word."[15] While the Parthenon provides a dramatic example of what rhetoric could accomplish in the ancient world, rhetoric's constitutive role extended beyond buildings and public works projects. Through rhetoric (as well its counterpart dialectic, a more rigorous attempt to get at probable truth that involved exchange of ideas), the ancients formed government and law. This activity prompted conflicts about the nature and role of truth in rhetoric and law, and ultimately about the nature of rhetoric and law themselves.

2.1. The role of truth in rhetoric and law

To understand what the ancients thought about truth in the legal sphere, one must first understand ancient legal custom and procedure. The Greek system differed in important respects from the Roman.

2.1.1. The Greek and Roman legal systems

The ancient Greek legal system was less a system and more a set of practices that emerged in response to local challenges. As democracy developed, citizens created processes to settle disputes over property ownership, criminal matters, and other pressing issues. There were no professional legal personnel during the classical period at Athens, nor were there police, criminal investigators, or public prosecutors.[16] Litigants were limited to freeborn male citizens of Athens who had reached the age of majority.[17] With the exception of women and slaves, whose cases had to be pled by a male relative or associate, parties were themselves responsible for gathering evidence and witnesses and presenting

15. The Rhetoric of Western Thought, *supra* note 7, at 39. Mention of Pericles is incomplete without noting the central role of Aspasia, his companion and a teacher and practitioner of rhetoric in her own right. She is one of the few women in the ancient world reported to have assumed a role in politics and public affairs. She was admired by Cicero and, according to Plato, known to Socrates. Some scholars consider Aspasia to be the author of Pericles' famous Funeral Oration. *See* Beth Waggenspack, *Women's Role in Rhetorical Traditions*, in The Rhetoric of Western Thought, *supra* note 7, at 43–45; The Rhetorical Tradition, *supra* note 8, at 53–58; Cheryl Glenn, Rhetoric Retold: Regendering the Tradition from Antiquity through the Renaissance 39–43 (1997).

16. Victor Bers & Adriaan Lanni, *An Introduction to the Athenian Legal System*, Dēmos: Classical Athenian Democracy 2 (March 13, 2003), https://www.stoa.org/demos/intro_legal_system.pdf.

17. *Id.*

their case to the courts.[18] This led to the need for rhetorical education. In the words of prominent scholar George Kennedy, the system "assumed that an ordinary citizen was competent to prosecute or defend a case,... [even though] a person with no previous experience in public speaking might find it difficult to address a large jury, explain the case clearly, and persuade the jury of the justice of the speaker's side of the issue."[19]

Trials consisted largely of the parties presenting their cases to a jury through speeches. The time of these speeches was limited and measured by a water-clock. Unlike trials in many countries today, where evidence enters the record through witness testimony in somewhat disjointed fashion, Athenian trials largely consisted of orderly presentations of the case by the parties themselves. At various points in time, there were limited procedures for witness testimony (without cross-examination), or for simpler witness corroboration of a party's statements. Athens lacked a developed system of binding law or legal precedent. While speakers could refer to past cases, juries were not bound to follow their results.

Athenian juries consisted of hundreds of members: 201 at minimum, and 501 or more in important cases. Athenian jurors decided questions of both fact, that is, questions about what happened, and law, that is questions about what rules should govern and how they should apply to the case. Consequently, scholars disagree whether they should be termed "jurors" or "judges."[20] Jurors voted by secret ballot, and parties needed to obtain a simple majority to win. In certain cases, a plaintiff who did not obtain at least a fifth of the jurors' votes was subject to fine for bringing a frivolous case. Indeed, the Athenian legal system employed several techniques to discourage litigants from bringing ill-supported cases, including pre-trial hearings to test the strength of a case, and a form of arbitration to resolve disputes before trial. There was no appeal from jury decisions.

Roman rhetoricians wrote about quite a different legal system. Much has been written about Roman law.[21] In considering how the Roman legal system influenced Roman legal rhetoric, two features of the legal system stand

18. KENNEDY, *supra* note 8, at 20; Bers & Lanni, *supra* note 16, at 3.

19. KENNEDY, *supra* note 8, at 21.

20. *Law and Courts in Ancient Athens: A Brief Overview*, THE KOSMOS SOCIETY (Sept. 20. 2018), https://kosmossociety.chs.harvard.edu/?p=40452#_ednref5.

21. *See, e.g.*, NICHOLAS BARRY, AN INTRODUCTION TO ROMAN LAW (2008); THE OXFORD HANDBOOK OF ROMAN LAW AND SOCIETY (Paul J. du Plessis et al., eds. 2016); ERNEST METZGER, LITIGATION IN ROMAN LAW (2005).

out. First, the concept of "law" itself was more permanent at Rome. Written law was more concrete and plentiful, and the Romans thought systematically and scientifically about law.[22] Written law came in several forms from different sources, and law covered subject matters that resemble modern legal categories, including family law, property, and contract. Over the past two millennia, many legal systems have imported concepts from Roman law, including civil law systems of Western Europe and elsewhere, and even the Anglo-American common law system, in certain respects.

Second, and most importantly, the legal system at Rome was professionalized. Litigants relied on lawyers to plead their causes, and the system had individuals working in various professional capacities, including as magistrates and others with judicial power. The more advanced and developed system of Roman law required a more sophisticated and systematized rhetoric to embody its practice. If the purpose of rhetoric at Greece was to prepare the average citizen to plead a case in the law courts, rhetoricians at Rome resembled legal educators, addressing their writing to lawyers who would be repeat players in the Roman legal system. Much foundational thought about rhetoric generally and legal rhetoric in particular comes from Greek writers, but the circumstances at Rome make Roman insights particularly important for modern lawyers and legal educators.

2.1.2. The nature of truth in ancient legal rhetoric and modern law

The requirement that litigants present their own cases to ancient Greek courts sparked the need to provide materials and instruction to assist citizens with this task. In this sense, the beginnings of the formal discipline of rhetoric and of rhetorical education coincide with the earliest legal education in the Greek world. The teachers and writers who developed forensic rhetoric at Greece advanced a probabilistic approach to truth that dovetails quite well with the needs of legal proceedings then and now.

A citizen untrained in advocacy had several options. One choice was to purchase a speech describing his case from a professional draftsperson known as a logographer. The citizen would then deliver the speech himself in sessions at court. Successful Greek orators, such as Demosthenes and Isocrates, found

22. Maria Panezi, *A Description of the Structure of the Hellenic Republic, the Greek Legal System, and Legal Research*, GLOBALEX 2.2 (November/December 2021), https://www.nyulawglobal.org/globalex/Greece1.html.

logography quite lucrative.[23] Alternatively, citizens could pursue rhetorical education by using either written materials for self-study or by working with a teacher.[24] Both the technical rhetoricians and the Sophists wrote treatises that outlined the art of persuasion in the law courts. In addition, famous teachers conducted classes in speechmaking for young and wealthy citizens for a fee. For instance, the Sophist Isocrates founded the first permanent institution of higher learning, a school of speech, at Athens in 392 BCE, five years before the establishment of Plato's Academy.[25]

Rhetorical education was expensive and therefore not available to those of modest means. However, it did serve to expand slightly the number of those who could participate in government beyond those of noble birth to those who could afford education. At a much later time period, this was the path taken by Cicero, who grew up about 70 miles from Rome in a wealthy but nonpolitical family. Sent as an adolescent to live in the home of a famous politician and orator at Rome, Cicero used his talents and education to "speak[ ] his way to the top."[26]

The teachings of the rhetorical handbooks were narrower in scope than later, theoretical treatments of rhetoric, such as those of Aristotle, Cicero, or Quintilian. Rhetorical handbooks, which continued to be written and to influence rhetorical writing throughout antiquity, guided readers in how to structure an oration and how to employ various persuasive techniques, and they also set out principles of public speaking.[27] The handbooks avoided larger ethical questions of which cases to argue, and they did not address questions about the limits of legitimate advocacy. Consequently, the handbooks tended to neglect concerns about the character of the speaker and the characteristics of the audience.

Socrates, as reported in Plato's *Phaedrus*, critiques the handbook tradition of rhetoric, including the technical rhetoricians and the Sophists, as holding "what is likely... in higher honor than what is true," and making "small things

---

23. THE RHETORIC OF WESTERN THOUGHT, *supra* note 7, at 37, 83. Later in life, Isocrates denied having been a logographer, a fact which suggests that the profession may have had a less-than-honorable reputation. *See* THE RHETORICAL TRADITION, *supra* note 8, at 84.

24. KENNEDY, *supra* note 8, at 25, 29.

25. THE RHETORIC OF WESTERN THOUGHT, *supra* note 7, at 83.

26. MARY BEARD, SPQR: A HISTORY OF ANCIENT ROME 28 (2015); James M. May, *Cicero: His Life and Career*, *in* BRILL'S COMPANION TO CICERO: ORATORY AND RHETORIC 2 (James M. May ed., 2002).

27. KENNEDY, *supra* note 7, at 22. Cicero's youthful effort, the *De Inventione*, may be placed in this category. *Id.* at 25–26.

appear great and great things small... by the power of their language."[28] Socrates' critique is even sharper in the *Gorgias*, where he terms legal rhetoric "quite worthless for getting at the truth" and alleges that legal rhetoric can be used to plead "in defense of injustice."[29] Socrates and Plato, in situations where probable knowledge was the best one could do, looked to the disciplined academic inquiry of dialectic, which attempts to establish propositions through the exchange of ideas among two or more speakers, often in question-and-answer format.[30]

When the rigorous analysis of dialectic is impossible or undesirable, rhetoric builds arguments, persuades, and appeals to the predispositions of an audience. The ancient teachers of rhetoric pursued a method of persuasion that has lasted in today's legal system. Modern standards of proof function by weighing probabilities: in a contemporary civil case, jurors assess liability according to a "preponderance of the evidence" standard, that is, by deciding which version of events is "more likely than not."[31] Criminal liability is of course assessed under the higher "beyond a reasonable doubt" standard. Evidence is weighed and contrasted, to be sure, but the jury is instructed to apply logic and common sense in making decisions. In this system, truth is contingent, and the decision-maker must be persuaded by the rhetorical argument of the parties.

In the modern world, absolute truth is not the sole goal of the legal system. In the United States, questions of fact are the province of the jury. However, many cases never reach a jury; they are either decided on dispositive motion or settled at earlier stages. Even at jury trials, absolute truth does not always emerge. For example, William Blackstone, in his highly influential *Commentaries on the Laws of England*, demanded exacting proof for conviction of a crime, stating that it is "[b]etter that ten guilty persons escape, than that one innocent suffer," suggesting that truth is not the only goal served by the criminal law.[32] Alternatively, consider *Mapp v. Ohio*, which prohibits the government from using evidence obtained in violation of the Fourth Amendment in a criminal

---

28. PLATO, PHAEDRUS (Alexander Nehamas and Paul Woodruff trans., 1995), *reprinted in* THE RHETORICAL TRADITION, *supra* note 8, 267a, at 189.

29. PLATO, GORGIAS (W.R.M. Lamb trans., 1925), *reprinted in* THE RHETORICAL TRADITION, *supra* note 8, 472a, 480b, at 121, 128.

30. THE RHETORIC OF WESTERN THOUGHT, *supra* note 7, at 53, 63–64.

31. *Evidentiary Standards and Burdens of Proof in Legal Proceedings*, JUSTIA (last visited Mar. 3, 2022, 11:47 PM), https://www.justia.com/trials-litigation/lawsuits-and-the-court-process/evidentiary-standards-and-burdens-of-proof.

32. WILLIAM BLACKSTONE, COMMENTARIES ON THE LAWS OF ENGLAND 352.

trial.[33] This case has set at least some guilty people free because it requires that criminal convictions be based on constitutionally adequate procedures in the gathering of evidence. Based on considerations of this sort, Prof. James Boyd White has gone so far as to claim that law's "main goal" is not truth but justice; while law is concerned with truth, justice is a "human value of at least equal dignity and importance."[34]

In view of the goals and methods of today's legal system, the Socratic critique that legal rhetoric insufficiently serves truth has endured. Lawyers are still sometimes slurred as hired guns, more interested in winning a case through deft manipulation of the rules than in pursuing truth and doing justice as the public responsibility of the legal profession seems to require. However, the modern legal system pursues reliable, fair, and credible outcomes by ensuring that evidence is gathered and presented according to fair procedure and by constraining a jury's impulses through standards of proof. As a result, it is perhaps not surprising that lawyers at times take advantage of design features of the legal system to obscure inconvenient facts and build rhetorical arguments that favor their clients' preferred outcomes. In so doing, they follow ancient models.

2.1.3. Reconciling rhetoric and truth: The Aristotelian model

The ancients worked to bridge the gap between philosophy's commitment to truth and rhetoric's capacity to build many linguistic arguments. Perhaps more than any other ancient Greek writer, Aristotle's view of rhetoric foresees the method of the western legal tradition. *On Rhetoric* is Aristotle's magnum opus on the subject; in it, he famously defines rhetoric in an encompassing way as "an ability, in each particular case, to see the available means of persuasion."[35] One commentator has described Aristotelian rhetoric as "a moral but practical art grounded in probability or the contingent nature of things."[36]

As a pedagogical matter, Aristotle advocates that a speaker "should be able to argue persuasively on either side of a question,"[37] thus recognizing that rhetoric speaks to circumstances where truth is contingent. Observing that some speakers will have stronger cases while others will have weaker, Aristotle views

33. Mapp v. Ohio, 367 U.S. 643, 655 (1961).

34. James Boyd White, Keep Law Alive 5–6 (2019).

35. Aristotle, On Rhetoric I.2.1, at 37 (George Kennedy, trans., Oxford University Press 2d ed. 2007).

36. The Rhetoric of Western Thought, *supra* note 7, at 68.

37. On Rhetoric, *supra* note 35, I.1.13, at 35.

rhetoric itself as a neutral tool and recognizes the risk that it can be used for harmful ends.[38] However, Aristotle sees mitigating factors that lead him not to condemn rhetoric. He observes that all arts can be misused and that true and just positions are by nature stronger than their opposites. Thus, he concludes the benefits of rhetoric outweigh its risk of misuse.[39] In some sense reflecting Aristotle's position, many thinkers justify the adversary system in the law of the United Kingdom and United States by arguing that it leads to outcomes that are most probably true in many if not all matters.[40]

For Cicero, rhetoric was a building block of the State. *De oratore* stands as Cicero's testament to the importance of rhetoric in the well-ordering of society, and it contains a systematic exposition of the orator's character, process, and techniques. In Book III, Crassus declares that rhetoric "establishes traditions, law, and legal arrangements, governs the State, and addresses with distinction and copiousness all questions belonging to any area whatsoever."[41]

Like Aristotle, Cicero appears to view the tools of rhetoric as neutral, that is, as capable of being used for just or unjust purposes. In considering the risks of rhetoric, Cicero's Crassus declares in the *De oratore* that students who do not have "integrity and the highest measure of good sense" may well do more harm than good.[42] Indeed, rhetorical education "will certainly not make orators of them, but will put weapons in the hands of madmen."[43]

For Cicero, however, true oratory is rooted in the speaker's knowledge, wisdom, and a commitment to the affairs of state. Speaking in his own voice in the prologue to Book II of *De oratore*, Cicero calls for the orator to combine "the whole of wisdom" with "rhetorical rules"; for Cicero, a speaker must know

38. *Id.* I.1.13, at 36.

39. *Id.* I.1.12–13, at 35–36; *see also, Aristotle's Rhetoric,* STANFORD ENCYCLOPEDIA OF PHILOSOPHY 4.2 (last visited Feb. 1, 2010), https://plato.stanford.edu/entries/aristotle-rhetoric/#4.2.

40. For a classic justification of the adversary system, *see* Lon L. Fuller & John D. Randall, *Professional Responsibility: Report of the Joint Conference of the ABA and AALS,* 44 A.B.A. JOURNAL 1159, 1160–61 (1958). Of course, this view has been critiqued. *See, e.g., David Luban, "Twenty Theses on Adversarial Ethics," in* BEYOND THE ADVERSARIAL SYSTEM 143–45 (Helen Stacy & Michael Lavarch, eds. 1999). Other theorists see the goal of the adversary system as protecting rights more than ferreting out truth. *See generally,* DEBORAH L. RHODE, IN THE INTERESTS OF JUSTICE 53–58 (2001).

41. CICERO, ON THE IDEAL ORATOR III.76, at 248 (James M. May and Jakob Wisse, trans., Oxford University Press, 2001) (55 B.C.E.).

42. *Id.* III.55, at 239.

43. *Id.*

his subject well to "maintain a claim to the title of eloquence."[44] His character Crassus declared that his teachers were "practical experience, the laws, the institutions of the Roman people, and the traditions of [his] ancestors."[45] Thus, Cicero's approach to rhetoric roots the discipline in deep knowledge of the speaker's subject matter and an orator's commitment to use speech for noble public purposes.

Much of Cicero's approach to oratory in the courts prefigures contemporary ideas about a lawyer's responsibility to her clients. Antonius, another character in the *De oratore* dialogue, is presented as a renowned legal advocate. Contemporary lawyers would recognize Antonius' methodical process for investigating a legal case: he begins with client intake interviews, gathers documents, and thoroughly investigates the matter.[46] For Antonius, the orator's presentation of a case comes from deep knowledge gained through assiduous investigation. Like his character Antonius, Cicero himself was a renowned orator who built his reputation through work in the courts.[47] Cicero considered his youthful defense of Sextus Roscius, in the *Pro Roscio,* to be the speech that established his reputation.[48] As a result, many have taken Antonius' views on lawyering to be Cicero's own.

Whether one accepts the Platonic critique that rhetoric does not lead to truth or whether one follows the paths forged by the Sophists, Aristotle, Cicero or others, the usefulness of rhetoric in the modern legal system should be apparent. The modern system, based on competing versions of fact and competing attempts to reason from the facts to appropriate legal conclusions, requires advocates to marshal all available means of persuasion in a way that reflects the complexity of the situation and the requirements of the law, in order to reach credible and reliable results.

---

44. *Id.* II.5, at 126.

45. *Id.* III.74, at 247.

46. *Id.* II.99–104, at 149–50.

47. *See* Michael J. Cedrone, *Cicero and Barack Obama: How to Defend the Republic without Losing your Head,* 20 Nev. L.J. 1177, 1182–84 (2020), and sources cited therein.

48. Stephen Usher, Cicero's Speeches: The Critic in Action 7 (2008) (citing Cicero, Brutus 312). *See also* William J. Dominik, T*he Development of Roman Rhetoric, in* The Oxford handbook of Rhetorical Studies 160 (Michael J. MacDonald ed., 2017) (Cicero's election to the highest political office in the Roman republic "owed much to the rhetorical and oratorical skills that he had acquired and displayed in his successful defense of prominent clients in the courts.").

2.2. The nature and status of rhetoric

A key dispute in the ancient debate between rhetoric and philosophy concerned whether rhetoric was sufficiently committed to philosophical truth or whether it was amoral and subject to misuse. This dispute was part of a larger struggle between rhetoric and philosophy over the nature of rhetoric itself. Attacks on the status of rhetoric continue today. Law, which is embodied, communicated, practiced, and enforced through language,[49] is subject to similar critiques as rhetoric. Understanding the terms of the ancient debate over the nature of rhetoric helps clarify contemporary critiques of law and make sense of the nature of law practice today.

The larger struggle over the nature of rhetoric in antiquity centered on the question whether rhetoric was an art. In the ancient world, a discipline could be called an "art" (in Greek, *techne*, in Latin, *ars*) if it was understood to be "a systematic body of real knowledge that constituted a reliable guide for attaining desired practical results."[50] Aristotle's definition from the *Nicomachean Ethics* is more concise and more focused on process than product: an art, he says, is a "reasoned habit of mind."[51]

In Plato's *Gorgias*, Socrates famously declares that rhetoric is not an art. Instead, he says, it is "part[ ] of the same practice" as "cookery."[52] Expanding the idea, Socrates declares:

> It seems to me... [that rhetoric is] a pursuit that is not a matter of art, but showing a shrewd, gallant spirit which has a natural bent for clever dealing with mankind, and I sum up its substance in the name "flattery."[53]

For Socrates, rhetoric in and of itself leads nowhere but to flattery and deceit. Thus, it poses great risks. The Sophists clung to an opposing view. They embraced the term "art" in referring to rhetoric, and indeed Isocrates went so

---

49. *See* White, *supra* note 34, at 82–85 ("I [see] law... as an activity of mind and language, a way of claiming meaning for experience and making that meaning real. It is not merely a system of rules,... but a structure of thought and expression that is built upon a set of inherently unstable, dynamic, and dialogic tensions. In this it is like a poem.").

50. James M. May & Jakob Wisse, *Introduction* to On the Ideal Orator, *supra* note 41, at 25.

51. Aristotle, Nicomachean Ethics 6.4, as quoted in On Rhetoric, *supra* note 35, at 31 n. 8.

52. Gorgias, *supra* note 29, 462c, at 115.

53. *Id.* 463a, at 115.

far as to claim that in teaching rhetoric he was teaching "philosophy," that is, "love of wisdom."[54]

Aristotle and Cicero again attempt to bridge the divide. In *On Rhetoric*, Aristotle asserts that rhetoric is an art.[55] It is possible that Aristotle's penchant to organize and systematize, combined with his experience lecturing about rhetoric at Plato's Academy in the mid-350s BCE, led him to claim rhetoric as an art.[56] In any event, Aristotle claims that his emphasis on artistic proofs will distinguish his rhetoric from that of others, whom he accuses of overly relying on emotion as a tool of persuasion.[57]

Cicero does not fully commit to the view that rhetoric is an art. In *De oratore*, Crassus declares that oratory may be considered an art "if not according to th[e] precise definition [of 'art'] then at least in the ordinary sense in which we use the word."[58] Like Aristotle, Cicero finds the work of his predecessors lacking: various characters in *De oratore* make fun of existing rhetorical rules, calling the teaching of rhetoricians of his day "utterly ridiculous."[59] Like the Sophists, however, Cicero's rhetoric was based on learning and wisdom. Some of that learning comes from outside the discipline of rhetoric itself, perhaps explaining why Cicero steps back from a full endorsement of rhetoric as an art. According to the *De oratore* discussants, knowledge of the civil law is essential for an orator, showing that, for Cicero, law and rhetoric were intertwined.[60]

The debate over whether rhetoric is an art capable of producing knowledge mirrors a contemporary problem in the modern legal system. The Platonic distinction between knowledge and its expression—which raises up the study of philosophy and denigrates the study of rhetoric—leads to a distinction between learning legal doctrine and learning lawyering skills.[61] This distinction finds its way into legal education in the way that "doctrinal" courses are distinguished from so-called "skills" classes, particularly legal writing courses and clinical legal education. The well-documented denigration of legal skills

---

54. *See* KENNEDY, *supra* note 8, at 39.

55. ON RHETORIC, *supra* note 35, I.1.2, at 31.

56. For more information about the development of Aristotle's ideas on rhetoric, *see* George A. Kennedy, *Introduction* to ON RHETORIC, *supra* note 35, at 4–5.

57. ON RHETORIC, *supra* note 35, I.1.3, at 31.

58. ON THE IDEAL ORATOR, *supra* note 41, I.109, at 82.

59. *See* Cedrone, *supra* note 47, at 1188–1189.

60. *See generally* ON THE IDEAL ORATOR, *supra* note 41, I.166–203, at 94–107.

61. On this point, see Kristen Tiscione & Amy Vorenburg, *Podia and Pens: Dismantling the Two-Track System for Legal Research and Writing Faculty*, 31 COLUM. J. GENDER & L. 47, 60 (2015).

in the law school curriculum contributes to hostility between legal academics and the practicing bar. In the legal academy, academic writing—in the pursuit of knowledge—is the coin of the realm, while practitioner writing is viewed as inferior. Within the law curriculum, discussion of rhetoric, when it is included at all, is relegated to skills and specialty classes, leading to an underappreciation of rhetoric's role in constructing law.

3. The ancient roots of modern legal rhetoric

The legacy of classical rhetoric to modern legal practice is vast. The ancient and traditional division of rhetoric into three species—forensic, deliberative, and epideictic—provides a lens for understanding the speech of modern lawyers, who communicate in writing and speech in each of these situations. Though time in the senses of chronos, or chronological sequences of events, and kairos, meaning "opportune moment" or "proper time,"[62] was not a central concept in the work of Aristotle, it too has ancient roots and modern branches. Some legal changes are only possible because of a combination of patient preparation (chronos) and the right opportunity (kairos). Moreover, the Aristotelian distinction among three appeals of artistic argument—based on logos, ethos, and pathos—has continuing vitality for modern lawyers. This section will examine how these three appeals work together to strengthen the Supreme Court's opinion in *Brown v. Board of Education*.

The ancient systems of oratory prefigure modern practice in even more detailed ways. Whether one looks to the differing advice of Corax or Aristotle or Cicero, the structural division of a formal oration prefigures lawyerly organization of memos, briefs and other analytic and argumentative documents. In short, and painting very broadly, for ancients and moderns, a narration of the facts is followed by a legal argument (which incorporates answers to counterarguments), and all of this is bookended by an introduction and conclusion. Ancients also explored what we might anachronistically call "the writing process," laying out a series of canons (in the case of Aristotle) or activities (in the case of Cicero) that guided their readers in how to construct (and deliver) orations.

62. *See* Clarke Rountree, *Kairos and American Legal Praxis*, 20 Nev. L.J. 855, 855 (2020).

3.1. The species of ancient rhetoric

In *On Rhetoric*, Aristotle identifies three species of rhetoric, the deliberative, judicial, and epideictic.[63] These three species address different subjects, embrace different objectives, arise for different purposes and occasions, and entail different audiences. Examining the circumstances of each species shows how each contributes to legal rhetoric.

Deliberative oratory is addressed to a judge of future happenings, for example a member of the democratic assembly.[64] Aristotle defines the subject of deliberative rhetoric as "the advantageous" and "the harmful," meaning policies the speaker exhorts the audience to follow in their own best interests, or policies the speaker dissuades the audience from adopting because of their danger or risk.[65] Other factors, such as the justice or injustice of a course of action, or the honor or disgrace involved in that course, are secondary concerns in a deliberative speech.[66] In addition, Aristotle bounds deliberative rhetoric by saying that it does not include matters on which advocacy would be futile: that is, matters that are impossible to bring about because they are certain to happen (or not happen), or because they are "contingent" on "the work of nature" or chance.[67] In short, deliberative rhetoric is focused on what's possible: "those [matters] that can both possibly come to pass or not."[68]

The audience for judicial rhetoric consists of judges of past actions.[69] The subject of judicial rhetoric is conceived in fairly narrow terms, primarily accusation and defense.[70] Aristotle views judicial rhetoric as inferior to

---

63. While the three species of rhetoric are most closely associated with Aristotle, he was most likely consolidating the work of earlier writers. *See* ON RHETORIC, *supra* note 35, I.3, at 46. The basic classification system was carried forward by later writers in antiquity, including Cicero and Quintilian. *See* ON THE IDEAL ORATOR, *supra* note 41, I.141, at 89; Quintilian, *Institutio Oratoria 3.4.9*, PERSEUS DIGITAL LIBRARY (Harold Edgeworth Butler, trans.), http://www.perseus.tufts.edu/hopper/text?doc=urn:cts:latinLit:phi1002.phi0013.perseus-eng1:4.9 (last visited Mar. 3, 2022).

64. ON RHETORIC, *supra* note 35, I.3.2, at 48.

65. *Id.* I.3.3, I.3.5, at 48, 49.

66. *Id.* I.3.5, at 49.

67. *Id.* I.4.3, at 53.

68. *Id.* I.4.1, at 52–53.

69. *Id.* I.3.3, at 48. Aristotle scholar George Kennedy discourages the use of the term "forensic" with respect to Aristotelian judicial rhetoric, for several reasons. *See* ON RHETORIC, *supra* note 35, at 47 n. 73 (primarily, both deliberative and judicial rhetoric took place in the forum. In addition, the English word "forensic" may refer to debates or to medical evidence, neither of which is illuminating in reading Aristotle.).

70. ON RHETORIC, *supra* note 35, I.3.4, I.10.1, at 49, 83.

deliberative; in addition to terming deliberative subjects "finer and more important to the state," he states that jurors may struggle to see the truth in legal cases because "friendliness and hostility and individual self-interest are often involved."[71] In addition, Aristotle repeatedly criticizes writers of rhetorical treatises for their too-heavy focus on judicial rhetoric at the expense of deliberative.[72] Perhaps Aristotle's distrust of judicial rhetoric came about because he himself had little personal experience with legal cases.[73] Thus, Aristotle's treatment of judicial rhetoric does not achieve the sophistication of Cicero and other ancient writers.

Aristotle's final category is epideictic rhetoric, which was, for him, primarily the rhetoric of praise or blame. For Aristotle, the audience for epideictic rhetoric is made up not of judges, but of observers.[74] The primary time the speaker is concerned with is the present, because an epideictic orator speaks about "existing qualities."[75] That said, Aristotle recognizes that such a speaker may recall past events and make predictions about the future, so the concept of time in this species of oration is elastic.[76]

While judicial oratory may seem the most obvious province of lawyers, in fact, all three species have implications for law. Aristotle himself includes "framing of the laws" as a subject for deliberative address. He explains that democracy is weakened when its principle of equality is relaxed, thus leading to oligarchy. On the other hand, if the equality principle is applied too rigidly, it risks depriving the state of leadership by the most qualified people and may cause the state to devolve into anarchy.[77] Modern lawyers and lawmakers struggle with these sorts of concerns in designing systems of government and in framing legal rules and rights in deliberative fora.

---

71. On Rhetoric, *supra* note 35, I.1.7, at 32. Not all of Aristotle's critiques are well-taken. For instance, Aristotle does not seem to perceive the public significance of important and finely-wrought speeches in trials. *Id.* at n. 18. Aristotle never revised and published his Rhetoric, so analysis that treats it as a coherent published work can easily be misguided. That said, John Rist calls chapters 5–15 of Book I, in which Aristotle discusses the three species of rhetoric, the "early core" of the work, John Rist, The Mind of Aristotle: A Study in Philosophical Growth 85 (1989), and Kennedy notes that in this section of the treatise, Aristotle "demotes" judicial rhetoric to third place, after both deliberative and epideictic, On Rhetoric, *supra* note 35, at 52 n.89.

72. On Rhetoric, *supra* note 35, I.1.10, at 33.

73. *Id.* at 32.

74. *Id.* I.3.2, at 48.

75. *Id.* I.3.4, at 48.

76. *Id.* I.3.4, at 48–49.

77. *Id.* I.4.2, at 55.

Aristotle's description of judicial rhetoric distinguishes common law and written law. For Aristotle, common law did not resemble the system of judge-made law that characterizes the Anglo-American legal tradition. Instead, it refers to cases not determined by written law, in which the Greek jury decided on an outcome in accordance with their "best understanding" of cultural norms, rooted in nature.[78] Aristotle's discussion of written law is sophisticated. He writes about the interpretation of ambiguity in legal text and the use of purpose to decide the meaning of that text.[79] These moves and techniques, while not encompassing all of a modern lawyer's tools, remain part of advocacy before a tribunal today.

Finally, even Aristotelian epideictic rhetoric can have important implications for the law. To take one prominent example of an epideictic speech from the nineteenth century, the lawyer-President Abraham Lincoln famously spoke at Gettysburg, Pennsylvania to praise deceased Civil War soldiers. His brief speech challenged listeners to dedicate themselves to the "unfinished work" of the Union soldiers, namely, "that this nation ... shall have a new birth of freedom."[80] Lincoln explicitly connected the new order of freedom to the soldiers' sacrifice; his invocation of this new understanding of freedom prefigured the changes to the constitutional order of the United States that would be embodied in the Reconstruction Amendments, adopted after the end of the Civil War.

3.2. Chronos and kairos

As is clear from the discussion above, Aristotle distinguished between deliberative, judicial, and epideictic rhetoric based on the chronological time periods each species addresses: deliberative rhetoric deals with proposals for the future, judicial rhetoric addresses past matters that are disputed, and epideictic rhetoric deals with praise or blame of figures in the present. Of course, these distinctions are not rigid; deliberative advocacy and epideictic speeches often involve arguments based on history.[81] Further, as systems of precedent have strengthened, judicial cases have come to be concerned about the implications of a ruling for future cases.

---

78. *Id.* I.15.5–6, at 103. *See also id.* I.10.3, at 84, I.13.1–2, at 97.

79. *See generally* I.15, at 102–110.

80. *The Gettysburg Address*, ABRAHAM LINCOLN ONLINE (last visited Mar. 3, 2022, 12:30 PM), http://www.abrahamlincolnonline.org/lincoln/speeches/gettysburg.htm.

81. ON RHETORIC, *supra* note 35, at 49, n. 81.

Our modern concept of time includes another meaning of ancient origin: kairos, or sense of occasion or opportune moment. Aristotle does not explore the term, but his discussion of audience and his emphasis on what is possible in defining the aim of deliberative rhetoric suggest that he understood that rhetoric's possibilities were bound by what could be accomplished in a given moment.[82] Such diverse writers as Gorgias, Isocrates, and even Plato in the *Phaedrus*, however, emphasized the importance of proper moments to deliver speeches and messages.[83] One prominent commentator notes that kairos is "Gorgias's most prominent rhetorical principle."[84] Isocrates, for instance, in *Against the Sophists*, identified "fitness for the occasion [kairos]" as a necessary ingredient for oratory to be "good."[85] Finally, in his vision of ideal rhetoric found at the end of *Phaedrus*, Plato's Socrates includes "a knowledge of the times for speaking and for keeping silence" as part of what is necessary to develop rhetorical art.[86]

For the modern lawyer, a more robust concept of kairos may help us understand the boundaries of legal argument.[87] Studying changes in law, especially those that happen rapidly, can help lawyers understand that the question of when to bring a case can be important to achieving a hoped-for outcome. For instance, in 1996, Congress passed the federal so-called Defense of Marriage Act (DOMA) by wide, bipartisan, veto-proof majorities, and it was signed into law by then-President Clinton.[88] Section 3 of the act amended federal law to provide that marriage is defined as "a legal union between one man and one

82. *See* Rountree, *supra* note 62, at 855, 859.

83. See *id.* at 858–59.

84. Bruce McComiskey, Gorgias and the New Sophistic Rhetoric 111 (2020).

85. Isocrates, *Against the Sophists 13.13* (trans. George Norlin), Perseus Digital Library (last visited Mar. 14, 2022, 2:36 PM), http://www.perseus.tufts.edu/hopper/text?doc=Perseus%3Atext%3A1999.01.0144%3Aspeech%3D13%3Asection%3D13; *see also* Isocrates, *Pangyricus, 4.9*, Perseus Digital Library (last visited Mar. 14, 2022, 2:38 PM), http://www.perseus.tufts.edu/hopper/text?doc=Perseus%3Atext%3A1999.01.0144%3Aspeech%3D4%3Asection%3D9 ("For the deeds of the past are, indeed, an inheritance common to us all; but the ability to make proper use of them at the appropriate time, to conceive the right sentiments about them in each instance, and to set them forth in finished phrase, is the peculiar gift of the wise.").

86. Plato, *Phaedrus 272a* (trans. Harold N. Fowler), Perseus Digital Library (last visited Mar. 14, 2022, 2:41 PM), http://data.perseus.org/citations/urn:cts:greekLit:tlg0059.tlg012.perseus-eng1:272a.

87. On this point, *see generally* Rountree, *supra* note 62.

88. Defense of Marriage Act, Pub. L. 104–199, 110 Stat. 2419 (1996).

woman as husband and wife," and limited the definition of spouse to "a person of the opposite sex."[89] Section 2 provided that states need not recognize marriages between persons of the same sex performed in other states.[90] At the time, no substantial question was raised as to the constitutionality of the statute. Indeed, prior to 2010, every federal court to examine the statute upheld its constitutionality.

However, on July 8, 2010, a pair of decisions issued the same day by a Massachusetts federal district court struck down Section 3.[91] Just three years later, the Supreme Court held the federal marriage definition unconstitutional in *United States v. Windsor*, concluding that the definition deprived gay and lesbian citizens equal protection of the laws.[92] Section 2 of DOMA, which was not at issue in *Windsor*, found its end in *Obergefell v. Hodges*, decided in 2015, which held that the Fourteenth Amendment requires all states to recognize same-sex marriages.[93]

Less than twenty years, from the 1996 enactment of DOMA to the 2015 holding in *Obergefell*, is a relatively short time for views of constitutionality of a federal statute to change. So, what happened? The answer is, of course, complicated.[94] At the state level, statutes and constitutional decisions and amendments were passed and issued in favor of and against marriage for the LGBTQ+ community during the years 1996–2010. During this period, proponents of marriage engaged in a chronological campaign to change the law. The resulting shift in public opinion in favor of gay rights, however, was dramatic

---

89. 1 U.S.C. § 7.

90. Defense of Marriage Act § 2.

91. *See* Gill v. Office of Pers. Mgmt., 699 F. Supp. 2d 374, 376 (D. Mass. 2010) (Tauro, J.). (holding DOMA unconstitutional under equal protection principles implicit in the Fifth Amendment Due Process Clause) and Mass. v. U.S. Dep't of Health and Hum. Svcs., 698 F. Supp. 2d 234, 235–36 (D. Mass. 2010) (holding DOMA unconstitutional under the Tenth Amendment and the Spending Clause). The First Circuit affirmed both decisions in Mass. v. U.S. Dep't of Health and Hum. Svcs., 682 F.3d 1, 17 (1st Cir. 2012), and the Supreme Court denied certiorari, 570 U.S. 931, following its decision in *Windsor*, discussed in the main text.

92. United States v. Windsor, 570 U.S. 744, 749–52, 774–75 (2013).

93. Obergefell v. Hodges, 576 U.S. 644, 681 (2015) ("The Court, in this decision, holds same-sex couples may exercise the fundamental right to marry in all States. It follows that the Court also must hold—and it now does hold—that there is no lawful basis for a State to refuse to recognize a lawful same-sex marriage performed in another State on the ground of its same-sex character.").

94. For the view of Evan Wolfson, founder of the Freedom to Marry coalition, *see Freedom to Marry's Ladder of Clarity: Lessons from a Winning Campaign (That Has Not Yet Won)*, 29 COLUM. J. GENDER & L. 236 (2015).

and swift,[95] and that shift created a climate in which Court action on DOMA and marriage equality issues became possible. In that sense, a kairic moment arrived for the Supreme Court to issue its decisions in *Windsor* and *Obergefell*. That moment was partly a product of changed cultural circumstances, which advocates of equal marriage themselves helped bring about.[96] Lawyers cannot always control when kairic moments arrive, but recognizing them and using them to advantage can be an important legal skill.

3.3. Ethos, pathos, and logos

In writing about the invention of arguments, Aristotle considers various means of persuasion,[97] and makes an initial division into two categories: inartistic and artistic. Inartistic proofs are those that are not created by the speaker, but merely used. Artistic proofs, on the other hand, are those created by the speaker.

For Aristotle, the category of inartistic proof includes what he considered matters of irrefutable fact: laws, witnesses, contracts, slave testimony extracted through torture (a subject about which Aristotle had mixed emotions), and statements made under oath.[98] Cicero holds that using inartistic means of proof requires "only average natural ability, but a really extraordinary amount of practice."[99] Lawyers at times construct cases from inartistic sources alone, but more often, artistic proof comes into play.

In Aristotle's view, artistic proofs are the product of three different appeals: ethos, pathos, and logos, which correspond to the "three constituents of the speech-act: speaker, audience, and speech, respectively."[100] Ethos concerns the character or trustworthiness of the speaker, pathos concerns the emotional response of the audience, and logos concerns the logic of the speech. Artistic

95. *See, e.g.*, *Attitudes on Same-Sex Marriage*, Pew Research (Mar. 3, 2022, 2:36 PM), https://www.pewforum.org/fact-sheet/changing-attitudes-on-gay-marriage.

96. For a thoughtful examination of how advocates can use kairic moments, *see* Rountree, *supra* note 62, at 873–76.

97. "Means of persuasion" attempts to capture the meaning of the Greek word *pisteis*, which is not easily rendered in English. For an older but still relevant scholarly discussion of how to translate *pisteis*, *see* G. H. Wikramanayake, *A Note on the Pisteis in Aristotle's Rhetoric*, 82 Am. J. Philology 193–196 (1961).

98. On Rhetoric, *supra* note 35, I.15, at 102–110.

99. On the Ideal Orator, *supra* note 41, 2.119, at 154–55.

100. Kennedy, *supra* note 8, at 82; *see also* On Rhetoric, *supra* note 35, I.2.3, at 38.

proofs based on these appeals are the most developed concept of proof in the ancient writing on rhetoric.

Much of law study and its practice in the modern world focuses on logical reasoning. Without logos, a speaker becomes what Cicero called a "ranter," making up in volume and fervor what is lacking in knowledge and worthy argument.[101] However, logos ends up somewhat overemphasized in contemporary legal rhetoric, at times to the exclusion or rhetorical rejection of ethos and pathos. Cicero and other ancient writers remind us that ethos and pathos must work together with logos to create effective argument.

3.3.1. Ethos

Ethos, like its counter-parts pathos and logos, meant different things to different writers in antiquity.[102] Aristotle regarded ethos as "the most authoritative form of persuasion."[103] His concept of ethos refers to the sense of self created by the speaker during the speech: the speaker creates and projects their own character "in such a way as to make the speaker worthy of credence."[104] For Aristotle, this mode of persuasion "should result from the speech [itself], not from a previous opinion that the speaker is a certain kind of person."[105] This approach is quite a different position from that of Isocrates, who emphasized that "the argument which is made by a man's life is of more weight than that which is furnished by words"; to Isocrates, an "honorable reputation" adds "greater persuasiveness" to the speaker's words and "greater lustre" to the speaker's deeds.[106]

---

101. On the Ideal Orator, *supra* note 41, I.202, at 106. To Crassus, a person active in the affairs of the State but lacking knowledge of laws and politics is but a "second-rate pleader, a shouter, or a ranter." Elsewhere, Antonius says that a person of no natural ability who nonetheless pursues a career as an orator "rant[s] in defiance of appropriateness and [his own] limitations" and "collect[s] as many witnesses of his own stupidity as he can." *Id.* II.86, at 146.

102. For a thoughtful discussion of ethos in ancient writers, *see* Melissa H. Weresh, *Ethos at the Intersection: Classical Insights for Contemporary Application*, 20 Nev. L.J. 877, 880–88 (2020).

103. On Rhetoric, *supra* note 35, I.2.4, at 39.

104. On Rhetoric, *supra* note 35, I.2.4, at 38.

105. *Id.*

106. Isocrates, *Antidosis 278* (George Norlin, trans.), Perseus Digital Library, http://data.perseus.org/citations/urn:cts:greekLit:tlg0010.tlg019.perseus-eng1:278 (last visited Mar. 4, 2022); Isocrates, *Antidosis 280* (George Norlin, trans.), Perseus Digital Library, http://data.perseus.org/citations/urn:cts:greekLit:tlg0010.tlg019.perseus-eng1:280 (last visited Mar. 4, 2022).

Prof. Melissa Weresh has characterized Aristotle's position as considering ethos to be an "appearance" that is "projected" during a speech, while Isocrates considers ethos to be "the actual character of the rhetor," and therefore a "possession" of the rhetor.[107] To be sure, Aristotle's view of ethos is not instrumental or amoral. He recognizes that ethos comes from the speaker's personal qualities of "practical wisdom, virtue, and good will,"[108] but his discussion of ethos emphasizes a speaker's demonstration of these qualities to the audience in the speech itself.

Cicero draws on both Isocratean and Aristotelian approaches to ethos. Following Aristotle, Cicero's character Antonius emphasizes that orators create ethos through their speeches, advising that "speaking thoughtfully and with a certain taste,... mold[s] an image of the character of the orator."[109] However, earlier in the very same passage, Antonius also notes that "the character, the customs, the deeds, and the life" of lawyers and clients contribute to "winning a case."[110] This Isocratean approach corresponds with the Roman view that character was a fixed characteristic, important for a person active in public life.[111] Quintilian goes even further than Cicero in embracing the Isocratic ideal, emphasizing the "good man skilled in speaking."[112] For Quintilian, "eloquence and ethics are inseparable."[113]

Scholars have speculated that differences in the Greek and Roman legal system may account in part for the difference between the Romans and Aristotle on ethos.[114] In Greece, as we have seen, litigants represented themselves, perhaps with the help of a logographer. As a result, there was no lawyerly class, meaning fewer repeat players and fewer well-known advocates in the culture. Even in the assembly, ordinary citizens spoke alongside noted people. Audience members were therefore less likely to recognize particular speakers and had to rely more on the speech itself for evidence of a speaker's character. Rome, on the other hand, had a professionalized group of lawyers; Cicero himself is the prime example of an advocate who could rely on his own repu-

107. Weresh, *supra* note 102, at 880.

108. On Rhetoric, *supra* note 35, II.1.5, at 112.

109. On the Ideal Orator, *supra* note 41, II.184, at 171.

110. *Id.*

111. *See* Weresh, *supra* note 102, at 886 (citing James M. May, Trials of Character: The Eloquence of Ciceronian Ethos 6 (1988)).

112. Quintilian, *Institutes of Oratory* (John Selby Watson, trans.), *in* The Rhetorical Tradition, *supra* note 8, XII.1.1, at 355.

113. Kirsten A. Dauphinais, *Quintilian's Curriculum*, 20 Nev. L.J. 917, 929 (2020).

114. *See generally* Weresh, *supra* note 102, at 886–87 and sources cited therein.

tation in advocating on behalf of clients. Thus, a fixed concept of the speaker's character, that transcended any individual oration, figured more prominently in Roman writing.

3.3.2. Pathos

For Aristotle, pathos is about emotion. He observes that decision makers who are "rejoicing" or "friendly" render more favorable judgments than those who are "grieved" or "hostile."[115] In a long section in Book II of *On Rhetoric*, Aristotle methodically examines human emotions with the purpose of guiding speakers in understanding how to move their audiences. This famous section of the book has been called "the earliest systematic discussion of human psychology."[116] Cicero also provides a tutorial on emotions as they were understood in his day, but his character Antonius also asks an orator to consider "whether or not the case demands" an appeal to pathos, noting that "insignificant matters" do not demand "oratorical firebrands."[117]

The ancients regarded the purpose of pathos as disposing the audience to accept a speaker's position. Aristotle and Cicero frame appeals to pathos as particularly useful in judicial rhetoric. Aristotle asserts that it is "useful in lawsuits... for the audience to be disposed in a certain way [i.e. to be moved by appeals to pathos]."[118] Cicero's Antonius frames his long introduction to the concept of pathos around his own experience in advocating cases to juries.[119]

Cicero recognizes that ethos and pathos can be "hard to keep... apart"; after all, effective ethotic persuasion should have an emotional effect on the audience, a topic within the traditional realm of pathos.[120] This problem is less present for Aristotle, whose concept of ethos is narrower. For Aristotle, ethos evokes a rational, unemotional assessment of the speaker by the audience. Pathos, on the other hand, is where Aristotle places all of a rhetor's (non-ethotic) devices that create an emotional response in the audience.[121] While recognizing some overlap between these concepts, it's easiest to distinguish those features of a speech that primarily construct or project the character of the speaker from those that primarily incite emotion in the audience.

---

115. On Rhetoric, *supra* note 35, I.2.5, at 39.
116. *Id.* at 113.
117. On the Ideal Orator, *supra* note 41, II.204, at 178.
118. On Rhetoric, *supra* note 35, II.1.4, at 112.
119. On the Ideal Orator, *supra* note 41, II.185–192, at 172–73.
120. *Id.* 2.211, at 180.
121. May & Wisse, *supra* note 50, at 34–35.

In the modern world, speakers sometimes denigrate pathos. Famously, Congresswoman Barbara Jordan disclaimed pathos as she spoke during the nationally televised Nixon impeachment hearings in July 1974. "It is reason, and not passion, which must guide our deliberations, guide our debate, and guide our decision," Jordan told her colleagues and the nation.[122] As the first African-American woman from the south elected to the House of Representatives since Reconstruction, Jordan took pains to elevate logos in her consideration of the charges against Nixon. Arguably, Jordan made a wise choice in considering the situation she faced; even ancient writings recognize that passion can lead to excess. However, Jordan's speech still aimed at prompting an emotional response from her audience. Rather than stirring up anger and outrage, Jordan, in her speech, asks House members and the country to reach a somber and sad conclusion that impeachment is required.

3.3.3. Logos

For Aristotle, logos consists of "show[ing] the truth or the apparent truth from what is persuasive in each case."[123] For Aristotle, the building blocks of logical argument grow out of inductive and deductive logic. Induction permits one to "show on the basis of many similar instances that something is so," while the deductive logic as expressed in the syllogism permits one to show "that if some premises are true, something else [the conclusion] beyond them results from the[m]."[124] Law uses both induction and deduction repeatedly. Lawyers who synthesize legal rules after reading multiple cases on a particular topic make use of inductive reasoning. Similarly, lawyers who apply rules to the facts at hand reason deductively and often use express or implied syllogisms.

In Aristotelian rhetoric, the "enthymeme" is a type of rhetorical syllogism used to establish premises.[125] There is an important difference between the syllogism as used in formal logic and the enthymeme as used in rhetoric. A syllogism in formal logic produces scientific truth: if the premises are indisputably true, the conclusion will be indisputably true. The enthymeme, on the other hand, employs premises that consist of probable truth or that rely on

---

122. *My Faith in the Constitution is whole; it is complete; it is total,* UVA Miller Center (Mar. 3, 2022, 2:45 PM), https://millercenter.org/the-presidency/impeachment/my-faith-constitution-whole-it-complete-it-total.

123. On Rhetoric, *supra* note 35, 1.2.6, at 39.

124. *Id.*, 1.2.8–9, at 40.

125. *Id.*

induction or audience knowledge; thus an enthymeme's conclusion is itself a probable truth, and a matter of persuasion.

3.3.4. A modern example

Modern lawyers use ethos, pathos, and logos in a wide variety of persuasive situations. Consider *Brown v. Board of Education*, which held that "separate but equal" education policies requiring black and white children to attend separate public schools violate the right of black children to equal protection of the laws.[126] The ultimate success of *Brown* is mixed. Constitutional law and public policy subsequent to *Brown* have betrayed many of the ideals of the 1954 opinion.[127] Sheryll Cashin has observed that even today, "our schools are [still] separate, but hardly equal."[128] The 1954 opinion itself is nonetheless remarkable. In a mere eleven pages of the United States Reports, Chief Justice Earl Warren aimed for a ruling that (in his own words) would be "short, readable by the lay public, non-rhetorical, unemotional and, above all, non-accusatory."[129]

Warren's decision to disclaim emotion and even rhetoric itself points to a gap between the perception and reality of rhetoric. When driven by emotion or consisting of clever language that obfuscates, rhetoric can be perceived as leading to poor decisions. The reality is that rhetoric is everywhere: even Warren's decision to describe his words as "non-rhetorical" is a persuasive rhetorical technique that elevates the status of the rhetor, advances a logical argument, and favorably disposes the audience to the message. While the opinion is "non-rhetorical" in the sense that it avoids flourishes of language and obvious displays of emotion, Warren uses rhetorical persuasion—including appeals to emotion—masterfully.

The ethos of the decision begins with identification of who is speaking. Chief Justice Warren, recognizing the importance of the case, wanted a unan-

---

126. Brown v. Board of Educ., 347 U.S. 483, 487, 495 (1954).

127. *See* SHERYLL CASHIN, THE FAILURES OF INTEGRATION: HOW RACE AND CLASS ARE UNDERMINING THE AMERICAN DREAM 208–16 (2004); SHERYLL CASHIN, PLACE NOT RACE: A NEW VISION OF OPPORTUNITY IN AMERICA 20–22 (2014). This sad legacy stems from many sources, not least the Supreme Court's reticence in 1955 to embrace a robust remedy in the *Brown* litigation.

128. CASHIN, FAILURES OF INTEGRATION, *supra* note 127, at 208.

129. *See* Lani Guinier, *Forward: Demosprudence Through Dissent*, 122 HARV. L. REV. 4, 52 (2008) (citing Memorandum from Justice Earl Warren to his colleagues concerning his draft opinion in Brown v. Board of Education (May 7, 1954)). *See also Brown v. Board of Education*, LIBRARY OF CONGRESS: BROWN V. BOARD AT FIFTY, https://www.loc.gov/exhibits/brown/brown-brown.html#obj80 (last visited Mar. 4, 2022).

imous decision.[130] When the Court speaks with one voice, devoid of dissent or separate concurrence, its decisions tend to resonate more loudly in the public sphere. Even current Chief Justice John Roberts has publicly stated that he prefers the Court to act unanimously, believing it lends greater legitimacy and credibility to the Court's decisions.[131] Legitimacy and credibility appear to be the prime goals Warren sought for the Court in *Brown*. The Court confines most of the supporting evidence for its views to footnotes. While this decision at first appears to be one of arrangement, and therefore logos, it also has ethotic implications. The Court's voice in this case is not dense or technical; rather, the Justices of the Court worked to create a brief and powerful statement that would resonate with the American people.

Pathos in the Court's decision is a subtler matter, given Chief Justice Warren's determination to be "unemotional" and "non-rhetorical."[132] Despite this denial, the *Brown* decision attempts to elicit an emotional response from its audience. Appealing to the audience's sense of fair play, the Court declares it "doubtful that any child may reasonably be expected to succeed in life if he is denied the opportunity of an education," and points out that segregation on the basis of race "generates a feeling of inferiority [in black children]... that may affect their hearts and minds in a way unlikely ever to be undone."[133] This language resonates with the ambitions many people have for themselves and their children: to receive an education, to succeed in life, and to belong to the American community.

The logos of the opinion is both straightforward and revolutionary. Though the Court does not frame it as an enthymeme, it may be understood as such. The Court relies on the Fourteenth Amendment's Equal Protec-

---

130. Charles Ogletree, All Deliberate Speed: Reflections on the First Half Century of Brown v. Board of Education 9 (2004).

131. Jeffrey Rosen, The Supreme Court: The Personalities and Rivalries that Defined America 226 (2006).

132. For an interesting analysis of pathos in constitutional decision making, *see generally* Jamal Greene, *Pathetic Argument in Constitutional Law*, 113 Colum. L. Rev. 1389 (2013), and Colin Starger, *Constitutional Law and Rhetoric*, 18 U. Pa. J. Const. Law 1347 (2016).

133. Brown v. Board of Educ., 347 U.S. 483, 489, 493–94 (1954). Of course, Justices of the Court are capable of overt displays of emotion in their opinions. For example, Justice Blackmun opens his dissent in *DeShaney v. Winnebago County Department of Social Services* with the famous outcry, "Poor Joshua!" 489 U.S. 189, 213 (1989) (dissenting from the Court's holding that a state's failure to protect a victim of severe child abuse did not violate that victim's due process rights).

tion Clause as its major premise. However, the Fourteenth Amendment had never been interpreted to require the integration of public schools. Thus, to establish its major premise, the Court rejected evidence of the original meaning of the Amendment. It called that evidence "inconclusive" because the system of public education was less developed and had a less prominent role in American life when the Amendment was written and ratified.[134] The Court also rejected its own prior holding in *Plessy v. Ferguson*[135] in favor of separate-but-equal facilities in transportation.[136] The Court argues in clear language, based on social science research, that segregated educational facilities—even where they are equal between racial groups—have a detrimental effect on minority children.[137] Thus, the enthymeme implicit in the opinion emerges: the major premise, newly-minted by the Court, requires equal treatment of students in public schools. This premise is supported by the broad language of the Fourteenth Amendment, by largely non-legal evidence and logic, and by ethos, pathos, and absolutely stunning kairos.[138] The minor premise observes that "separate educational facilities are inherently unequal,"[139] and the conclusion inexorably follows: "the doctrine of 'separate but equal' has no place" in public education.[140]

In sum, study of ethos, logos, and pathos in *Brown v. Board of Education* shows that the three appeals work together to create a powerful text that sets forth a new dimension of meaning to the Fourteenth Amendment's equality principle.

---

134. *Brown*, 347 U.S. at 489, 493.

135. Plessy v. Ferguson,163 U.S. 537 (1896).

136. *Brown*, 347 U.S. at 488.

137. *Id.* at 494. This portion of the opinion has been much re-examined over the years. The progress of research after the decision called into question some of the specific psychological studies on which the Court relied. *See generally* John P. Jackson, Jr., *The triumph of the segregationists? A historiographical inquiry into psychology and the Brown litigation*, 3 Hist. Psych. 239–261 (2000). However, educational theorists and others have vindicated the Court's ultimate position by documenting the harms of segregated schooling. *See generally* Sabrina Zirkel & Nancy Cantor, *50 Years After Brown v. Board of Education: The Promise and Challenge of Multicultural Education*, 60 J. Soc. Issues 1–15 (2004).

138. I am grateful to Prof. Linda Berger for this observation.

139. *Brown*, 347 U.S. at 495.

140. *Id.* at 495. The Court does not speak of major or minor premises, but its logic can be understood in these terms. *Cf.* On Rhetoric, *supra* note 35, II.22.3, at 169 (noting that the enthymeme can omit or imply various propositions).

3.4. The structure of ancient oration and the writing of modern lawyers

The basic pattern of the ancient oration is a form that is quite recognizable to modern lawyers. Aristotle claims that only two parts of the oration are essential: a statement (prothesis) and its proof (pisteis).[141] He recognizes other parts, such as an introduction, conclusion, narration of facts, and the like, but suggests that they are not universally required in rhetoric. Even in judicial rhetoric, a conclusion may not be necessary, says Aristotle, "if the speech is short, or if the subject is easily remembered."[142]

Early Greek writers on rhetoric prescribed an introduction, a narration of facts, a statement of position and proof, and an epilogue.[143] Aristotle says that these four parts "at the most" are required.[144] He recognizes the importance of counterarguments, but regards them as part of the proof.[145] This ancient form of persuasion was present in the culture before writers on rhetoric described it. Consider Odysseus' famous speech to Achilles in Book IX of the *Iliad*, in which Odysseus attempts to persuade the offended Achilles to return to battle, lest the Trojans destroy Greek ships.[146] After an introduction, Odysseus narrates the desperate situation of the Greeks, then launches into reasons designed to convince Achilles to fight, culminating in a conclusion designed to elicit pathos on the part of Achilles.

Roman oratory in the judicial forum was more important, and Roman writers addressed the form and structure of judicial rhetoric more extensively. Cicero describes the parts of a speech as follows:

- Introduction (exordium)
- Statement of facts (narratio)
- Statement of position (partitio—a dividing of the matter into issues to be proved)

---

141. On Rhetoric, *supra* note 35, III.13.1, at 230.

142. *Id.*, III.13.3, at 230.

143. On Rhetoric, *supra* note 35, at 229, 296.

144. *Id.* III.13.4, at 230–31.

145. *Id.*

146. Homer, *Iliad IX*. 225–306 (A.T. Murray, trans.), Perseus Digital Library, http://data.perseus.org/citations/urn:cts:greekLit:tlg0012.tlg001.perseus-eng1:9.205-9.243 (last visited August 16, 2021); see also Kennedy, *supra* note 8, at 8–9 for a structural analysis of Odysseus' speech.

- Proof/support (confirmatio)
- Answer to Counterarguments (refutatio)
- Conclusion (conclusio).[147]

Within this frame, Cicero and other ancient writers urge flexibility. The unknown author of the *Rhetorica ad Herennium* asserts that the parts of an oration can be "accommodated to circumstance in accordance with the speaker's judgment" when the speaker's "cause demands" such variation.[148]

Both the author of the *Rhetorica ad Herennium* and Cicero advise readers about the order in which a speaker should place arguments in the "proof" section of a speech. The *Rhetorica ad Herennium* urges that strongest arguments should come at the beginning and end of the proof and refutation, while weaker arguments should be placed in the middle.[149] In *De oratore*, Cicero's Antonius echoes this advice, telling his audience that strong points be placed at the beginning so that "the audience's expectations should be met as quickly as possible," while "some... excellent resources should also be reserved for the end."[150] Faulty arguments should be omitted entirely, while "points of moderate strength... should be thrown into the common crowd in the middle."[151]

In modern approaches to legal writing, the basic format of the ancients—introduction, statement of facts, argument, answer to counterargument, and conclusion—describes many traditional forms of legal communication.[152] Briefs to the Supreme Court of the United States are governed by the Supreme Court Rules.[153] Rule 24 prescribes the following sections among others for briefs on the merits of cases:

---

147. Cicero, *De Inventione* (H. M. Hubbell, trans.), *in* The Rhetorical Tradition, *supra* note 8, at I.19, at 258, and On the Ideal Orator, *supra* note 35, I.143, at 89–90 (for a fuller treatment of the various parts of a speech, see *id.* II.307–349, at 208–18). *See also* Kennedy, *supra* note 8, at 103–06.

148. Rhetorica ad Herennium III.9, at 185–87 (Harry Caplan, trans., Harvard Univ. Press 1954). *See also* Kennedy, *supra* note 8, at 108–09; The Rhetorical Tradition, *supra* note 8, at 241 (describing authorship debate). For Cicero's take on flexibility, *see* On the Ideal Orator, *supra* note 41, II.307–308, at 208.

149. Rhetorica ad Herennium, *supra* note 148, X.18, at 189; *see also*, Kennedy, *supra* note 8, at 109.

150. On the Ideal Orator, *supra* note 41, II.314, at 209.

151. On the Ideal Orator, *supra* note 41, II.314, at 209.

152. Kristen Konrad Tiscione, Legal Writing: From Advice to Advocacy 41 (2021).

153. *See Rules and Guidance*, Supreme Court of the United States, https://www.supremecourt.gov/filingandrules/rules_guidance.aspx (last visited Mar. 4, 2022).

- the question presented for review
- a list of all parties
- a table of contents and a table of cited authorities
- a concise statement of material facts
- a summary of the argument
- the argument and
- a conclusion.[154]

This structure resembles Cicero's parts of a speech: an introduction, a fact statement, a legal argument, and a conclusion.

Memos, emails, and briefs of many varieties follow this same pattern, at least superficially. Moreover, the legal analysis or argument itself often begins with a Ciceronian partitio—a roadmap or umbrella paragraph stating the various propositions the document needs to establish in order to prove its point.[155] Many other forms of legal communication, such as the email, the demand letter, and even contracts of various sorts, follow the general introduction-facts-legal analysis or argument-conclusion model.

Moreover, the flexibility urged by ancient rhetoricians can also be found in modern times. Organization in modern legal writing is not a formalist matter of filling in required sections. Instead, lawyers adapt the conventional forms and at times depart from expectations to present arguments in a way best suited to the case. In *Endrew F. v. Douglas County School District RE 1*, the Supreme Court decided how to apply the "free, appropriate, public education" (FAPE) requirement of the Individuals with Disabilities Education Act (IDEA).[156] In the 1982 *Rowley* case, the Supreme Court had held that the FAPE requirement was satisfied by an educational program that provided "some educational benefits" to children with disabilities.[157] In Endrew F.'s case, the local school district argued (and the Tenth Circuit held) that *Rowley* was satisfied by education that provided "merely . . . more than de minimis" benefits.[158] The petitioner-plaintiff

154. Sup. Ct. R. 24.

155. On this point, *see* Tiscione, *supra* note 152, at 263 (memos), and 356 (briefs).

156. Endrew F. v. Douglas Cnty. Sch. Dist. RE 1, 137 S. Ct. 988, 993 (2017) (considering a challenge under the Individuals with Disabilities Education Act, 20 U.S.C. §§ 1400–1482). The free, appropriate, public education requirement is found at 20 U.S.C. § 1412(a)(1).

157. Board of Educ. v. Rowley, 458 U.S. 176, 200 (1982) (Rehnquist, J.)

158. Brief for Respondent at 10, *Endrew F.*, 137 S. Ct. 988 (No. 15-827) (local school district's position); Endrew F. v. Douglas Cnty. Sch. Dist. RE 1, 798 F.3d 1329, 1338 (10th Cir. 2015) (Tenth Circuit holding).

Endrew F. argued that FAPE required that he should be provided "substantially equal opportunities to achieve academic success, attain self-sufficiency, and contribute to society."[159]

Beginning with their statements of facts, the parties' briefs use organization to present two very different versions of the case to the Court. Both parties depart from the conventional function of a statement of facts by including extended treatment of the complicated statutory context. The petitioner Endrew F.'s brief includes a twelve-page section titled "Statement of the Case," which spends nearly equal space on "Legal background," summarizing IDEA and its varied requirements, and on "Factual and procedural background," summarizing Endrew F.'s situation.[160] The respondent school district's brief, on the other hand, contains a just-over-seven-page section merely titled "Statement," which includes five pages of "Statutory Background" and two and one-half pages of "Procedural History."[161] The respondent includes no facts relating Endrew F.'s situation beyond what is necessary for its brief procedural history. The respondent is clear throughout its brief that it is less concerned with the specific facts of Endrew F.'s claim and more concerned about the burden a heightened standard would impose on every state and school district in the country.[162] While Endrew F. focuses on the injustice of his particular situation, the school district dispenses with the facts of his claim almost entirely in order to maintain focus on systemic concerns.

Organizational differences similarly pervade the Argument sections of the two briefs. Endrew F's brief focuses on the text, purpose, and structure of IDEA and sidelines the Supreme Court's 1982 decision in *Rowley.*[163] The School District's argument section, on the other hand, begins with the following brief paragraph:

159. Brief for Petitioner at 14, *Endrew F.,* 137 S. Ct. 988 (No.15-827). The federal government as amicus curiae argued that FAPE required that children with disabilities have the opportunity to make "significant educational progress." Brief for the United States as Amicus Curiae in Support of Petitioner at 9.

160. Brief for Petitioner at 2–13, *Endrew F.,* 137 S. Ct. 988 (No. 15-827).

161. Brief for Respondent at 3–10, *Endrew F.*, 137 S. Ct. 988 (No. 15-827).

162. *Id.* at 2 ("The Court cannot surprise participating States by superimposing on this scheme a substantive condition of which they had no notice.").

163. *See* Brief for Petitioner at ii-iii (Table of Contents), *Endrew F.*, 137 S. Ct. 988 (No.15-827); Board of Educ. v. Rowley, 458 U.S. 176, 200 (1982) (Rehnquist, J.).

> Petitioner asks this Court to decide what "level of educational benefit" an IEP must aim to provide to satisfy the IDEA's FAPE requirement.... The Court answered that question 34 years ago in *Rowley.*[164]

The brief then spends twelve pages explicating *Rowley*, arguing that *Rowley*'s holding governs Endrew F.'s case, that any other standard would be inconsistent with *Rowley*, and that stare decisis requires adherence to *Rowley*.[165] The brief moves consideration of the statute itself into a secondary position in its argument, as it is focused mainly on urging the Court not to revisit the standard articulated in *Rowley*.[166]

In its decision in the case, a unanimous Supreme Court, per Chief Justice Roberts, positioned itself as giving neither party what it was looking for.[167] Instead, it requires school districts to provide students with disabilities with an education that is "reasonably calculated to enable [that] child to make progress appropriate in light of [that] child's circumstances."[168] The Court charted a middle course through the arguments of the parties by rooting its approach in the statute and in *Rowley*. In doing so, the Court purported to articulate a standard that will serve the "wide spectrum" of children with disabilities who fall within the statute.[169] Whether it has succeeded must be the subject of empirical study of educational outcomes under the statute.

In this case, organization may well have been a deciding factor. The school district minimized the facts of the particular case and rooted its argument in *Rowley*. This approach did not succeed. Endrew F.'s approach, based on the broad language of the statute without attending to the lengthy history of judicial interpretation and experience with the statute, also did not succeed. The Court merged both organizational schemas to craft an updated standard that respects the statute and precedent.

---

164. Brief for Respondent at 13, *Endrew F.*, 137 S. Ct. 988 (No. 15-827).

165. *Id.* at 13–25.

166. Brief for Respondents at 25–51, *Endrew F.*, 137 S. Ct. 988 (No.15-827).

167. *Endrew F.,* 137 S. Ct. at 998 ("We cannot accept the school district's reading of *Rowley*."), 1001 (declining to adopt the petitioner and government's standards because they are "plainly at odds" with *Rowley*, noting that Congress has not changed the statutory requirements despite amending the statute twice since *Rowley* was decided).

168. *Id.* at 999.

169. *Id.*

3.5. The ancient canons, the activities of an orator, and the modern writing process

In describing rhetoric, ancient writers distinguished various of its aspects as separate "canons." The five canons of classical rhetoric were:

- Invention,
- Arrangement,
- Style,
- Memory, and
- Delivery.

Like most of classical rhetoric's precepts, these concepts originate in Aristotle.[170] Aristotle's *On Rhetoric* does not discuss the canons per se, but Books I and II provide an exhaustive taxonomy of methods of persuasion (pisteis). In that sense, they are a study of invention. Book III begins with a brief discussion of delivery, then proceeds to examine style and arrangement. For Aristotle, invention involved devising arguments, and arrangement dealt with organizing them into the parts of the speech outlined in Section 3.4, above. Aristotle does not treat memory in *On Rhetoric.*

Over the centuries of the classical period, rhetoricians' understandings of these categories varied. The relationship between invention and arrangement, as any experienced writer recognizes, is particularly complex. The meanings of these terms expanded and contracted in the work of various writers. Some later ancient writers abandoned Aristotle's systematic approach to persuasion and instead viewed invention as a process of creating the structural parts of a speech.[171] This approach leaves the category of arrangement fairly empty, and these authors venture only a few remarks about the best way to order arguments when they discuss arrangement.[172]

---

170. May & Wisse, *supra* note 50, at 29–30. The ideas in this section derive from Sections 7.2 and 7.3 of May & Wisse's excellent introductory essay to their translation of Cicero's *On the Ideal Orator*; *see id.* at 32–38. There is also a useful outline of Aristotle's *On Rhetoric* that relates to the canons found in George Kennedy's introduction to his translation. *See* Kennedy, *Introduction*, *supra* note 56, at 24–25.

171. May & Wisse, *supra* note 50, at 31.

172. *Id.*; *see* discussion *supra* Section 3.4, for what Cicero and the *Rhetorica ad Herennium* have to say about organization of strong, medium, and weak arguments.

In *De oratore*, Cicero returns to the Aristotelian model, presenting a fully developed system of invention which encompasses persuasion based on ethos, pathos, and logos, along with many ideas about how to develop argument. Much of Cicero's contribution in this area is directed toward judicial rhetoric. He rejects the standard approach of his day, which was to produce lists of preformulated arguments called "commonplaces" or "topics," as too rigid.[173] Instead, again modeling, adapting, and developing Aristotelian ideas, Cicero presents "abstract argument patterns," which comprise stasis theory.[174] Stasis theory taxonomizes legal issues of the day, describing many disputes in ways that modern lawyers will recognize: disputes of fact and law, matters of how law applies to fact, questions of procedure.[175] In that sense, Cicero prefigures lawyers whose arguments fall into recognizable patterns, for example, those based on the credibility of a witness, or on the logic and common sense of a jury, or on the proper interpretation of a legal text. Beyond that, Cicero's mature "view of the process of composition centers not on rules, but on the personal skills and activities of the orator."[176] In that sense, Cicero was an early explainer of the writing process—a systematic approach of flexible yet articulated stages through which a creator passes in putting together a speech.

Taken as a whole, the ancient canons did not describe a coherent writing process, but rather gave people a way to talk about different aspects of the creation and delivery of a speech. Modern attempts to describe the writing process lead to great variety. Lawyers and composition theorists have articulated the writing process in different ways. A classical formulation, adapted to legal writing by Professors Mary Ray and Jill Ramsfield, consists of prewriting, writing, rewriting, revising, and polishing.[177] The legal writing process has also been described as a mostly-research stage, a mostly-writing stage, and a mostly-revision stage.[178] In any event, the stages for most modern writers are recursive: one may be revising a document only to discover that further

173. *Id.* at 34.

174. *Id.*

175. For a description of stasis theory in chart form, *see id.* at 33; *see also* The Rhetoric of Western Thought, supra note 7, at 86–87. *See also* Susan E. Provenzano & Brian N. Larsen, *Civil Procedure as a Critical Discussion*, 20 Nev. L.J. 967, 986–1004 (2020).

176. May & Wisse, *supra* note 50 at 10 (Introduction).

177. *See* Mary Barnard Ray & Jill J. Ramsfield, Legal Writing: Getting It Right and Getting It Written 614–15 (6th ed. 2018).

178. Elizabeth Fajans & Mary R. Falk, Scholarly Writing for Law Students: Seminar Papers, Law Review Notes and Law Review Competition Papers 52 (4th ed., 2017).

research is needed to shore up an argument that appears weak on rereading. The modern world's focus on the written word leads to less attention given to memory and delivery, but invention, arrangement, and style remain central concerns in the writing process as writers plan, craft and revise their texts. Ancient insights in these areas can contribute much to our understanding of the process.

4. Conclusion

As the western world passed from the classical period to the early Christian era, the central occasions for rhetoric shifted. The role of rhetoric as a tool of government and a means for the citizen to participate in democracy gave way to the need for the Church to teach scripture and the truths of faith. Thus, the sophistic and Aristotelian commitments to contingent truth, so foundational to the legal system, gave way to rhetoric concerned with conveying doctrine and teaching faith with clarity. Thus, it is appropriate to end our consideration of the legal foundations of rhetorical history at the close of the classical era, and to next turn our attention to modern lawyers and their development of modern rhetorical tools.

Summing It Up

- Many modern rhetorical theories and techniques have their roots in the ancient world.
- Ancient rhetoric developed in the context of ancient culture. As literacy spread in the ancient world, citizens were expected to use words in judicial, political, and ceremonial settings. These contexts produced different species of rhetoric: forensic or judicial, deliberative, and epideictic.
- The ancient world differed widely from the modern world. The ancients' understandings of citizenship, inclusion, and equality differed from our own. While we practice rhetoric in a different social and cultural context, there is much to be gained from examining the continuing legacy and vitality of ancient rhetoric.
- Ancient judicial rhetoric advanced a probabilistic approach to truth: in situations where absolute truth was not ascertainable, rhetoric

sought to convince the hearer that a situation was most likely to be true. This probabilistic conception of truth is a foundation on which the modern legal system is built.

- Aristotle defined rhetoric as "an ability, in each particular case, to see the available means of persuasion." He urged speakers to learn to argue both sides of a question and believed that rhetoric itself was a neutral tool that could be used for constructive or harmful ends.
- Rhetoric occurs in chronological time (chronos) and also includes the concept of delivering a message at its opportune moment (kairos).
- Aristotle divides various means of persuasion into two categories: inartistic and artistic. Inartistic proofs are those not created by the speaker, but merely used. Artistic proofs are those created by the speaker.
- Artistic proofs are the product of three different appeals: ethos, pathos, and logos. Ethos concerns the character or trustworthiness of the speaker; pathos concerns the emotional response of the audience, and logos concerns the logic of the speech.
- Ancient orations were often structured to include an Introduction, Statement of Facts, Statement of Position, Proof, Answer to Counterarguments, and Conclusion. This classic formulation is derived from the work of Cicero, but many ancient writers advised similar patterns.
- The five canons of classical rhetoric were: Invention, Arrangement, Style, Memory, and Delivery.

Suggestions for Further Reading

Primary Sources

ARISTOTLE, ON RHETORIC (George Kennedy, trans., Oxford University Press 2d ed. 2007).

CICERO, ON THE IDEAL ORATOR (James M. May & Jakob Wisse, trans., Oxford University Press, 2001).

QUINTILIAN, *Institutio Oratoria*, PERSEUS DIGITAL LIBRARY (Harold Edgeworth Butler, trans.), http://www.perseus.tufts.edu/hopper/text?doc=Perseus%3Atext%3A2007.01.0060%3Abook%3D1.

RHETORICA AD HERENNIUM (Harry Caplan, trans., Harvard Univ. Press 1954).

Secondary Sources

NICHOLAS BARRY, AN INTRODUCTION TO ROMAN LAW (2008).

MARY BEARD, SPQR: A HISTORY OF ANCIENT ROME (2015).

Victor Bers & Adriaan Lanni, *An Introduction to the Athenian Legal System*, DĒMOS: CLASSICAL ATHENIAN DEMOCRACY, https://www.stoa.org/demos/intro_legal_system.pdf.

Classical Rhetoric as a Lens for Contemporary Legal Praxis, NEVADA LAW JOURNAL, Vol. 20, Issue 3 (2020).

CHERYL GLENN, RHETORIC RETOLD: REGENDERING THE TRADITION FROM ANTIQUITY THROUGH THE RENAISSANCE (1997).

GEORGE A. KENNEDY, CLASSICAL RHETORIC AND ITS CHRISTIAN AND SECULAR TRADITION FROM ANCIENT TO MODERN TIMES (2d ed. 1999).

THE RHETORIC OF WESTERN THOUGHT (James L. Golden et al., eds., 10th ed. 2011).

THE RHETORICAL TRADITION: READINGS FROM CLASSICAL TIMES TO THE PRESENT (Patricia Bizzell et al., eds., 3d ed. 2020).

PART TWO

PART TWO

Introduction

Modern Rhetorical Theories & the Practice of Law

DELIA B. CONTI

A distinction between the classical origins of law and rhetoric and the contribution of modern theories of rhetoric to the practice of the law is both a practical division and a theoretical construct. While classical rhetorical theories permeate all of persuasion and the practice of the law, modern rhetorical theories most aptly illuminate specific practices in the law. This section will continue to apply rhetorical theories to legal concepts and specific cases, in doing so highlighting the impact of persuasive ideologies.

Chapter 3, featuring the rhetorical theories of Stephen Toulmin, Chaim Perelman, and Richard Weaver, is most closely associated with what we traditionally think of as argumentation, reasoning, and the principles underlying critical thinking. Issue identification is fundamental to legal argument and case law. An understanding of analogy is critical in assessing precedents. Issues of interpretation are preeminent in examining conflict of laws. When we talk about conditions in the law, about precedents, about intricate distinctions between specific cases, we are talking about the rhetorical principles in this chapter.

Chapter 4 focuses on narrative theory. We persuade each other through the telling of stories. Humans are storytellers. The theory of the case is premised on building a coherent narrative structure, and thus the paradox. Courtroom rules are premised on minimizing the ability to weave a lengthy story. The effectiveness of storytelling is minimized through the dismissal of the appeal to emotions and the artificial separation between reason and emotions. Kenneth Burke, often called the preeminent rhetorical theorist of the twentieth century, writes about the importance of narrative form and the potency of the hierarchical nature of language. Jerome Bruner considers the connection between logic and narrative. Walter Fisher discusses what makes stories powerful: narrative probability and narrative fidelity. It is plausibility and coherence that make arguments persuasive, building narratives out of individual facts. The chapter includes examples of storytelling to illustrate these modern rhetorical theories. All examples show skilled legal storytellers at work. It is the nature of humans as storytellers that reveals the overarching pull to create a theory of the case and to build a compelling story in favor of the client. Understanding the theories of dramatism and narrative illuminate not just how to be an effective trial lawyer, but most critically what compels humans to come together to build a common foundation for society.

Chapter 5 discusses metaphor and analogy in the law, and especially their role in providing persuasive frames for legal problems and issues. Metaphor and analogy rely on our capacity to see one thing as another. This capacity to make mental connections, finding similarities across differences, is central to our everyday thinking and decision making. By providing meaningful frames for legal questions, metaphor and analogy help the reader make the leap between the current legal problem and an image or example that leads to a favorable result for an advocate's client. Once the initial mental connection has been made, the reader or listener may be unconsciously persuaded that other consequences will naturally follow. The chapter traces the development of rhetorical theory on metaphor through Aristotle, I.A. Richards, Max Black, and Michael Osborn; describes the cognitive metaphor theory studied and popularized by George Lakoff, Mark Johnson, and Raymond Gibbs; and explains the cognitive research on analogy and metaphor conducted by Dedre Gentner and her colleagues. The chapter then illustrates how metaphor and analogy (1) contributed directly to First Amendment doctrine by providing essential images and examples and (2) indirectly influenced First Amendment jurisprudence through accompanying scripts that provided settings and roles for the various participants while also carrying over emotions, values, attitudes, and beliefs that influenced legal decisionmakers and the public.

Chapter 6 moves from our focus on cases and trials to the individuated nature of the law—to what comes before the hallowed ground of the courtroom trial. The Rhetorical Situation, premised on the work of Lloyd Bitzer, and Rhetorical Sensitivity, premised on the work of Rod Hart and Don Burks, emphasize the roles we possess. These roles affect our personal and our professional lives. Focusing on the law, they encourage us to think before we speak, to understand the roles we possess as lawyers and the roles our clients inhabit. Our professional personas can be daunting as we learn and as we practice the profession. It would serve us well to remember the initial reverence we held as we learned the structure of the law, and it is even more critical to remember that our clients are confronted with a web of unfamiliar and often frightening situations. We should also remember the initial impetus for a legal case. The rhetorical situation posits an exigence, or issue, that can be resolved through talk. How we identify and define this issue is critical to its resolution. In short, in the entire practice of law we must critically examine the roles we have and that we present to the client, to opposing counsel, to the jury, and to the judge.

This section of the primer examines the rhetorical foundations of the law that underscore the importance of character, of community, of form, of structure and of narrative to the larger questions of justice beyond individual cases and specific statutes. An understanding of the fields of law and of rhetoric, including metaphor, narrative, ethics, and interpersonal communication, is essential to building a successful case, one premised on the fundamentals of language usage and theory.

Chapter Three

Argumentation

MELISSA LOVE KOENIG

---

1. Introduction

Why do lawyers argue? Argument is central to the craft of lawyering.[1] We argue because, as lawyers, our role is to advise our clients and to protect and advance their interests—and argument helps us achieve those objectives. When we argue, we consider and acknowledge the dispute at the center of a case, as well as our role in advocating for our clients.

Justice Oliver Wendell Holmes Jr. expressed the importance of argument to the practice of law as a profession:

> When we study law we are not studying a mystery but a well-known profession. We are studying what we shall want in order to appear before judges, or to advise people in such a way as to keep them out of court. The reason why it is a profession, why people will pay lawyers to argue for them or to advise them, is that in societies like ours the command of the public force is intrusted to the judges in certain cases, and the whole power of the state will be put forth, if necessary, to carry out their judgments and decrees.[2]

As the "public force," as Justice Holmes described our legal system, bears down on our clients, the sword and shield of our arguments must protect and empower our clients in that arena. Our arguments on behalf of our clients, when they are most vulnerable and in need of representation, are what elevate our work to a profession. Our arguments are the path through which we zealously advocate for our clients.[3]

Arguments breathe life into the law, and so argumentation—the process of creating and delivering an argument—is inextricably intertwined with the practice of law itself. James Boyd White, a professor of law and English, a literary critic, and a rhetoric scholar, has long recognized the connection between language-as-argument and the law: when he was in law school, he "saw the law as a wonderful system in which power worked through conversation, through open argument and persuasion";[4] later, when he practiced law, White saw the law as "an activity of mind and language: a kind of trans-

---

1. *See* Brett G. Scharffs, *Law as Craft*, 54 Vand. L. Rev. 2245, 2276 (2001).

2. Oliver Wendell Holmes Jr., *The Path of the Law*, 10 Harv. L. Rev. 457, 457 (1897), *reprinted in The Path of the Law After 100 Years*, 110 Harv. L. Rev. 989, 991 (1997).

3. *See* Model Rules of Prof'l Conduct pmbl. (Am. Bar Ass'n 2018).

4. James Boyd White, *An Old-Fashioned View of the Nature of Law*, 12 Theoretical Inquiries L. 381, 385 (2011).

lation, a way of claiming meaning for experience and making that meaning real."[5] Law, he therefore concluded, "is not a system of rules, . . . but a structure of thought and expression built upon a set of inherently unstable, dynamic, and dialogic tensions."[6]

How to define the dialogic tensions inherent in the law has been a source of differing views—views that shape approaches to argumentation.[7] Reason and experience are two of the varying traditional perspectives. One way of looking at law is as a form of reasoning, according to Sir Edward Coke, who was an English lawyer and judge: "Reason is the life of the law; nay, the common law itself is nothing but reason."[8] A focus on reason as the life of the law reflects the importance of legal logic, according to Justice William J. Brennan Jr.[9] Legal logic is important because, as Judge Ruggero Aldisert remarked, law "must embody reason" to gain respect and acceptance by a legal audience.[10] Another approach to the law is experience, as famously asserted by Justice Holmes:

> The life of the law [is] not . . . logic; it [is] experience. The felt necessities of the time, the prevalent moral and political theories, institutions of public policy, avowed or unconscious, . . . have had a good deal more to do than the syllogism in determining the rules by which men should be governed.[11]

Whether viewed as grounded in reason or experience, legal argumentation is practical argumentation.[12] Contemporary rhetorical theory reflects Aristotle's teaching that arguments about human disputes—in contrast to formal logic and mathematics—are informal and establish "probable or reasonable" outcomes, as opposed to certain results or "absolute truths."[13]

---

5. *Id.* at 386.

6. *Id.*

7. Wilson Huhn, *The Use and Limits of Syllogistic Reasoning in Briefing Cases*, 42 SANTA CLARA L. REV. 813, 815–17 (2002).

8. *Id.* at 815 n.7 (quoting SIR EDWARD COKE, COMMENTARY UPON LITTLETON 97b (Charles Butler ed., Legal Classics Library 18th ed. 1985) (1628)).

9. William J. Brennan Jr., *Foreword* to RUGGERO J. ALDISERT, LOGIC FOR LAWYERS: A GUIDE TO CLEAR LEGAL THINKING, at xix, xix (3d ed. 1997) (recognizing, at the same time, the importance of Justice Holmes's view of the law as experience).

10. *Id.* (quoting Judge Aldisert).

11. Huhn, *supra* note 7, at 816, 816 n.11 (quoting Justice Holmes).

12. Kurt M. Saunders, *Law as Rhetoric, Rhetoric as Argument*, 44 J. LEGAL EDUC. 566, 567 (1994).

13. *Id.* (also referring to the work of Chaïm Perelman and Stephen Toulmin for their studies of legal reasoning as examples of practical argumentation).

Argument can be defined as "a set of conceptual lenses persons use to examine rhetorical events."[14] When we think of lenses as a metaphor for argument, we can see that we need a way to build those lenses and focus them to respond to the underlying conflict; these lenses act as perspective in rhetoric.[15] Applying this metaphor to legal arguments, an advocate presents a client's perspective to a court in the form of persuasive legal reasoning that is organized and delivered in writing or via oral argument. Notice, too, that we are talking about multiple lenses because a legal argument is a multifaceted construct supported by multiple legal points.[16] In fact, an argument has also been described as a strong cable "that weaves together the different types of legal argument," instead of as a linear, breakable chain.[17]

Authors Sonja K. Foss, Karen A. Foss, and Robert Trapp asserted that "rhetoric . . . is characterized by the uniquely human ability to use symbols to communicate with one another."[18] Therefore, a rhetorical event is a space where humans communicate. In the law, that rhetorical event often centers on a dispute between parties. Going back to the definition of an argument, then, an argument is a set of conceptual lenses through which an advocate communicates with an intent to persuade in the course of a dispute. Others present in the rhetorical event—such as opposing counsel and judges—also provide arguments in support of their positions or rulings.

And, as White noted, within the conflict of a legal dispute is a cooperation of sorts between both sides—an agreement between parties about an argument's materials and procedure.[19] The practice of law, in resolving disputes through argument, is thus a practice in the "art of rhetoric" because law is "an art of language and judgment, an art of the maintenance and repair of human culture and community."[20] Lawyers can argue about the law because legal principles

---

14. Sonja K. Foss, Karen A. Foss & Robert Trapp, Contemporary Perspectives on Rhetoric 252 (1985) (citing Wayne Brockriede, *Where Is Argument*, 11 J. Am. Forensic Ass'n 179, 179–82 (1975)). Foss, Foss, and Trapp characterized rhetoric starting in the twentieth century as contemporary; accordingly, this chapter uses the term *contemporary* when referring to the rhetorical theories of Perelman, Toulmin, and Richard M. Weaver. *Id.* at 10.

15. *See id.* at 13.

16. Wilson Huhn, The Five Types of Legal Argument 85 (2002).

17. *Id.* (discussing the cable metaphor in William N. Eskridge Jr. & Philip P. Frickey, *Statutory Interpretation as Practical Reasoning*, 42 Stan. L. Rev. 331, 351 n.2 (1990)).

18. Foss, Foss & Trapp, *supra* note 14, at 13; *see also* Julie A. Oseid, *infra* chapter 4.

19. White, *supra* note 4, at 391.

20. James Boyd White, Keep Law Alive 102 (2019).

are malleable and language is imperfect in its ability to reflect legal relationships.[21] Therefore, the central job of lawyers is to make arguments about the meaning of the language that governs the most significant relationships among individuals, organizations, and governments within our society.[22]

What becomes evident from these definitions is that argumentation is a complicated, multifaceted human endeavor—but one critical to the practice of law for the successful advocacy of clients. As such, argumentation as a means of persuasion is worthy of study. Much has been written about how to compose and evaluate legal arguments. This chapter examines, and illustrates, methods of developing and organizing legal arguments through the lens of contemporary rhetorical theory.[23]

This chapter begins by briefly discussing how classical rhetoric informs concepts central to a contemporary view of legal argumentation. The chapter next moves into the crux of the discussion: contemporary rhetoric and legal argumentation. To examine how arguments are constructed to be persuasive, this chapter explores the themes that emerge in the written work of three contemporary rhetoricians who thought carefully about the complexities of human argumentation: Chaïm Perelman, Stephen Toulmin, and Richard M. Weaver. Their work, which broadly focuses on how to create and present an argument, goes a long way toward resolving the tensions inherent in the varying perspectives of argumentation, such as appeals to reason and experience, with which students of the law have wrestled for centuries. Finally, this chapter highlights the application of these contemporary rhetorical theories of argumentation by examining Ruth Bader Ginsburg's writings—first as an advocate before the U.S. Supreme Court and then as a justice on the Court—to demonstrate her effective use of the powerful rhetorical principles set out by Perelman, Toulmin, and Weaver.

---

21. *See* Melissa H. Weresh, *Stargate: Malleability as a Threshold Concept in Legal Education*, 63 J. Legal Educ. 689, 719 (2014).

22. *See* Melissa H. Weresh, Kristen K. Tiscione, Kirsten K. Davis, Threshold Concepts in Legal Writing (Ruth Anne Robbins, Linda L. Berger, David Thomson, contributing eds.) (forthcoming 2023).

23. *See* Foss, Foss & Trapp, *supra* note 14, at 9 (quoting preacher and rhetorician Richard Whately for his view that the finding and arrangement of an argument are the proper focus of rhetoric). Many authors have written about the process of writing and evaluating legal arguments; this chapter focuses on contemporary rhetorical theory and research to enrich the reader's understanding of the developmental process and organization of legal argumentation.

The review of Perelman, Toulmin, and Weaver and the analysis of their methods make clear that argumentation is both direct and fluid. Rhetorical principles of argumentation are flexible and yet guide an advocate to focus on the most important and essential methods to create a powerful argument. As a lawyer, you will be able to implement these principles and use them to hone your advocacy for your clients.

2. Classical rhetoric and legal argumentation

[A] society cannot live without rhetoric.

—Richard M. Weaver[24]

The focus of this book is on contemporary rhetoric, but it is worth considering the backdrop of classical rhetorical tradition as it pertains to legal argumentation[25] because contemporary rhetorical theories of argumentation rest, in part, on the foundations laid by classical rhetoric.[26] For this task, we must explore Aristotle, the ancient Greek philosopher, discussed in chapter 2, who first categorized a process of rhetoric in *Rhetoric*.[27] According to Aristotle, an advocate must "invent" (or find or create) arguments and "arrange" (or organize) them.[28] In addition to invention and arrangement, Aristotle identified style and delivery as part of composing a speech;[29] these four processes plus memory developed into five canons of rhetoric by the time of the Romans.[30] The canons of rhetoric survive today in law school classrooms because they are timeless methods of persuasion. In chapter 2, Michael Cedrone explained that the relationship between invention and arrangement is complex, and that these

24. Richard M. Weaver, *The Cultural Role of Rhetoric*, *in* Language Is Sermonic 161, 174 (Richard L. Johannesen, Rennard Strickland & Ralph T. Eubanks eds., 1970).

25. Michael H. Frost, Introduction to Classical Rhetoric: A Lost Heritage 23 (2005).

26. Foss, Foss & Trapp, *supra* note 14, at 10; *see also* Linda Levine & Kurt M. Saunders, *Thinking Like a Rhetor*, 43 J. Legal Educ. 108, 109 (1993).

27. Foss, Foss & Trapp, *supra* note 14, at 4; *see also* Michael J. Cedrone, *supra* chapter 2.

28. Foss, Foss & Trapp, *supra* note 14, at 5.

29. *Id.* (noting that Aristotle did not discuss the canon of memory in *Rhetoric*).

30. The Rhetorical Tradition: Readings from Classical Times to the Present 31 (Patricia Bizzell & Bruce Herzberg eds., 2d ed. 2001).

categories expanded and contracted in the work of various ancient theorists.[31] To this day, invention and arrangement are the foundation of how arguments are devised. Invention and arrangement are the focus of this chapter because these canons address the "substance" and "action" of legal argumentation.[32]

2.1. Invention

According to classical rhetoric, invention, or the process of finding or discovering a persuasive argument,[33] demands consideration of a number of elements, including an analysis of the facts of a case and an assessment of how common types of arguments, called *topoi*, or *topics of invention*, could be used to uncover specific arguments in that case.[34] When an advocate properly invents an argument, the law and the facts of the case line up precisely and accurately like overlapping lattices, such that the court can confidently understand how the law resolves the legal issues in favor of the client.

Aristotle identified the process of invention as developing an argument that draws upon three types of "'artistic'...proofs," as he called them: (1) ethos, or ethical argument; (2) pathos, or emotional argument; and (3) logos, or logical argument.[35] An advocate should strive to use all three artistic proofs in making an argument.

Of utmost importance in legal argumentation, an advocate needs to demonstrate ethos, or ethics, in an argument by being "credible and honest."[36] An advocate must be aware, for instance, of balancing zealous advocacy with a

---

31. Michael J. Cedrone, *supra* chapter 2. The meaning of *invention* and *arrangement* varied among the classical writers. *See id.* section 3.5. Notwithstanding these differences, the process of creating and organizing arguments is as relevant for modern lawyers as it was for their ancient forebears.

32. *See* Foss, Foss & Trapp, *supra* note 14, at 10 (referring to rhetoric as "more than simply the expression of ideas or considerations of style apart from substance or action"); *see also* Linda L. Berger, *Studying and Teaching "Law as Rhetoric": A Place to Stand*, 16 J. Legal Writing Inst. 3, 48 (2010) ("In the twentieth century, New Rhetoric sought to re-discover the importance of rhetoric and the central role of persuasion and argument in building understanding.").

33. Frost, *supra* note 25, at 4.

34. *Id.*; *see also* Berger, *supra* note 32, at 48–49.

35. Kristen Konrad Robbins-Tiscione, Rhetoric for Legal Writers: The Theory and Practice of Analysis and Persuasion 18 (2009) (quoting Aristotle).

36. *Id.* at 203; *see also* Michael J. Cedrone, *supra* chapter 2, section 3.3.1.

duty of "candor to the tribunal" and must follow the *Model Rules of Professional Conduct*.[37] An advocate must also adequately and properly cite sources.

Arguments based on pathos speak to the fact that emotions are powerful, and a good advocate knows how to appeal not only to the mind but also to the heart.[38] Appeals to emotion motivate an audience to be receptive to an argument.[39]

Logos, the appeal to logic, specifically incorporates two types of reasoning: inductive reasoning and deductive reasoning. In inventing or developing a logical legal argument, an advocate uses inductive reasoning to determine what the rule is and then deductive reasoning to apply the rule to facts to arrive at a conclusion.[40] These proofs, or "enthymemes," as they are called, mimic syllogisms but are not true syllogisms as defined in formal logic.[41] This is because human facts are often contested and therefore are not indisputably true, and the rules being applied to those facts are debatable and continue to evolve.[42]

As part of his discussion of logos, Aristotle identified a number of lines of arguments, topoi, to help an advocate discover how to fit a case within potential types of arguments.[43] Some examples of topoi include definition, precedent, and cause and effect.[44] Michael H. Frost described topoi as "invaluable short-cuts": by considering how a case might fit into common types of arguments, an advocate in Greece or Rome could more easily develop a persuasive and complete argument.[45] And, more specifically, in a case of statutory interpreta-

---

37. ROBBINS-TISCIONE, *supra* note 35, at 208; *see* MODEL RULES OF PRO. CONDUCT r. 3.3 (AM. BAR ASS'N 2018) ("Candor Toward the Tribunal").

38. MICHAEL R. SMITH, ADVANCED LEGAL WRITING: THEORIES AND STRATEGIES IN PERSUASIVE WRITING 104 (3d ed. 2013) (discussing how strategies employing pathos use appeals to emotions and values to persuade).

39. ROBBINS-TISCIONE, *supra* note 35, at 179.

40. *Id.* at 137–38.

41. *Id.* at 138 (describing an enthymeme as a rhetorical syllogism); *see also* THE RHETORICAL TRADITION, *supra* note 30, at 171–72. In legal argument today, an argument is presented in the form of an enthymeme if a premise or conclusion is not stated because it is "obvious and understood." ALDISERT, *supra* note 9, at 61–62; *see also* Berger, *supra* note 32, at 50 (describing an enthymeme as containing a conclusion and a premise, with "the other premise being implied and both premises being only presumably true," providing only a probable conclusion).

42. *See* FROST, *supra* note 25, at 34 (discussing how affirmative arguments and refutations both deal with probabilities).

43. *Id.* at 27.

44. *Id.* at 27–28.

45. *Id.* at 27.

tion, the topoi could aid an advocate in developing the major premise, or rule, of a syllogism.[46]

Wilson Huhn identified five types of arguments that serve as modern legal topoi; these arguments are based on (1) the text of the Constitution, statutes, ordinances, or other codes; (2) the intent of the author of the text; (3) precedent reflecting on the text; (4) the tradition of the community; and (5) policy.[47] Huhn presented these arguments in this order, and they essentially proceed from narrow to broad.[48]

Today, in considering what arguments to present to a court, an advocate must think about whether the case presents an application of well-settled law to a new fact pattern at the trial court level, or whether the issue presents an opportunity for an appellate court to modify existing law. An appellate court may also consider a case of first impression (in other words, a case where no legal standards exist to answer the question); in that instance, a court must weave together sometimes-disparate sources to create new law.

2.2. Arrangement

Arrangement refers to the organization of the document being crafted and the order of the component parts of the particular document.[49] Arrangement is important to persuasion because a well-structured brief is one that will enable a judge to better comprehend an argument. A modern brief presented to a court still includes the same sections as would have been included in a speech in ancient Greece: introduction, facts, argument, and conclusion.[50] Each section of a brief serves a purpose; when the sections work together, they highlight what is most compelling in an argument.

One hallmark of persuasive legal writing is that the conclusion being advocated for is stated up front.[51] Similarly, in a classical argument, the summary at

46. *Id.* at 30.

47. HUHN, *supra* note 16, at 13; *see also* FROST, *supra* note 25, at 36–37 (discussing Huhn's five types of arguments as modern topics of invention).

48. *See* HUHN, *supra* note 16, at 15.

49. ROBBINS-TISCIONE, *supra* note 35, at 213.

50. *Id.*; FROST, *supra* note 25, at 45. The Romans later added a summary of the argument in oratory, which is now commonly used in appellate briefs and in some trial-level briefs. FROST, *supra* note 25, at 45.

51. *See* JOAN M. ROCKLIN, ROBERT B. ROCKLIN, CHRISTINE COUGHLIN & SANDY PATRICK, AN ADVOCATE PERSUADES 131 (2016).

the beginning of the argument created a prime location for an advocate to state the advocate's conclusion and relay key supporting arguments.[52]

Another feature of modern legal writing is that key points are repeated to provide emphasis.[53] Similarly, in classical rhetoric, the conclusion at the end of the argument was a place for dramatic repetition of arguments.[54]

Modern legal writers, following in the footsteps of the classical rhetoricians, typically begin with the strongest argument first.[55] Moreover, an argument's arrangement should consider not only the position of arguments supporting a client but also how to frame responses to the points of tension among the arguments of the parties. In other words, advocates should heed Aristotle's advice to "first present your own argument, and then meet the opposing argument by direct refutation or by pulling them to pieces in advance."[56] Arguments that are arranged well steers a court to the points of tension between both sides' arguments, guiding the court to an understanding of why the client's position is better reasoned and why the other side's assertions fall short.

3. A contemporary rhetorical view of argumentation

> *Rhetoric moves the soul with a movement which cannot finally be justified logically.*
>
> —Richard M. Weaver[57]

The classical rhetorical approaches to invention and arrangement provided a strong basis for contemporary rhetoricians Chaïm Perelman, Stephen Toulmin, and Richard M. Weaver.[58] These contemporary rhetoricians, like Aristo-

---

52. FROST, *supra* note 25, at 50 (noting that the purpose of the summary is "to focus the court's attention on the most important points and to limit the scope of the argument"); *see also* Michael J. Cedrone, *supra* chapter 2, section 3.4.

53. ROBBINS-TISCIONE, *supra* note 35, at 213.

54. FROST, *supra* note 25, at 54.

55. *Id.* at 52.

56. *Id.* at 52–53 (quoting ARISTOTLE, RHETORIC 235–36).

57. RICHARD M. WEAVER, *The* Phaedrus *and the Nature of Rhetoric*, *in* LANGUAGE IS SERMONIC, *supra* note 24, at 57, 80.

58. ROBBINS-TISCIONE, *supra* note 35, at 66 (noting that Aristotle's work served as a basis for the work of Perelman and Toulmin). Weaver's rhetorical work reflects the work of

tle, sought to understand how to create and develop an argument to persuade an audience.[59] The rhetorical theories of Perelman, Toulmin, and Weaver are wide-ranging and deep. This chapter specifically reflects the intersection of their theories on argument invention and arrangement; some rhetorical theories are not necessarily distinct to one area of focus—a theory might apply to both invention and arrangement, for instance, or to priming[60] or preparing an audience in addition to invention and/or arrangement. Each of these rhetoricians grappled with how best to develop arguments for presentation and how to structure arguments effectively. These are the very tools of invention and arrangement that every lawyer struggles to master.

3.1. Contemporary rhetoricians

Perelman, Toulmin, and Weaver have been described as "taking an 'argumentative' perspective on rhetoric," meaning that their work focuses on how to develop a persuasive argument.[61] Their perspectives on the use of arguments to *persuade* unite them in this chapter, although each made unique contributions to the study of rhetorical theories of argumentation. While whole volumes have been written by and about these rhetoricians, this chapter seeks to highlight only those ideas that have practical application in legal argumentation.

Central to an argument is the reasoning supporting the argument, which gets at how and why a conclusion is correct. Perelman and Toulmin were concerned with practical reasoning, which relates to the reasoning associated with human problems and how people reason through and solve disputes, as opposed to the rigid reasoning in formal logic.[62] Perelman, along with his coauthor, Lucie Olbrechts-Tyteca, studied the methods through which an advocate could seek

---

Aristotle as well as that of Plato. *E.g.*, WEAVER, *supra* note 24, at 171; RICHARD M. WEAVER, *Language Is Sermonic*, *in* LANGUAGE IS SERMONIC, *supra* note 24, at 201, 205–06.

59. FOSS, FOSS & TRAPP, *supra* note 14, at 14; ROBBINS-TISCIONE, *supra* note 35, at 66 (noting that Perelman and Toulmin viewed arguments as a means to create ideas).

60. LINDA L. BERGER & KATHRYN M. STANCHI, LEGAL PERSUASION: A RHETORICAL APPROACH TO THE SCIENCE 107–08 (2018) (Law, Language & Communication Series).

61. FOSS, FOSS & TRAPP, *supra* note 14, at 14. Foss, Foss, and Trap used the term *perspective* to emphasize rhetoricians' unique interpretations of rhetoric and the "conceptual lenses" through which rhetoricians view the topic of rhetoric. *Id.* That definition is adopted here.

62. ROBBINS-TISCIONE, *supra* note 35, at 66.

"audience adherence" to a position.[63] Toulmin developed a layout for a non-formal logical argument using a grounds-warrant-claim scheme.[64] Weaver focused on the power of language and the ethics of argumentation.[65]

3.1.1. Chaïm Perelman

Perelman (1912–1984) was born in Warsaw and studied in Belgium.[66] A lawyer,[67] Perelman was interested in "a logic of value judgments" (where a value is an opinion that expresses a preference), and that led him to rhetoric.[68] Perelman recognized that the reasoning used in philosophy was rooted in formal logic.[69] As such, arguments considering value judgments were not found in philosophy, and Perelman needed to seek elsewhere.[70] Perelman and Lucie Olbrechts-Tyteca researched the arguments made in the law by judges, as well as arguments made by others such as those in the law and politics.[71] From this research, Perelman articulated a rhetorical theory of argumentation, and Olbrechts-Tyteca contributed examples of the theory.[72] Perelman and Olbrechts-Tyteca found that the argument types used in value judgments paralleled those of the topoi in classical rhetoric.[73] Perelman and Olbrechts-Tyteca laid out their theories of argumentation in *The New Rhetoric: A Treatise on Argumentation*.[74] In *The Realm of Rhetoric*, Perelman updated those theories and presented them in a concise way.[75] Perelman's recognition of the informal nature of argumentation and acceptance of ambi-

63. Saunders, *supra* note 12, at 572 (quoting CHAÏM PERELMAN & LUCIE OLBRECHTS-TYTECA, THE NEW RHETORIC: A TREATISE ON ARGUMENTATION 4 (John Wilkinson & Purcell Weaver trans., Univ. of Notre Dame Press 1969) (1958)).

64. *Id.* at 568.

65. ROBBINS-TISCIONE, *supra* note 35, at 64.

66. THE RHETORICAL TRADITION, *supra* note 30, at 1372.

67. Saunders, *supra* note 12, at 572.

68. THE RHETORICAL TRADITION, *supra* note 30, at 1372 (quoting Chaïm Perelman, *Philosophy, Rhetoric, Commonplaces*, *in* THE NEW RHETORIC AND THE HUMANITIES 52, 56 (D. Reidel Publ'g Co. 1979) (trans. of *Philosophie, Rhétorique, Lieux Commune*, BULLETIN DE L'ACADEMIE ROYALE DE BELGIQUE 144–56 (1972)).

69. *Id.*

70. *Id.*

71. *Id.*

72. *Id.*

73. *Id.*

74. PERELMAN & OLBRECHTS-TYTECA, *supra* note 63.

75. CHAÏM PERELMAN, THE REALM OF RHETORIC (William Kluback trans., Univ. of Notre Dame Press 1982) (1977).

guity in argument fit well with legal argumentation, according to Kurt M. Saunders.[76] Furthermore, the concept of adherence to an audience directly speaks to the role of a lawyer advocating for a client before a judge or jury.[77] When an advocate seeks an audience's adherence to an argument, the outcome is necessarily probable, not certain,[78] and this difference between probable and certain outcomes speaks to the very reason why the outcome in a legal dispute is not assured.

Perelman and Olbrechts-Tyteca identified their "new rhetoric" as a break with centuries of reasoning established by René Descartes.[79] Descartes's philosophy emphasized rational reasoning through logic, not argument based on plausibility;[80] and during Descartes's time, methods to advocate for an audience's adherence to an argument were completely neglected.[81] Arguing against Descartes, Perelman and Olbrechts-Tyteca asserted that the "domain of argumentation" is not those propositions that are self-evident "since no one deliberates where the solution is necessary or argues against what is self-evident."[82] Instead, argumentation's province is "the credible, the plausible, the probable, to the degree that the latter eludes the certainty of calculations."[83] Perelman and Olbrechts-Tyteca sought to fill what they saw as a void in argumentation: how to argue when propositions are not self-evident and instead relate to value judgments.[84] The "new rhetoric," as Perelman defined it, is "concerned with discourse addressed to *any sort of audience*"[85] with the audience's adherence as the goal of the discourse.

In developing the new rhetoric and differentiating argumentation from self-evident propositions, Perelman took great care to distinguish practical argumentation from formal logic such as mathematics. Mathematical demon-

---

76. Saunders, *supra* note 12, at 572.

77. *Id.* at 572–73.

78. Berger, *supra* note 32, at 54; *see also* Michael D. Murray, *After the Great Recession: Law and Economics' Topics of Invention and Arrangement & Tropes of Style*, 58 LOY. L. REV. 897, 908 (2012).

79. PERELMAN & OLBRECHTS-TYTECA, *supra* note 63, at 1.

80. *Id.*

81. *Id.*

82. *Id.*

83. *Id.*

84. *See id.* at 3–4; *see also* PERELMAN, *supra* note 75, at 34 ("Every argument implies a preliminary selection of facts and values, their specific description in a given language, and an emphasis which varies with the importance given them.").

85. PERELMAN, *supra* note 75, at 5 (emphasis in original).

stration relies on signs "free from ambiguity," but argumentation uses language that naturally contains ambiguities.[86] Mathematics and argumentation therefore have different starting points, with mathematics using self-evident axioms and argumentation presupposing a meeting of the minds as a goal.[87]

The new rhetoric is also premised on Perelman's view that rhetoric and dialectic are used together when an advocate argues for audience adherence to points that are not self-evident.[88] Perelman distinguished dialectic reasoning, which pertains to "justifiable opinion," from formal analytic (logical) reasoning, which deals with "truth."[89] Dialectic had come to be separated, or divided, from formal logic in the modern world;[90] and, for that reason, Perelman argued, rhetoric had lost its connection to practical reasoning: "[t]he contempt for rhetoric and the eclipse of the theory of argumentation have led to the negation of practical reason."[91]

By bringing rhetoric and dialectic back together in the new rhetoric, Perelman asserted, "all who believe in the existence of reasonable choice, preceded by deliberation or discussion where different solutions confront each other, cannot avoid a theory of argumentation such as the new rhetoric presents."[92] Accordingly, argumentation has a role in practical reasoning, and rhetoric has both practical and theoretical applications.[93]

Perelman identified arguments in terms of forms of discourse, where each side presents a competing thesis.[94] Each person in the audience must decide with which thesis to agree, considering the costs and benefits of each argument and "the value of the solution" that each argument presented.[95] Perelman classified different forms or types of arguments.[96] One form is a *liaison*, which he defined as a "transference to the conclusion of the adherence accorded to the premises."[97] When an argument takes the form of a liaison, therefore, the conclusion can be agreed upon through agreement to each of the premises,

---

86. *Id.* at 9.
87. *Id.*
88. The Rhetorical Tradition, *supra* note 30, at 1373.
89. Perelman, *supra* note 75, at 3.
90. *Id.* at 4.
91. *Id.* at 7.
92. *Id.* at 7–8.
93. *Id.* at 8.
94. *Id.* at 49.
95. *Id.*
96. *Id.*
97. *Id.*

or elements, of that argument.[98] The other form is a *dissociation*, which he said "aims at separating elements which language or a recognized tradition have previously tied together."[99] When an argument is made by dissociation, a single concept is split "into two independent, but related concepts"[100] that can both be used to organize new data or argumentative concepts.[101]

Perelman further identified three types of liaisons: quasi-logical arguments, arguments based on the structure of reality, and arguments that establish the structure of reality.[102] Quasi-logical arguments are similar to logical formal thinking but use a nonformal thesis.[103] For instance, in an argument by division, an advocate shows how a conclusion about the whole can be drawn after reasoning about the parts.[104] Arguments based on the structure of reality are ones where an advocate relies on "the existence of agreements which are not questioned" in reality, such as causality.[105] Closely related, then, are arguments that establish the structure of reality: "those, which, starting from a known specific case, allow the establishment of a precedent, model, or general rule, such as enable reasoning by model or example."[106] Perelman's classification of different forms of arguments helps an advocate to consider whether to build up an argument from parts or split an argument into related concepts; these forms can aid an advocate in both inventing and structuring an argument.

3.1.2. Stephen Toulmin

Toulmin (1922–2009) was an English philosopher who worked at universities in England and the United States.[107] Toulmin was concerned with integrating logic, which he felt had become overly abstract and formalistic, into human endeavors such as law.[108] While Toulmin saw himself primarily as a philosopher, his work has been influential in the field of rhetoric.[109]

98. Berger, *supra* note 32, at 55.
99. PERELMAN, *supra* note 75, at 49.
100. Berger, *supra* note 32, at 55.
101. PERELMAN, *supra* note 75, at 52.
102. *Id.* at 50.
103. *Id.*
104. *Id.*
105. *Id.* at 50–51.
106. *Id.* at 51.
107. THE RHETORICAL TRADITION, *supra* note 30, at 1410.
108. *Id.*
109. *Id.*

Toulmin's most important work is *The Uses of Argument*, where he set forth practical reasoning as an alternative to the formal logic that had developed over the centuries.[110] This structure shows the movement[111] from initial grounds to a claim using a warrant and also incorporates the concepts of backing for the warrant, qualifiers, and rebuttal.[112] Toulmin was also concerned with the extent to which "the same sort of canons or standards of arguments" can be used across arguments when a person is analyzing an argument's merits.[113] To create a way of thinking about "how far there are common standards applicable in the criticism of arguments taken from different fields," Toulmin divided arguments into those that are field invariant and those that are field dependent.[114] When two arguments each contain grounds and conclusions that "are of the same logical type," Toulmin identified them as being in the same field.[115] Conversely, arguments that are not in the same field are those where the backing and conclusions do not share "the same logical type."[116] Some arguments are field dependent—that is, there is a different way of assessing arguments when comparing arguments made in different fields.[117] If arguments are field invariant, the standards for assessing arguments and qualifying conclusions remain the same.[118] Identifying whether the standards for assessing an argument are field dependent or field invariant allows the person evaluating the argument to consider whether common standards apply across arguments from different fields.[119] Toulmin's work in developing a logical structure for practical reasoning and identifying field-dependent and field-invariant arguments serves as a useful framework for an advocate to both create and evaluate legal arguments.[120]

---

110. *Id.*
111. Saunders, *supra* note 12, at 568.
112. *Id.* at 568–69.
113. Stephen Toulmin, The Uses of Argument 14 (8th prtg. 2008).
114. *Id.* at 15.
115. *Id.* at 14.
116. *Id.*
117. *Id.* at 15.
118. *Id.*
119. *Id.*; *see also* Brian N. Larson, *Law's Enterprise: Argumentation Schemes & Legal Analogy*, 87 Univ. Cin. L. Rev. 664, 695 (2018) (commenting that the reasonableness of a legal argument is field dependent because the various areas of law may use different standards).
120. Berger, *supra* note 32, at 52.

Toulmin's practical reasoning accounts for complex arguments better than the traditional logical syllogism, which Toulmin found to be too limited.[121] He, like Perelman, was concerned that the study of logic had become overly formal and centered on demonstration, as opposed to critical analysis of argument.[122] At the same time, Toulmin "sought to extend the rigor of formal logic" to law and other fields "of greater uncertainty."[123] Saunders identified Toulmin's layout of an argument as especially well-suited to legal argument because it is flexible.[124] That flexibility comes from the model's ability to address inference, judicial uncertainty, and rebuttal.[125]

Indeed, Toulmin recognized the close connection between his argument layout and the law:

> Logic (we may say) is generalized jurisprudence. Arguments can be compared with law-suits, and the claims we make and argue for in extra-legal contexts with claims made in the courts, while the cases we present in making good each kind of claim can be compared with each other. A main task of jurisprudence is to characterize the essentials of the legal process: the procedures by which claims-at-law are put forward, disputed and determined, and the categories in terms of which this is done. Our own inquiry is a parallel one: we shall aim, in a similar way, to characterize what may be called "the rational process", the procedures and categories by using which claims-in-general can be argued for and settled.[126]

Toulmin viewed his structure for analyzing arguments as "logically candid,"[127] but he described the nature of his structure as being more complex than traditional logic:

> The form of analysis arrived at is decidedly more complex than that which logicians have customarily employed, and forces on us a number of distinctions for which the normal analysis leaves no room; too many different things (I will suggest) have been run together in the past under the name of "major premisses", and a single division of arguments into

---

121. The Rhetorical Tradition, *supra* note 30, at 1410.
122. *Id.*
123. *Id.* at 1195.
124. Saunders, *supra* note 12, at 571.
125. *Id.*
126. Toulmin, *supra* note 113, at 7.
127. *Id.* at 8 (emphasis omitted).

> "deductive" and "inductive" has been relied on to mark at least four different distinctions. When these various distinctions are separated out, it begins to look as though formal logic has indeed lost touch with its application, and as if a systematic divergence has in fact grown up between the categories of logical practice and the analyses given of them in logicians' textbooks and treatises.[128]

Toulmin saw a double standard between what he called the philosopher's ideal and the ordinary person's questions.[129] The layout of arguments that he proposed aids nonphilosophers working in real-world problems of humanity, offering them a way to sort out and think critically about the logic of the arguments to solve those problems.[130]

3.1.3. Richard M. Weaver

Weaver (1910–1963) grew up in North Carolina and spent his summers on the family farm in Weaverville, North Carolina.[131] Weaver was known for his conservativism, although he started out as a Socialist,[132] and his Platonist and agrarian ideals.[133] Like Perelman, Weaver saw a close connection between rhetoric and dialectic.[134] Yet, unlike Perelman or Toulmin, who can be viewed as having developed an integrated rhetorical theory in their approaches to practical reasoning, Weaver's life work in rhetorical theory is hard to neatly encapsulate.[135] Weaver commented on the recent decline of rhetoric as a discipline; Foss, Foss, and Trapp noted that Weaver saw a parallel between "cultural degeneration" and the decline of rhetoric.[136] Yet, Weaver also saw the poten-

---

128. *Id.*

129. *Id.* at 9.

130. *See id.* at 9–10.

131. THE RHETORICAL TRADITION, *supra* note 30, at 1348 (also noting that Weaver spent most of his career at the University of Chicago).

132. *Id.*

133. Richard L. Johannesen, Rennard Strickland & Ralph T. Eubanks, *Richard M. Weaver on the Nature of Rhetoric: An Interpretation*, *in* LANGUAGE IS SERMONIC, *supra* note 24, at 10–11.

134. *Id.* at 19.

135. FOSS, FOSS & TRAPP, *supra* note 14, at 72.

136. *Id.* at 67.

tial for hope.[137] Weaver's best-known works are collections of essays, including *Language Is Sermonic*[138] and *The Ethics of Rhetoric*.[139]

Weaver recognized the longstanding definition of *rhetoric* as "the art of persuasion,"[140] as others have, and "truth plus its artful presentation."[141] The purpose of rhetoric, according to Weaver, is to produce movement by persuading a person to change an attitude or to take action:

> This art, whether it presents itself in linguistic or in other form ... meets the person to whom it is addressed and takes him where the rhetor wishes him to go, even if that "going" is nothing more than an intensification of feeling about something. This means that rhetoric, consciously employed, is never innocent of intention, but always has as its object the exerting of some kind of compulsion.[142]

A complete rhetorician has both knowledge and "certain arts of appeal which have to do with the inspiring of feeling."[143] Weaver explained that to move an audience, rhetoric must account in concrete ways for how the communication is directed to the audience and situation in time.[144]

Weaver believed that society needed rhetoric to give it direction and create cohesion.[145] In adding artful presentation to truth,[146] a rhetorician becomes "a noble lover of the good, who works through dialectic and through poetic or analogical association."[147] Moreover, rhetoric itself has a "passion for the actual," which reflects the reality of human passion.[148] Accordingly, rhetoric has the power to move the soul.[149]

---

137. *Id.* at 69.

138. LANGUAGE IS SERMONIC, *supra* note 24.

139. RICHARD M. WEAVER, THE ETHICS OF RHETORIC (1985).

140. RICHARD M. WEAVER, *Concealed Rhetoric in Scientistic Sociology*, *in* LANGUAGE IS SERMONIC, *supra* note 24, at 139, 140.

141. WEAVER, *supra* note 139, at 15.

142. WEAVER, *supra* note 140, at 140.

143. *Id.* at 140–41.

144. WEAVER, *Language Is Sermonic*, *supra* note 58, at 206.

145. WEAVER, *supra* note 24, at 174–75.

146. WEAVER, *supra* note 57, at 71.

147. *Id.* at 74–75.

148. *Id.* at 77–78.

149. *Id.* at 80.

3.2. Contemporary rhetorical theories on composing an argument

Composing a legal argument is a process that can and should be guided by rhetorical principles.[150] Perelman, Toulmin, and Weaver contributed important theories to the world of rhetoric with regard to the development and organization of arguments. These theories are equally important to legal argumentation because, together, the perspectives that they espouse cover the issues that lawyers must consider when crafting arguments. In particular, in developing and organizing an argument, a lawyer must consider the power of language, audience adherence to an argument, sources for invention, the layout of an argument, and arrangement.

Perelman, Toulmin, and Weaver wrote about many facets of the composition process, and the following sections have been selected and ordered to provide a sense of how their rhetorical theories can work together in an integrated taxonomy.[151] First, Weaver's assessment of the power of language and Perelman's consideration of audience are part of the way that a legal advocate primes an argument—the initial considerations of how to shape an argument and the thematic narrative that will drive the argument.[152] Then, Weaver's sources of an argument and Toulmin's layout of an argument aid an advocate in considering how to invent and structure an argument, as well as how to critique an argument. Finally, Perelman's guidance on argument speaks to how the structure and order of an argument draw in an audience and focus on what is most important and beneficial to persuade. These theories lead an advocate through the process of priming, invention, and arrangement as a form of composition.

3.2.1. The power of language

Words are the ultimate tool of any lawyer's trade. The starting point for an advocate must be the carefully chosen words used to shape the terms of a contract, the closing argument to a jury, or the persuasive elements of a brief. Weaver cared deeply about language and words and their power over an audience. Weaver's essays speak to a skill that all attorneys must master: the ability to name and describe a concept accurately and precisely with words. In "The

---

150. Berger, *supra* note 32, at 47.

151. Levine & Saunders, *supra* note 26, at 122 (discussing the new rhetoric as offering a "taxonomy" of reasoning).

152. Berger & Stanchi, *supra* note 60, at 108.

Power of the Word," Weaver acknowledged that a person who masters the power of language has control.[153] For example, a definition requires an analogy of one thing to another.[154] Therefore, "words, each containing its universal, are our reminders of knowledge."[155] Weaver's focus on the power of words parallels a concept in legal advocacy called *priming*.[156] Priming is a technique of persuasion that relates to first impressions: according to Kathryn Stanchi, priming is "a process in which a person's response to later information is influenced by exposure to prior information."[157] So, for instance, if an advocate can control a jury's first impression of a case using a theme that evokes a particular emotion or cognitive reaction, the jury will see the witness testimony and evidence in the trial in light of that theme.[158]

President Abraham Lincoln, a lawyer, understood the importance of priming when he began the Gettysburg Address with the following line: "Four score and seven years ago our fathers brought forth on this continent, a new nation, conceived in Liberty, and dedicated to the proposition that all men are created equal."[159] Here, at the Gettysburg battlefield, Lincoln reminded his audience of the Declaration of Independence with his use of the word *Liberty* and the phrase *all men are created equal*.[160] He primed his audience with these powerful words to view the battles fought in the Civil War as a fight for the ideals on which the United States was founded.[161]

Language, Weaver asserted, can be described as "a great storehouse of universal memory," or as a net that helps us to see both the present meaning and the experiences of others carried in that meaning.[162] Because of their "common currency," words have a greater significance than can be attributed to a single user in a single situation.[163] For that reason, "[t]he community of lan-

153. Richard M. Weaver, *The Power of the Word*, *in* Language Is Sermonic, *supra* note 24, at 33, 33.

154. *Id.* at 41.

155. *Id.* at 44.

156. Kathryn M. Stanchi, *The Power of Priming in Legal Advocacy: Using the Science of First Impressions to Persuade the Reader*, 89 Or. L. Rev. 305, 307–12 (2010) (defining *priming*).

157. *Id.* at 306.

158. *Id.* at 312.

159. President Abraham Lincoln, Gettysburg Address (Nov. 19, 1863), *quoted in* Diana Schaub, His Greatest Speeches: How Lincoln Moved the Nation 60 (2021).

160. Schaub, *supra* note 159, at 75–80.

161. *See also id.* (offering several interpretations of Lincoln's words).

162. Weaver, *supra* note 153, at 44.

163. *Id.*

guage gives one access to significances at which he cannot otherwise arrive."[164] By connecting the battle at Gettysburg to the Declaration of Independence and the founding of the nation on the ideals of freedom, Lincoln showed the greater significance of the moment: this was not a single battle; it was a battle to protect the common currency of life, liberty, and the pursuit of happiness.

In fact, Diana Schaub asserted, the Gettysburg Address was a war speech—a rallying cry.[165] This "rallying cry" approach is particularly evident in the last sentence in the Gettysburg Address:

> It is rather for us to be here dedicated to the great task remaining before us—that from these honored dead we take increased devotion to that cause for which they gave the last full measure of devotion—that we here highly resolve that these dead shall not have died in vain—that this nation, under God, shall have a new birth of freedom—and that government of the people, by the people, for the people, shall not perish from the earth.[166]

Lincoln drew upon the great storehouse of Americans' universal memory of the United States' founding to spur on the war effort and to connect the present battles to a memory of the Declaration of Independence and the nation's birth.[167]

The brevity of Lincoln's speech even further distills the meaning of the words and increases their potency.[168] So, too, can a lawyer distill the essence of the client's side of the case by using a theme word or phrase early in a brief or trial and weaving the theme throughout the rest of the document or trial testimony and closing argument.[169] Indeed, some attorneys consider the opening sentence of the trial to be the most important because that is where the theme is established. A theme can also be developed through the story being told, which primes the audience's emotions.[170] An advocate must carefully choose words that evoke emotions in telling the story.[171]

---

164. *Id.* at 45.

165. SCHAUB, *supra* note 159, at 64.

166. President Abraham Lincoln, Gettysburg Address (Nov. 19, 1863), *quoted in* SCHAUB, *supra* note 159, at 60–61.

167. SCHAUB, *supra* note 159, at 71–72.

168. *Id.* at 93; *see also* Julie A. Oseid, *The Power of Brevity: Adopt Abraham Lincoln's Habits*, 6 J. ASS'N LEGAL WRITING DIRS. 28, 39–41 (Fall 2009).

169. Stanchi, *supra* note 156, at 312.

170. *Id.* at 313.

171. *Id.* at 325.

How an advocate develops a theme implicates Weaver's description of language as "a social and cultural creation."[172] The forces within, not without—the "psychic constitution" of the people using words—determine the scope of the words' references.[173] Accordingly, Weaver saw communication and cognition as being closely related.[174] Humans create understanding and comprehension: "[t]he problem of deciding upon the correct meaning of words, then, is not one of external measurement, but one of internal receptivity or capability."[175] Language is a "humanistic creation" that creates an important bond—a "covenant among those who use it."[176]

For example, John Roberts, who later became a chief justice of the U.S. Supreme Court, was an attorney in practice representing the State of Alaska when he wrote the following passage in the factual section of a brief before the Court in *Alaska Department of Environmental Conservation v. Environmental Protection Agency*:

> For generations, Inupiat Eskimos hunting and fishing in the DeLong Mountains in Northwest Alaska had been aware of orange- and red-stained creekbeds in which fish could not survive. In the 1960's, a bush pilot and part-time prospector by the name of Bob Baker noticed striking discolorations in the hills and creekbeds of a wide valley in the western DeLongs. Unable to land his plane on the rocky tundra to investigate, Baker alerted the U.S. Geological Survey. Exploration of the area eventually led to the discovery of a wealth of zinc and lead deposits. Although Baker died before the significance of his observations became known, his faithful traveling companion—an Irish Setter who often flew shotgun—was immortalized by a geologist who dubbed the creek Baker had spotted "Red Dog" Creek.[177]

---

172. Richard M. Weaver, *Relativism and the Use of Language*, *in* Language Is Sermonic, *supra* note 24, at 115, 120–21.

173. *Id.* at 121.

174. *Id.*

175. *Id.* at 123.

176. *Id.* at 122, 136.

177. Brief for Petitioner at 7–8, Alaska Dep't of Env't Conservation v. Env't Prot. Agency, 540 U.S. 461 (2004) (No. 02-658), https://www.findlawimages.com/efile/supreme/briefs/02-658/02-658.mer.pet.pdf; Melissa Love Koenig, Julie A. Oseid & Amy Vorenberg, *OK, Google, Will Artificial Intelligence Replace Human Lawyering?*, 102 Marq. L. Rev. 1269, 1296–97 (2019) (quoting petitioner's brief for *Alaska Dep't of Env't Conservation*, 540 U.S. 461 (No. 02-658)); Ross Guberman, Point Made: How to Write Like the Nation's Top Advocates 59 (2d ed. 2014) (same).

Surely, the visually compelling words that Roberts used to describe the area and the almost nostalgic way that he described Baker—the bush pilot and part-time prospector, flying over the DeLong Mountains with his Irish setter—were meant to capture the essence of this part of Alaska. As Ross Guberman noted, Roberts was visually depicting the place and people of Alaska in a photojournalistic way in this federalism dispute because, after all, "[w]ho knows more about what a mine means to nearby residents than the local and state officials close to the ground?"[178] Roberts sought to bring Alaska close to the Supreme Court justices reading the brief in Washington, D.C., with vivid, concrete words that created a bond between the place and the reader.[179]

Weaver explained that language can affect us in three ways: (1) it can move us toward good, (2) it can move us toward evil, or (3) it can fail to move us.[180] Persuasive or rhetorical language draws from "small nuances" and is particular to each situation, in contrast to what Weaver called *utility language*, which is general and whose meaning can be easily created through paraphrase.[181] Weaver saw persuasive language as having a power that is "a kind of 'love.'"[182] A rhetorician's speech, therefore, has a passion that is both revolutionary and serves a practical end.[183]

Such powerful, passionate language moved the U.S. Supreme Court to change the rules on custodial interrogation in its decision in *Miranda v. Arizona*.[184] In *Miranda*, the Court announced a new requirement that custodial interrogation must be preceded with a statement by police about the nature and purpose of the interrogation, which is now commonly known as providing Miranda rights.[185] The petitioner's brief filed in the Court on behalf of Mr. Miranda, undoubtedly one of the factors leading to the Court's decision, exemplifies the kind of language that can move us toward good.[186] In particular, the

178. GUBERMAN, *supra* note 177, at 59.

179. *See id.* at 59–60 (describing the passage as an example of how writing should "show," not "tell"); *see also* Love Koenig, Oseid & Vorenberg, *supra* note 177, at 1296.

180. WEAVER, *supra* note 57, at 60 (drawing on Plato's description of the lover and the nonlover).

181. *Id.* at 63.

182. *Id.* at 69.

183. *Id.* at 70.

184. Miranda v. Arizona, 384 U.S. 436, 467–68 (1966).

185. *Id.*

186. Brief for Petitioner at 9–10, *Miranda*, 384 U.S. 436 (No. 759); *see also* Linda H. Edwards, *Once Upon a Time in Law: Myth, Metaphor, and Authority*, 77 TENN. L. REV. 883, 891–98 (2010) (describing the petitioner's brief as a birth or creation story because the

last paragraph in the "Summary of Argument" section of the brief captures the artful way that counsel used emotional priming and thematic argument:

> When this defendant went into Interrogation Room 2, instead of having "the guiding hand of counsel" to which we believe the principles of *Powell v. Alabama* entitled him, he had the guiding hand of two policemen. When [he] came out of Interrogation Room 2, there was no longer any point in giving him counsel—his case was over. We believe that such practices are barred by the Sixth and Fourteenth Amendments to the Constitution of the United States.[187]

This language bears the hallmarks of both being a call to action to the Court and serving a practical end by connecting the Court's prior precedent in *Powell* to the legal question then before the Court.

The single most important decision that an advocate can make is what words to use to convey a point on behalf of a client. That choice must always be the starting point for a lawyer. In addition to using words precisely (a legal dictionary should never be far from a lawyer) and reading them carefully in court opinions, statutes, and transactional documents, a lawyer must consider the emotional, persuasive power of language. The care that a lawyer takes in using words will reflect the attorney's abilities and affect his or her reputation.

3.2.2. Audience adherence to an argument

President Ronald Reagan, a former actor, had a special ability to connect with an audience. His most memorable line in office arguably was "Mr. Gorbachev, tear down this wall!"[188] This line, part of his Address at the Brandenburg Gate on June 12, 1987, discussing the issue of the Berlin Wall,[189] appealed to the emotions of his audience. In fact, almost from the beginning of the speech, he elicited audience adherence to his message:

> Our gathering today is being broadcast throughout Western Europe and North America. I understand that it is being seen and heard as well in the

---

petitioner showed how the constitutional protection of the right to counsel was ready to be developed "or birthed").

187. Brief for Petitioner, *supra* note 186, at 9.

188. President Ronald Reagan, Address at the Brandenburg Gate (June 12, 1987), *quoted in* Craig Fehrman, The Best Presidential Writing: From 1789 to the Present 407 (2020).

189. *Id.*

> east. To those listening throughout Eastern Europe, I extend my warmest greetings and the good will of the American people. To those listening in East Berlin, a special word: Although I cannot be with you, I address my remarks to you just as surely as to those standing here before me. For I join you, as I join your fellow countrymen in the west, in this firm, this unalterable belief: Es gibt nur ein Berlin [*There is only one Berlin*].[190]

Reagan publicly acknowledged the people in the West and in the East together, part of his message of solidarity across the Iron Curtain divide. In connecting with an audience that spanned both sides of the Berlin Wall, Reagan established a commonality between the two groups of people receiving his message.

Likewise, the audience is central to Perelman's rhetorical theory. An advocate persuades, according to Perelman, by seeking "to elicit or increase adherence of the members of an audience to theses presented for their consent," based on a meeting of the minds between the advocate and the recipient of the argument (i.e., the audience).[191]

The goal of audience adherence, Perelman said, is to "incit[e] action."[192] To incite action in an audience, an advocate must understand what emotions to elicit in the audience.[193] Linda L. Berger and Kathryn M. Stanchi noted the close relationship between priming theory and Perelman and Olbrechts-Tyteca's study of value-based arguments.[194] In presenting an argument, an advocate seeks to use discourse to "modify an audience's convictions," Perelman reflected in *Realm of Rhetoric*.[195] A persuasive argument "tries to gain a meeting of the minds instead of imposing its will through constraint or conditioning."[196]

Thus, the audience—which, in the case of legal argumentation, consists of the judge, the jury, and/or opposing counsel—is critical to the strategies employed in an argument and, ultimately, to the advocate's success in persuading and inciting action. Whether an argument is being given to a specific audience or a universal audience, for instance, can affect persuasion.[197] Reagan used his knowledge that thousands of people around the world would be

190. *Id.* at 405.
191. Perelman, *supra* note 75, at 9.
192. *Id.* at 12.
193. Berger & Stanchi, *supra* note 60, at 108.
194. *Id.*
195. Perelman, *supra* note 75, at 11.
196. *Id.*
197. *Id.* at 17–18.

listening to his Address at the Brandenburg Gate to electrify his message to Gorbachev. Similarly, Perelman noted that according to Aristotle, the character of an audience gives an advocate insight into how to excite the group's passions and emotions.[198] Therefore, an advocate must find ways to identify an audience's composition and character to achieve a meeting of the minds with the audience.

When presenting an argument to a jury, for instance, an advocate tries to learn about the background and viewpoints of the potential jurors in the jury pool through a series of questions posed to jurors in voir dire. Likewise, good advocates appearing before a single trial court judge or a panel of appellate judges study the judges' prior rulings in an attempt to ascertain what kinds of arguments will best play to the court. An effective appellate argument may refer a court back to its previous decisions, such as in the opening two paragraphs of the "Argument" section in the petitioner's brief in *Miranda*:

> When Miranda walked out of Interrogation Room 2 on March 13, 1963, his life for all practical purposes was over. Whatever happened later was inevitable; the die had been cast in that room at that time. There was no duress, no brutality. Yet when Miranda finished his conversation with Officers Cooley and Young, only the ceremonies of the law remained; in any realistic sense, his case was done. We have here the clearest possible example of Justice Douglas' observation, "what takes place in the secret confines of the police station may be more critical than what takes place at the trial." *Crooker v. California* [dissenting opinion].
>
> The question presented is whether a defendant in such circumstances is entitled to be told of his right to counsel and to have a meaningful opportunity to consult counsel before the law disposes of him. For "what use is a defendant's right to effective counsel at every stage of a criminal case if, while he is held awaiting trial, he can be questioned in the absence of counsel until he confesses?" Justices Douglas, Black, and Brennan in *Spano v. New York*.[199]

The Court in the late 1960s was poised to move in the direction of establishing a warning for custodial interrogation, and a large part of the brief is

---

198. *Id.* at 18.

199. Brief for Petitioner, *supra* note 186, at 10 (citations omitted); *see also* BERGER & STANCHI, *supra* note 60, at 35 (describing Interrogation Room 2 as the "space that captured the essence of Miranda's argument").

devoted to showing the movement in the law—a progression in values that the citations to *Crooker* and *Spano* highlight at the outset of the petitioner's brief.

In addition to studying the audience, Perelman said that before beginning an argument, an advocate must consider the thesis, presumptions, and values related to the argument.[200] First, an effective advocate must adapt the thesis of the argument to the audience so that an audience is more likely to receive the thesis favorably.[201] A thesis will be rejected by an audience if the audience finds it unacceptable;[202] moreover, an argument's purpose is to obtain adherence to a thesis, and, therefore, an advocate must not present a thesis as already accepted.[203] Second, along with facts and truths—which an audience has to understand and interpret in a way that is favorable to the advocate's position[204]—an advocate relies on presumptions (which can be contradicted by the facts).[205] Presumptions are based on what is considered normal, but people can differ over what is considered normal.[206] Finally, argumentation requires both universal and concrete values, but an advocate will emphasize one over the other during the course of an argument.[207] An advocate must think ahead carefully about how these pieces of the argument will play to the audience in order to present a winning argument.

Returning to Reagan's Address at the Brandenburg Gate, Reagan presented his thesis on the question of the Berlin Wall to his audience clearly:

> Today I say: As long as this gate is closed, as long as this scar of a wall is permitted to stand, it is not the German question alone that remains open, but the question of freedom for all mankind. Yet I do not come here to lament. For I find in Berlin a message of hope, even in the shadow of this wall, a message of triumph.[208]

In presenting his thesis, Reagan sought a meeting of the minds of the Berliners on either side of the Wall by using the metaphor of a scar: if the Berlin Wall would come down, the scar would heal.

---

200. PERELMAN, *supra* note 75, at 21, 24–25, 26–29.
201. *Id.* at 21.
202. *Id.*
203. *Id.* at 22.
204. *Id.* at 23–24.
205. *Id.* at 24–25.
206. *Id.* at 25.
207. *Id.* at 28.
208. President Ronald Reagan, Address at the Brandenburg Gate, *quoted in* FEHRMAN, *supra* note 188, at 405.

In the law, the question presented in a brief exemplifies the way that an advocate must carefully focus a court's attention on a thesis presented for consent. The question presented comes at the beginning of a brief, typically as a separate section of the brief, and is often referred to in the body of the argument. The question is the pivotal point of the argument, the point of tension between the two parties' contentions. Framing the question correctly aids a court in understanding both the ambiguity in the current state of the law and a potential path forward for a solution.[209] In the petitioner's brief in *Miranda*, for instance, the question is properly stated to highlight the pivotal facts and legal issue: "Whether the confession of a poorly educated, mentally abnormal, indigent defendant, not told of his right to counsel, taken while he is in police custody and without the assistance of counsel, which was not requested, can be admitted into evidence over specific objection based on the absence of counsel."[210] This question precedes an emotionally primed description of the facts. Those primed facts include, at the beginning of the argument section, that "when Miranda finished his conversation with Officers Cooley and Young, only the ceremonies of the law remained; in any realistic sense, his case was done."[211] These facts prepare a reader for the viewpoint that without a warning prior to custodial interrogation, an arrested individual has no chance.

An advocate also must consider how to keep an audience's attention focused on the key points of an argument. To command such audience focus, Perelman said, an advocate must make important choices in selecting the facts and values to present in an argument.[212] The elements of an argument are interdependent,[213] and rhetoric is the art of creating presence in that argument.[214] Perelman noted that presence is created when an advocate "prolongs the attention given" to elements of an argument to influence an audience's emotional response.[215] For example, the petitioner's brief in *Miranda* holds readers' attention by making them feel like they just walked out of Interrogation Room 2. Perelman suggested several techniques that can be used to focus an audience's attention: repeat key points and words, accumulate details, and accentuate pas-

209. *See* Saunders, *supra* note 12, at 574.
210. Brief for Petitioner, *supra* note 186, at 2.
211. *Id.* at 10.
212. Perelman, *supra* note 75, at 34; *see also* Saunders, *supra* note 12, at 573–74.
213. Perelman, *supra* note 75, at 33.
214. *Id.* at 37.
215. *Id.*

sages.[216] Likewise, in brief writing, an advocate should not be afraid to repeat key points in headings and summary paragraphs as points of emphasis. An advocate in court can use repetition and points of emphasis in oral argument, as well.

Perelman observed that an audience needs more than just words to understand an oral argument—it needs nonverbal language to provide cues.[217] Traditional nonverbal oral-presentation cues, of course, are not available in written arguments, but writing can include nonverbal signposting to help a reader focus and understand the significance of the facts and arguments. In today's briefs, for example, advocates are increasingly using nonverbal visual cues, such as graphs, charts, diagrams, and embedded pictures, to enhance their briefs. Even hyperlinks to authorities increase the functionality of a brief. These additions serve as modern forms of visual rhetoric in written advocacy that can strengthen a brief.[218]

3.2.3. Sources for invention

The most challenging part of argumentation is how to invent the argument—how to find the right path among all of the possible avenues for persuasive discourse. Berger and Stanchi identified invention as "perhaps the most critical step in legal persuasion,"[219] reflecting the strategic and creative process of developing an argument that considers the law and unique facts of a case. An advocate benefits from understanding and having a working knowledge of the "range and contours"[220] of common types of arguments. Ancient rhetoricians developed lists of topoi, or topics of common arguments, from which an advocate could invent an argument.[221] Weaver expanded on that con-

---

216. *Id.*

217. *Id.* at 44.

218. Michael Murray, *Visual Rhetoric: Topics of Invention and Arrangement and Tropes of Style*, 21 J. Legal Writing Inst. 1, 2 (2016); Guberman, *supra* note 177, at 293–94; Steve Johansen & Ruth Anne Robbins, *Art-iculating the Analysis: Systemizing the Decision to Use Visuals as Legal Reasoning*, 20 J. Legal Writing Inst. 57, 66–67 (2015); Lucille A. Jewel, *Through a Glass Darkly: Using Brain Science and Visual Rhetoric to Gain a Professional Perspective on Visual Advocacy*, 19 S. Cal. Interdisc. L.J. 237, 241 (2010).

219. Berger & Stanchi, *supra* note 60, at 162.

220. Susan E. Provenzano & Brian N. Larson, *Civil Procedure as a Critical Discussion*, 20 Nev. L.J. 967, 971 (2020) (noting that when working with the Federal Rules of Civil Procedure, advocates do not have such guidance across cases).

221. Frost, *supra* note 25, at 27.

cept in his contemporary rhetorical theory. Weaver's topoi provide a useful "taxonomy"[222] for an advocate to invent an argument.

In *Language Is Sermonic*, Weaver quoted Cicero's definition of *topic of invention* as "the seat of an argument," recounting how speakers in ancient Greece and Rome would use the topoi to invent an argument.[223] Weaver then transferred that idea to a contemporary rhetorical view of argumentation, using philosophy as a foundation. In philosophy, the topics, or ideas, are being, cause, relationship, and testimony and authority.[224] Weaver adapted these concepts to identify four sources used in interpreting a subject: definition, comparison of similarities and differences, cause-and-effect framework, and testimony or authority.[225] Argument from circumstance is a subset topic of cause.[226] The first three sources of interpretation (definition, comparison/analogy, and cause and effect) are internal ways to examine a subject, while the fourth (testimony or authority) is an external method.[227] Weaver placed these topics in an ethical hierarchy, starting with definition and followed by analogy; then cause and effect; and, finally, testimony or authority.[228]

Definition. Weaver found argument by definition to be the most ethical type of argument because a definitional argument presents an argument relating to the genus or "the nature of the thing."[229] An argument from definition is founded on a "single postulate," which relies on the concept that the object

---

222. Scholars have used the concept of a taxonomy as a way for law students and practicing lawyers to see relationships and the bigger picture in the study of law and assessment of legal strategies. Provenzano & Larson, *supra* note 220, at 971 (proposing a taxonomy of common litigation arguments consistent with the goals of the Federal Rules of Civil Procedure); Christine M. Venter, *Analyze This: Using Taxonomies to "Scaffold" Students' Legal Thinking and Writing Skills*, 57 Mercer L. Rev. 621, 637–38 (2006) (describing how Bloom's taxonomy helps students use metacognition in developing their legal analysis and writing skills); Levine & Saunders, *supra* note 26, at 122 (stating that an integrated study of rhetoric in law school can "offer students a taxonomy for understanding reasoning both inside and outside the legal community").

223. Weaver, *Language Is Sermonic*, *supra* note 58, at 208 (quoting Cicero).

224. *Id.* at 209.

225. *Id.*

226. Richard M. Weaver, A Rhetoric and Composition Handbook 141 (reprt. 1974) (1967).

227. Weaver, *Language Is Sermonic*, *supra* note 58, at 209.

228. Robbins-Tiscione, *supra* note 35, at 64–65.

229. Weaver, *supra* note 139, at 86; *see also* The Rhetorical Tradition, *supra* note 30, at 1349; Schaub, *supra* note 159, at 95.

being defined belongs to a class that is "determinate and therefore predictable."[230]

Weaver observed that Lincoln argued consistently from definition.[231] For instance, in Lincoln's First Inaugural Address, given on March 4, 1861, just a few weeks before the beginning of the Civil War,[232] Lincoln described the perpetual nature of the United States:

> I hold that in contemplation of universal law, and of the Constitution, the Union of these states is perpetual. Perpetuity is implied, if not expressed, in the fundamental law of all national governments. It is safe to assert that no government proper ever had a provision in its organic law for its own termination. Continue to execute all the express provisions of our national Constitution and the Union will endure forever—it being impossible to destroy it except by some action not provided for in the instrument itself.[233]

Weaver identified this argument as an argument from definition.[234] The nature of all governments is self-preservation: to protect themselves from destruction from outside forces or within.[235] Lincoln made that argument, Weaver said, in response to the seceding states' argument that the United States was not authorized to use force against those states.[236]

A definition is a primary source for a legal argument, as well. In fact, Weaver noted that Lincoln's arguments were for that reason lawyerly: "[i]t can hardly be overlooked that this concentration upon definition produces a strongly legalistic speech, if we may conceive law as a process of defining actions."[237]

Courts also use definitions at the core of their reasoning. For example, in *Gideon v. Wainwright*, the U.S. Supreme Court concluded that under the Sixth Amendment, an individual has the right to appointed counsel in a state criminal prosecution through the Due Process Clause of the Fourteenth Amendment.[238] The Court quoted its decision in *Johnson v. Zerbst* for the proposition that the

---

230. WEAVER, *supra* note 139, at 86.

231. *Id.*

232. President Abraham Lincoln, First Inaugural Address (Mar. 4, 1861), *quoted in* FEHRMAN, *supra* note 188, at 128–30.

233. *Id.* at 130.

234. WEAVER, *supra* note 139, at 97.

235. *Id.*

236. *Id.*

237. *Id.* at 99.

238. Gideon v. Wainwright, 372 U.S. 335, 341–43 (1963).

right to counsel under the Sixth Amendment safeguards "fundamental human rights of life and liberty."[239] The Court looked to the "fundamental nature" of the Bill of Rights to show that those rights are so fundamental that they must be applied at the state level, in addition to being a federal guarantee.[240] The Court's reflection on the fundamental nature of the Bill of Rights speaks to the very point of Weaver's discussion on definition and genus: an argument must begin by defining or describing the nature of the concept under consideration.

Beginning with definition, Weaver's taxonomy for inventing an argument runs parallel to other taxonomies for inventing an argument that modern legal scholars have described. Those taxonomies demonstrate the close relationship between rhetoric and legal argumentation.[241] Susan E. Provenzano and Brian N. Larson, for example, detailed the taxonomy of a civil case using stasis theory.[242] *Stases* are "a method of invention and a means of locating the central points of the adjudication along with commonplace arguments."[243] Provenzano and Larson looked to Roman rhetoric, which divided the stases of a case into conjecture, definition, and quality.[244] These stases each have their own topics of invention.[245] When considering definition in the context of a modern civil case, parties look to the "observable content of authoritative legal texts" and "debate linguistic meaning, particularly in litigation over statutes."[246] This type of debate centers on "sources of ordinary meaning" such as dictionaries.[247] Another type of definitional argument relies on "legal standards to interpret, categorize, and apply that content," such as canons of construction, other statutory interpretive tools, and legislative history.[248]

Similarly, Wilson Huhn's taxonomy of five types of arguments begins with argument based on text. The text of the law is a source of a legal argument based on what Weaver called the "nature of the thing." Huhn noted that a textual argument can be made on the law itself—the federal Constitution or state constitutions, statutes, administrative regulations, or municipal codes—or on

239. *Id.* at 343 (quoting Johnson v. Zerbst, 304 U.S. 458, 462 (1938)).

240. *Id.* at 341.

241. *E.g.*, Provenzano & Larson, *supra* note 220, at 971; Venter, *supra* note 222, at 638; Levine & Saunders, *supra* note 26, at 122.

242. Provenzano & Larson, *supra* note 220, at 972.

243. *Id.* at 991.

244. *Id.* at 992.

245. *Id.* at 995.

246. *Id.* at 1025.

247. *Id.* at 1026.

248. *Id.*

the basis of the text of privately written documents such as wills and contracts.[249] As with the definitional argument described by Provenzano and Larson, Huhn's description of textual argument outlines plain meaning;[250] canons of construction;[251] and intratextual arguments[252] as ways to support a textual argument.

Comparison. Weaver viewed comparison as an important source of argument[253] because an advocate uses a standard to compare the nature of two things.[254] When drawing an analogy, an advocate "invoke[s] essential (though not exhaustive) correspondences," Weaver said.[255]

As Weaver noted, Lincoln used comparison in the Gettysburg Address to inspire the Union to continue fighting.[256] The opening line reminded the audience that eighty-seven years before, the nation had been "brought forth... conceived in Liberty."[257] Now was a parallel time in this country's life to have a "new birth of freedom," through the resolve of the people who died at Gettysburg and the strength of those remaining to see the war to its finish.[258]

Advocates routinely use analogies to compare the similarities of a precedent case to the current case or to distinguish precedent if the precedent is unfavorable.[259] Advocates may also compare arguments, hypotheticals, statutes, or any text to build a persuasive argument. The challenge in drawing an analogy or distinction is in finding the best point of comparison that connects to the argument at hand. A well-crafted comparison of precedent must be specific in lining up the relevant facts, holding, and court's reasoning for both cases being compared.

Courts also use comparisons. In *Carpenter v. United States*, for instance, the U.S. Supreme Court held that the government could not obtain data of a

---

249. Huhn, *supra* note 16, at 17.

250. *Id.* at 19–22.

251. *Id.* at 22–24.

252. *Id.* at 25–29.

253. Weaver, *supra* note 139, at 56.

254. The Rhetorical Tradition, *supra* note 30, at 1349.

255. Weaver, *supra* note 139, at 56–57.

256. *See id.* at 109; *see also* Schaub, *supra* note 159, at 95.

257. Weaver, *supra* note 139, at 109 (quoting President Abraham Lincoln, Gettysburg Address (Nov. 19, 1863)).

258. Schaub, *supra* note 159, at 74–76 (quoting President Abraham Lincoln, Gettysburg Address (Nov. 19, 1863)).

259. Huhn, *supra* note 16, at 42–43.

person's location from wireless carrier cell-site records without a warrant.[260] In that case, the Court had to consider a novel fact pattern—cell phones—and compare it to the Court's assessment of previous technologies based on Fourth Amendment doctrine.[261] The Court determined that "even greater privacy concerns" exist when considering cell phone records:

> In fact, historical cell-site records present even greater privacy concerns than the GPS monitoring of a vehicle we considered in *Jones*. Unlike the bugged container in *Knotts* or the car in *Jones*, a cell phone—almost a "feature of human anatomy," *Riley*—tracks nearly exactly the movements of its owner. While individuals regularly leave their vehicles, they compulsively carry cell phones with them all the time. A cell phone faithfully follows its owner beyond public thoroughfares and into private residences, doctor's offices, political headquarters, and other potentially revealing locales.[262]

The Court's comparison of cell phones to GPS monitoring and bugged containers demonstrated the need for even greater Fourth Amendment protection in the form of a warrant. Analogies aid an advocate or court in building a three-dimensional argument that takes into account the unique facts presented in a case.

Cause and effect. Policy arguments can be viewed as a type of argument employing cause and effect. Huhn described policy arguments as "look[ing] to the future for confirmation."[263]

As an example, the petitioner in *Miranda* devoted a portion of the latter part of the brief to quelling concerns that extending the right to counsel would create burdens on the police or justice system.[264] Under the heading, "Practical Considerations of Law Enforcement Accord With Giving the Sixth Amendment Its Full Meaning,"[265] the petitioner addressed two potential concerns related to implementing a warning: (1) cost of administration and (2) the inability to detect and punish crime.[266] The petitioner acknowledged that members of the Supreme Court had expressed concern with these practical implications in

260. Carpenter v. United States, 138 S. Ct. 2206, 2220–21 (2018).
261. *Id.* at 2217–19.
262. *Id.* at 2218 (internal citations omitted).
263. HUHN, *supra* note 16, at 51.
264. Brief for Petitioner, *supra* note 186, at 35–48.
265. *Id.* at 35.
266. *Id.* at 37.

their dissents in *Escobedo v. Illinois* and *Massiah v. United States*, and therefore those issues needed to be discussed directly in the brief in *Miranda*.[267] This comment exemplifies the importance of dissents to the discussion of the evolving nature of the law.[268]

Responding first to the concern that extending the right to counsel would cost the public defender system more money, the petitioner asserted that

> [t]here are undoubtedly cheaper methods of law enforcement than those contemplated by the American Constitution. While some critics have contested the right to counsel in cost terms, no member of this Court has ever attempted to put a price tag on constitutional rights. Pepper in the eyes is cheaper than a fair trial and respect for constitutional rights in law enforcement will inescapably cost money.
>
> Let it.[269]

The analogy and the short, two-word paragraph used by the petitioner accentuate the forcefulness of the response: a price tag cannot be put on the Constitution.

Regarding concerns about law enforcement being hindered by the rule sought in *Miranda*, the petitioner used a variety of sources in response, including commentary from judges, academia, the Senate, and the Department of Justice, among others.[270] The volume of sources and the specificity of the commentary over several pages of the brief provide an excellent example of how to gather sources to dispel public policy concerns and address the importance of balancing policy concerns and interests.[271]

Circumstance. An advocate argues from circumstance when the "facts" or "situation," as Weaver described, "dictate the decision."[272] Weaver said that this form of argument suggests an argument of expediency and urgency from the "present circumstance."[273] For instance, in the *Carpenter* decision, the Court

---

267. *Id.* at 36–37; *see* Escobedo v. Illinois, 378 U.S. 478 (1964); Massiah v. United States, 377 U.S. 201 (1964).

268. *See* Mark A. Hannah & Susie Salmon, *Against the Grain: The Secret Role of Dissents in Integrating Rhetoric Across the Curriculum*, 20 Nev. L.J. 935, 943–44 (Spring 2020) (discussing the persuasive force of dissents).

269. Brief for Petitioner, *supra* note 186, at 38–39.

270. *Id.* at 39–42.

271. *Id.*

272. Weaver, *supra* note 139, at 57.

273. *Id.*

commented about how it must account for the advancing technology of cell-site location information (CSLI):

> While the records in this case reflect the state of technology at the start of the decade, the accuracy of the technology of CSLI is rapidly approaching GPS-level precision. As the number of cell sites has proliferated, the geographic area covered by each cell sector has shrunk, particularly in urban areas. In addition, with new technology measuring the time and angle of signals hitting their towers, wireless carriers already have the capability to pinpoint a phone's location within 50 meters.[274]

Here, the Court considered the present and soon-to-be-present circumstances of technology as a practical matter.

In a more heartfelt and sensitive matter, Thurgood Marshall, before his appointment to the U.S. Supreme Court, wrote a thirteen-page brief in *Brown v. Board of Education*, presenting the factual reality of Black children's lives in the United States under *Plessy v. Ferguson*.[275] In his brief, Marshall showed the fundamental unfairness and damaging nature of the separate-but-equal system of education.[276] Marshall's brief brought home to the Court the state of the situation for Black children by discussing a doll study.[277] In that study, children were shown a white doll and a Black doll.[278] Repeatedly, Black children preferred the white doll.[279] Dr. Kenneth Clark concluded from the study that the children felt inadequate and inferior, and those feelings became "integrated into the very structure of personality as it's developing."[280] The study demonstrated the urgent need for change, Marshall argued, because segregation "[i]nterferes with motivation for learning and instills in [a Black child] a feeling of inferiority resulting in a personal insecurity, confusion, and frustration that condemns [the child] to an ineffective role as a citizen and member of soci-

---

274. Carpenter v. United States, 138 S. Ct. 2206, 2219 (2018) (internal citation omitted).

275. Love Koenig, Oseid & Vorenberg, *supra* note 177, at 1284; *see* Plessy v. Ferguson, 163 U.S. 537 (1896).

276. Love Koenig, Oseid & Vorenberg, *supra* note 177, at 1281.

277. *Id.* at 1284–85.

278. *Id.* at 1284.

279. *Id.*

280. *Id.* (quoting RICHARD KLUGER, SIMPLE JUSTICE: THE HISTORY OF BROWN V. BOARD OF EDUCATION AND BLACK AMERICA'S STRUGGLE FOR EQUALITY 315 (1975)).

ety."[281] In some arguments, such as Marshall's argument in *Brown*, the facts themselves can be the most persuasive motivator for change.

Testimony or authority. Arguments from testimony or authority have a natural connection to the rationale supporting an advocate's brief and later the court's decision. Weaver noted that testimony and authority present external sources, while the other topics for argument discussed above are internal.[282] By that he meant that an internal source "is a direct perception by us of an aspect of phenomena," while an external source is someone else's "reported perception."[283] An example of testimony in a criminal matter is a police report,[284] while an affidavit or deposition transcript can serve as testimony in a civil matter. Weaver observed that testimony "affirm[s] that someone else affirms it."[285] In the course of a legal case, that affirmation is tested by cross-examination.

Weaver defined an argument from authority as "bring[ing] in a great name or some other exalted source whose word on the subject in question is regarded as final."[286] The four sources of law—constitutions, statutes, case precedent, and administrative materials—are primary authorities to which the courts in a corresponding jurisdiction must adhere. Secondary sources—commentary on the law such as treatises and law review articles—may be persuasive but are not binding on a court.

3.2.4. The layout of an argument

Lawyers need to know how to think critically about an argument. A lawyer should be able to identify the component parts of an argument and should have the tools to assess the argument's strengths, weaknesses, and potential fallacies. As part of his theory of practical reasoning, Toulmin created a framework for laying out an argument, seeking to develop a logic that would capture the sophistication of practical arguments such as those made by lawyers.[287] Syllogisms, Toulmin noted, were the customary form of logic relied upon by logicians to analyze arguments when Toulmin first published *The Uses*

---

281. *Id.* (quoting Brief for Appellants at 13, Brown v. Bd. of Educ., 347 U.S. 483 (1954) (No. 1)).

282. Weaver, *supra* note 226, at 145.

283. *Id.*

284. *Id.*

285. *Id.*

286. *Id.*

287. Foss, Foss & Trapp, *supra* note 14, at 79.

of Argument, his major work on logical argumentation, in 1958.[288] Toulmin was critical of the extensive overreliance on syllogisms as laid out by Aristotle, however, because he felt that they were too simple as a logical form: in his view, the major-premise/minor-premise/conclusion format of a syllogism did not adequately capture the range of variables presented by practical arguments,[289] which are based on what is probable and not what is absolute.[290] Toulmin viewed mathematical and jurisprudential logic as "rival methods," and he favored jurisprudential logic for its ability to handle complexity.[291] Just as in law, where an argument is presented to justify a position being advanced in court, the layout of a practical argument as created by Toulmin represents the process of justifying a claim.[292] Justifying a claim is a retrospective process of presenting and communicating supporting arguments (and testing them), while inferring an argument from evidence is a prospective endeavor.[293]

Toulmin's layout of an argument contains the following six concepts: claim, grounds, warrant, backing, qualifier, and rebuttal.[294] Every argument contains a claim, grounds, and warrant.[295] The backing, qualifier, and rebuttal, Toulmin asserted, are optional components that add to an argument's persuasive appeal.[296] The advantage of this layout over a formal syllogism is that it

---

288. Toulmin, *supra* note 113, at 89.

289. *Id.* It is worth noting the enthymeme here, also laid out by Aristotle and which is a "rhetorical equivalent of the syllogism." Edward P. J. Corbett, Classical Rhetoric for the Modern Student 60 (3d ed. 1990). An enthymeme is a "truncated syllogism" that contains a conclusion and one premise, while the other unstated premise is implied. *Id.* While a syllogism results in a firm conclusion, an enthymeme results in a "tentative conclusion from probable premises." *Id.* The enthymeme is a useful construct for creating an argument based on the probabilities of human activity, *id.* at 61, but the focus of Toulmin's work in *The Uses of Argument* is on creating a layout that adds new components for identifying and analyzing a claim.

290. *See* Toulmin, *supra* note 113, at 137; *see also* Michael D. Murray, *The Great Recession and the Rhetorical Canons of Law and Economics*, 58 Loyola L. Rev. 615, 624 n.21 (2012); Foss, Foss & Trapp, *supra* note 14, at 83.

291. Toulmin, *supra* note 113, at 88.

292. *Id.* at 6; Foss, Foss & Trapp, *supra* note 14, at 84–85 (citing Toulmin, *supra* note 113, at 6).

293. Foss, Foss & Trapp, *supra* note 14, at 85 (quoting Stephen Toulmin, Richard Rieke & Allan Janik, Introduction to Reasoning 9 (2d ed. 1984)); Berger & Stanchi, *supra* note 60, at 123.

294. Paul T. Wangerin, *A Multidisciplinary Analysis of the Structure of Persuasive Arguments*, 16 Harv. J.L. & Pub. Pol'y 294, 205 (1993).

295. *Id.*

296. *Id.*

more accurately and fully describes how the parts of a persuasive argument fit together and how deductive and inductive arguments blend in such arguments.[297] Toulmin used diagrams to visually depict the way that the component parts of his layout work, and some of those diagrams are presented here.[298]

The first three components—grounds, warrant, claim—depict the movement through an argument:

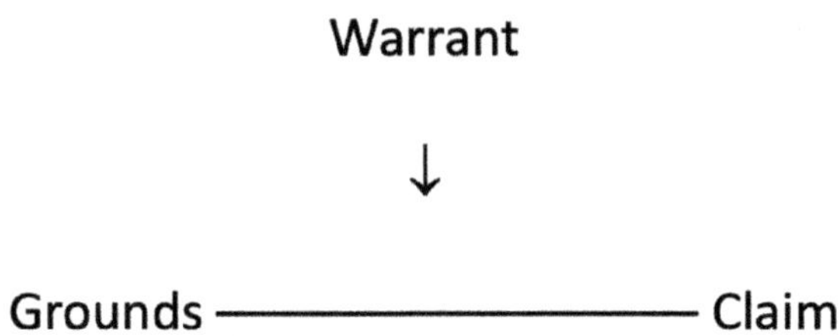

This diagram shows that an argument moves from the grounds through a warrant to the claim,[299] and Toulmin described those terms as follows:

- *Grounds* refers to the factual evidence, the "data, observations, personal opinions or factual materials relevant to an issue being considered."[300] More modern sources use the word *grounds*,[301] while Toulmin originally used the term *data*,[302] which he defined as the "facts we appeal to as a foundation for the claim."[303]
- Claim means a "conclusion whose merits we are seeking to establish."[304] A claim pertains to a matter in controversy and is associated with the words therefore or because.[305]

---

297. *Id.* at 203.

298. Toulmin, *supra* note 113, at 92.

299. Wayne Brockriede & Douglas Ehninger, *Toulmin on Argument: An Interpretation and Application*, 46 Q.J. Speech, 44, 44 (1960).

300. Wangerin, *supra* note 294, at 204.

301. *Id.*

302. Toulmin, *supra* note 113, at 90; Brockriede & Ehninger, *supra* note 299, at 45.

303. Toulmin, *supra* note 113, at 90.

304. *Id.*

305. Brockriede & Ehninger, *supra* note 299, at 45–46.

- Warrant is a proposition, a hypothetical statement, that serves as a bridge that can "authorize the sort of step to which our particular argument commits us."[306] A step is the link between the grounds and claim. A step requires us to ask, "How did you get there?"[307] Therefore, a warrant provides legitimacy to the step.[308] As in legal logic, Toulmin recognized the importance of justifying the step by showing that the step from the grounds to the claim is appropriate and legitimate.[309]

Grounds, warrants, and claims correspond to deductive—i.e., rule-based—reasoning in traditional logic, so a persuasive argument must include these components.[310] In legal rules-based reasoning, noted Paul Wangerin, the rules of law fill the role of a warrant.[311] However, added Wangerin, in terms of warrants, Toulmin's work also invokes case-based reasoning, a form of reasoning where an advocate looks back to previous precedent that is similar to the present situation to extrapolate from that precedent how to solve the current legal issue.[312] Wangerin noted the interesting relationship between rule- and case-based reasoning: "[r]ules often are nothing more than a synthesis of the results in a number of past cases."[313] Nonetheless, there is a difference between a lower court applying well-settled law and established rules articulated in the precedent in a trial-level brief and an appellate court seeking to establish a new legal standard or warrant. Although a rule is a compilation of legal principles that have been synthesized from multiple cases, when a court on appeal must identify the new rule to fill a gap in the law, then a case-based reasoning approach, often supplemented by other forms of reasoning such as policy-based reasoning, is used to develop the new rule.

For instance, in *Carpenter*, the petitioner's Summary of Argument started with the following paragraphs:

---

306. Toulmin, *supra* note 113, at 91.

307. *Id.* at 90–91.

308. *Id.* at 92.

309. *Id.*; *see also* Berger, *supra* note 32, at 51 (discussing the inferential leap from grounds to a conclusion).

310. Wangerin, *supra* note 294, at 204, 211.

311. *Id.* at 210.

312. *Id.* at 213.

313. *Id.* at 215 (noting additionally that "to use Toulmin's terminology, a warrant is a synthesis of the various things that serve as the backing for the warrant").

> I. Under this Court's recent Fourth Amendment cases, the government conducted a search when it obtained 127 days of petitioner's cell phone location records from his cellular service provider.
>
> A. When the government employs new technology to obtain sensitive personal information in a way that diminishes the degree of privacy that individuals reasonably expected prior to the technology's adoption, it conducts a search under the Fourth Amendment. Applying this principle in *United States v. Jones*, five Justices concluded that longer-term GPS tracking of a car violates reasonable expectations of privacy. Tracing a person's geographical movements reveals highly sensitive personal information, and prior to the digital age, people reasonably expected that police in most investigations would not have followed a person and recorded her every movement for days or weeks on end.
>
> The same analysis controls this case. CSLI exposes a great volume of highly sensitive information about a person, revealing where she has been and whom she has been with throughout each day. And as acute as that concern is today, it will only sharpen over time, as the volume and precision of CSLI records steadily increases. Furthermore, just as with GPS tracking, the government prior to the widespread proliferation of cell phones could have obtained only very limited information about a person's past geographical movements. Police officers could have, for example, interviewed witnesses, sought security camera footage, or examined store receipts near the scene of a crime. But these tactics pale in comparison to the unprecedent surveillance time machine that CSLI provides.[314]

Here, Carpenter, the petitioner, used case-based reasoning to support the argument that the Supreme Court should apply the same conceptual framework from *Jones*, based on an inference of the similarity in technology between the information provided by GPS location services and that provided by CSLI.

Toulmin's layout adds three other components not found in a classical syllogism: qualifier, backing, and rebuttal, as depicted in this diagram:

In brief, this diagram illustrates the following:

314. Brief for Petitioner at 10–11, Carpenter v. United States, 138 S. Ct. 2206 (2018) (No. 16-402) (citation omitted).

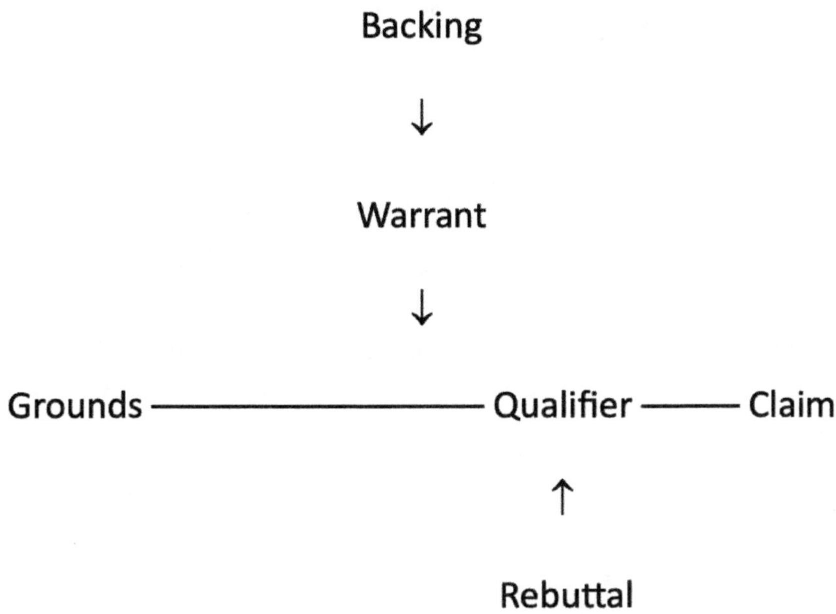

- *Qualifier* describes a degree of force.[315] Qualifiers explain whether a case is an exception to a rule because of "special facts," for instance.[316] They also show a warrant's strength on a step.[317]
- *Backing* is what supports a warrant. Additional facts can provide further grounds or confirm or rebut whether a warrant should be used.[318] Warrants also can be backed by "categorical statements of fact" and the grounds directly supporting conclusions.[319] Grounds and warrants can be confused,[320] and warrants need to be kept separate from backing.[321] Toulmin stated that we "gloss over ... the transition from backing to warrant.... [F]or philosophical purposes it leaves the effec-

315. Toulmin, *supra* note 113, at 93 (examples of qualifiers include "necessarily" and "probably").

316. *Id.*

317. *Id.* at 94.

318. *Id.* at 95–96.

319. *Id.* at 98.

320. *Id.*

321. *Id.* at 100.

tive structure of our arguments insufficiently candid."[322] Accordingly, the reality is that a practical argument requires more than simply a major premise and a minor premise; a practical argument also needs grounds, conclusions, warrants, and backing "to do justice to the situation."[323]

- *Rebuttal* refers to "circumstances in which the general authority of the warrant would have to be set aside."[324] A qualifier identifies situations where a "claim will not hold good or will hold good only in a qualified and restricted way."[325]

The warrant, grounds, and claim roughly correspond to the major premise, minor premise, and conclusion in a syllogism,[326] and yet the addition of the qualifier, backing, and rebuttal provides the extra categories needed to tackle the complexity of the working logic of human arguments.[327] Toulmin explained that formal logic and its application had diverged such that formal logic could no longer adequately express the working logic of human arguments.[328] Wayne Brockriede and Douglas Ehninger identified seven advantages to Toulmin's layout of an argument over formal logic: (1) it allows for warrant-establishing arguments (where backing is used to establish the "validity of the assumption underlying the inference"), (2) it highlights the inferences and relationships among the components of an argument, (3) it provides a framework for arguments based on probability, (4) it emphasizes movement from grounds through warrant to claim and how each part of the argument works together, (5) it lays open each component of the argument to be reviewed critically, (6) it permits an analysis of weaknesses in the argument, and (7) it addresses material validity in an argument.[329]

Toulmin looked to jurisprudence in developing the layout of an argument;[330] and, in turn, these categories form a useful framework for considering how to

322. *Id.* at 104.

323. *Id.* at 106.

324. *Id.* at 94.

325. Brockriede & Ehninger, *supra* note 299, at 45 (accordingly, "the rebuttal anticipates certain objections which might otherwise be advanced against the argument").

326. Wangerin, *supra* note 294, at 205.

327. Toulmin, *supra* note 113, at 100, 131; *see also* Saunders, *supra* note 12, at 571 (describing the flexibility of Toulmin's layout of an argument).

328. Toulmin, *supra* note 113, at 8–9.

329. Brockriede & Ehninger, *supra* note 299, at 46–47.

330. Toulmin, *supra* note 113, at 131; *see also* Berger, *supra* note 32, at 52.

develop a legal argument.[331] Moreover, practical legal arguments are not based on indisputably true premises, as in a formal syllogism—the grounds and claims are often subject to debate among parties. Accordingly, Toulmin's layout allows an advocate to think critically about an argument without being constrained by an overly rigid framework,[332] as well as to generate arguments.[333]

3.2.5. Arrangement

In addition to laying out an argument to create logical soundness, an advocate must consider how to arrange the argument to emphasize its persuasive force. In other words, the order in which arguments are presented should show the arguments in their best light. However, the order and structure of arguments vary depending on the type of argument being made.[334]

General order. Perelman began his comments on persuasion through structure by expressing the importance of what he called the *exordia*, or prelude or introduction.[335] The exordia should foster goodwill and win over the audience.[336] According to Aristotle, Perelman noted, the exordia can reduce or eliminate prejudice.[337]

President John F. Kennedy displayed his understanding of the importance of a good introduction in his Address on Communism and Germany in 1963. In that address in West Berlin, he began: "Two thousand years ago the proud boast was 'civis Romanus sum.' Today, in the world of freedom, the proudest boast is 'Ich bin ein Berliner.'"[338] This famous line, "Ich bin ein Berliner," captured the ears and hearts of the Berliners listening to his speech.

Similarly, an advocate writing a brief must understand the paramount importance of the brief's introduction. There, an advocate needs to clearly articulate the relief sought and provide context about the nature of the motion and parties so that the judge can quickly grasp the nature of the motion and

331. Saunders, *supra* note 12, at 569–71 (describing the different stages of litigation where the layout can aid a lawyer in analyzing a case).

332. *Id.* at 571 ("The grounds-warrant-claim model is more flexible than the syllogism because, by recognizing qualifiers, it accounts for the place of inference and uncertainty in judicial reasoning and decision-making.").

333. Berger, *supra* note 32, at 52.

334. PERELMAN, *supra* note 75, at 146.

335. *Id.* at 147.

336. *Id.*

337. *Id.*

338. President John F. Kennedy, Address on Communism and Germany (June 26, 1963), *quoted in* FEHRMAN, *supra* note 188, at 335.

the grounds for it.[339] On appeal, the "Summary of Argument" section creates a space for an advocate to provide a "'holistic' picture of the case," where the court can return for a critical overview of the argument.[340]

Thereafter, the order of the arguments can proceed in three ways, according to Perelman: (1) the strongest argument can be placed first, (2) the strongest argument can be placed last, or (3) the strongest arguments can be placed at the beginning and at the end.[341] To decide how to order arguments, an advocate should consider placing each argument "at the moment of greatest impact" and adapting to the audience.[342]

For instance, in the respondent's brief in *MCI Telecommunications Corp. v. American Telephone & Telegraph Co.*, a statutory interpretation case before the Supreme Court, AT&T's counsel used the following main-point headings:

I. The Language and Structure of The Act Do Not Permit The FCC To Eliminate The Requirement That All Rates Be Filed

II. This Court's Consistent Decisions For A Century Foreclose The FCC's Claim That Section 203(b)(2) Can Be Construed To Uphold A Detariffing Rule

III. Congress Has Ratified The D.C. Circuit's Interpretation Of The Act And It Is To Congress That Petitioners Must Turn[343]

Consistent with Perelman's ordering of arguments and Huhn's five types of arguments, the first argument in the respondent's brief relies on the text of the Communications Act as the strongest argument, followed by an argument based on precedent, and then a legislative history argument.

Strength of an argument. Clearly, then, an advocate must evaluate the fullness and strength of an argument, noted Perelman, when determining an argument's persuasive effect.[344] This is not true of mathematical demonstration, in contrast, where the elegance of a proof relates to how efficiently it is presented.[345]

---

339. Richard K. Neumann Jr. & Sheila Simon, Legal Writing 186 (2008).

340. Mary Beth Beazley, A Practical Guide to Advocacy 214 (4th ed. 2014).

341. Perelman, *supra* note 75, at 148.

342. *Id.* at 149.

343. Respondent's Brief at ii–iii, MCI Telecomms. Corp. v. Am. Tel. & Tel. Co., 512 U.S. 218 (1994) (Nos. 93-356, 93-521) (subheadings omitted).

344. Perelman, *supra* note 75, at 138.

345. *Id.*

Perelman asked, "Is the strong argument the one that persuades effectively, or is it the one that must convince every reasonable mind?"[346] Strength is assessed by considering an argument's efficacy and validity.[347] Strength depends on adherence of the listeners to the premises of the argument, on the pertinence of the premises, on the close or distant relationship of the premises to the defended thesis, on the objections that can be brought against the argument, and on the manner in which the objections can be refuted.[348] A worn argument is weaker than a new, novel succinct argument; therefore, when introducing a weak argument, an advocate should mention that it is a subsidiary argument.[349]

Moreover, strength is "a function of the audience, of its convictions, of its traditions, and of the methods of reasoning appropriate to it."[350] Thus, an advocate must reinforce an argument with the end goal of capturing the audience's hearts and minds.[351] An argument not adapted to the audience can reflect negatively on the speaker's ethos.[352]

Perelman noted that an argument's fullness may result not only from presentation but also from repetition, from the amplification of an argument.[353] President Lyndon Johnson used repetition to great effect in his State of the Union address in 1964, in which he declared an "unconditional war on poverty in America."[354] Johnson enumerated a list of action items, starting each sentence with the phrase *We must*:

> We must expand our small but our successful area redevelopment program.
>
> We must enact youth employment legislation to put jobless, aimless, hopeless youngsters to work on useful projects.
>
> We must distribute more food to the needy through a broader food stamp program....[355]

---

346. *Id.* at 140.
347. *Id.*
348. *Id.*
349. *Id.* at 141, 144.
350. *Id.* at 140.
351. *Id.* at 138.
352. *Id.* at 139.
353. *Id.* at 144.
354. President Lyndon Johnson, State of the Union Address (Jan. 8, 1964), *quoted in* FEHRMAN, *supra* note 188, at 342.
355. *Id.* at 343–44.

Johnson identified a total of thirteen separate points starting with *We must*.[356] The repetition of those words created a cadence that built in intensity to the final point: "[a]bove all, we must release $11 billion of tax reduction into the private spending stream to create new jobs and new markets in every area of this land."[357] In brief writing, the repetition of certain words, especially theme words, can unify an argument and focus a reader's attention. The proper use of headings, summary paragraphs, thesis sentences, and wrap-up sentences can help an advocate to draw a reader's attention and maintain it.

However, although repetition can give presence to certain arguments, it can be tedious.[358] Similarly, the quantity of arguments is not dispositive: psychological, social, and economic limits prevent advocates from amplifying discourse.[359] Therefore, an advocate must make choices on how to limit arguments in terms of time and the number of arguments presented to an audience.[360]

Sometimes less is more in other ways too. An advocate can allude to an argument without fully developing it: some arguments should be left to the audience's imagination.[361] And sometimes giving up an argument is advantageous because it shows that the remaining arguments are plentiful and strong, and "a concession is proof of goodwill."[362] Alternatively, an advocate can concede a point but then present an even stronger argument.[363] These points are true for both written and oral advocacy in persuasion.

Finally, Perelman cautioned that advocates tend to overvalue their arguments and undervalue their opponents' arguments.[364] Thus, an advocate should consider using opponents' own analogies against them.[365] While strategizing and crafting a brief, then, an advocate must consider both sides of the argument. To do this, it can be helpful to chart the arguments in favor of a client's position, as well as likely counterarguments. An advocate should consider how to weaken an opposing party's analogies by arguing that a different case makes

356. *Id.*
357. *Id.* at 344.
358. PERELMAN, *supra* note 75, at 144.
359. *Id.* at 139.
360. *Id.*
361. *Id.* at 144.
362. *Id.*
363. *Id.* at 144–45.
364. *Id.* at 141.
365. *Id.* at 142.

for a better comparison or that the analogy presented by the opposing party presents a weak or flawed comparison.

****

In sum, the rhetorical process of composing an argument is multifaceted; the theories of Perelman, Toulmin, and Weaver can assist an advocate in creating, drafting, and evaluating a persuasive argument at each step in that process.

4. Argumentation in action

> *There is one special virtue in the parallel between logic and jurisprudence: it helps to keep in the centre of the picture the* **critical** *function of the reason.*
>
> —Stephen Toulmin[366]

Legal argumentation is a locus of rhetorical theories in action. In particular, the writings of Ruth Bader Ginsburg as an attorney and as a U.S. Supreme Court justice solidly illustrate contemporary rhetorical theories of argumentation.

Ginsburg's advocacy as an attorney on behalf of gender equality is a natural fit for a chapter on legal argumentation because her reasoning was fully developed and clearly articulated. She established rock-solid foundations for her arguments and then explained those arguments in a way that would compel the Court to rule in her clients' favor. Ginsburg's arguments overcame inertia when she represented the party seeking to overturn a decision, and her arguments were equally compelling when supporting the position of the responding party.

Similarly, Ginsburg's writings as a justice on the Court were effective because she did not take for granted that the reader knew each step in the discussion—she backed up each statement with authority and explanation, much like a teacher explaining something to a student.

Each example below spotlights a key rhetorical theory, illustrated through Ginsburg's advocacy or her argumentation as the author of a Supreme Court opinion. First, Perelman's directive for audience adherence to an argument takes center stage in Ginsburg's briefing in *Reed v. Reed*.[367] Second, Toulmin's

---

366. TOULMIN, *supra* note 113, at 7.
367. 404 U.S. 71 (1971).

practical reasoning becomes theory in practice in Ginsburg's application of it to argue for a warrant in *Weinberger v. Wiesenfeld*.[368] And third, in *Yates v. United States*, Weaver's method of invention sets the foundation for Justice Ginsburg's consideration of the power of words in her statutory interpretation.[369]

4.1. Audience adherence: A call to action in *Reed v. Reed*

> *The preeminent realm of argumentation, dialectic, and rhetoric is that in which values come into play.*
>
> —Chaïm Perelman[370]

Reed v. Reed, one of a series of cases on which Ginsburg worked in the 1970s in an effort to gain equal protection for women—and men—under the Constitution, presented Ginsburg with an opportunity to consider the Equal Protection Clause's application to gender.[371] Simultaneous to a national movement to ratify the Equal Rights Amendment, Ginsburg aimed for the U.S. Supreme Court to establish a strict scrutiny standard of review for cases involving gender classification.[372] *Reed* was one of those cases.[373]

The writing by Ginsburg and her cocounsel[374] on behalf of Sally Reed is passionate and compelling. It is a call to action in the very best rhetorical tradition, as described by Perelman. The arguments for Sally perfectly exemplify Perelman's view that rhetorical argumentation "elicit[s] or increase[s] the adherence of the members of an audience to theses that are presented for their consent."[375] That adherence is evident in the Court's decision in *Reed*, which tracks the language of Ginsburg's argument. Surely, Sally's counsel achieved a meeting of the minds with the Court.

368. 420 U.S. 636 (1975).

369. 574 U.S. 528 (2015).

370. Perelman, *supra* note 75, at 160.

371. *Reed*, 404 U.S. at 74.

372. Love Koenig, Oseid & Vorenberg, *supra* note 177, at 1287–88.

373. *See id.*

374. Ginsburg's cocounsel were Allen R. Derr, Dorothy Kenyon, Pauli Murray, and Melvin L. Wulf.

375. Perelman, *supra* note 75, at 9.

4.1.1. Background of the case

Reed involved a dispute between two parents over the administration of their deceased minor son's estate in Idaho.[376] The parents, Sally Reed and Cecil Reed, had separated prior to their son's passing, and they both sought to be the administrator of his estate.[377]

The probate court ordered that Cecil, the father, be appointed.[378] The probate court read two statutes of the Idaho Code as controlling, and read those statutes to provide a preference for Cecil—as a male—to be the administrator.[379] One statute allowed for the father or mother to administer the estate of an intestate person, but the other statute expressly provided that "males must be preferred to females" in naming an administrator.[380] The probate court, in naming Cecil, noted that both parents were equally entitled to the position but that the father was to be preferred under the statute.[381] The probate court therefore did not assess the parties' individual capabilities to perform the functions of administrator.[382]

On appeal, the Idaho Supreme Court held that the statute preferring male administrators was "mandatory" and left no room for a probate court's discretion.[383] The Idaho Supreme Court rejected Sally's argument that the statute violated the Equal Protection Clause.[384] Sally then sought review by the U.S. Supreme Court.[385]

4.1.2. Arguments before the Court

Using methods cited by Perelman as effective ways to gain audience adherence, Sally's opening brief and reply brief seek adherence from the Court—that is, the audience—and present a call to action. Sally's briefing presents a compelling thesis by establishing premises about gender equality and using arguments that speak to a change in value judgments.

376. *Reed*, 404 U.S. at 73–74.
377. *Id.* at 71–72.
378. *Id.* at 72.
379. *Id.*
380. *Id.* at 73.
381. *Id.*
382. *Id.*
383. *Id.* at 74.
384. *Id.*
385. *Id.*

What is notable about these briefs is that in addition to using established precedent and authority to support Sally's position, the advocates presented arguments to move the Court to push past accepted notions of the day (regarding, for instance, the inherent competence or expertise of a man or woman in handling the administration of an estate) and focus on the kernel of the issue: the Equal Protection Clause does not allow men and women to be treated differently under the law when the legislation considers them to be similarly situated.[386] Although the advocates sought a change in the current position, they created a rhetorically strong argument by spotlighting the ideal of upholding constitutional law and thus embracing a technique endorsed by Perelman: targeting audience values.[387]

Sally's opening brief begins by embracing another rhetorical technique recognized by Perelman: establishing premises about which the audience can agree as a foundation for later agreement on some type of action. Specifically, the brief seeks a meeting of the minds with the Court that one of the Idaho statutes drew a line "mandating subordination of women to men without regard to individual capacity"[388]—and that this line required close judicial scrutiny.[389] This sex line,

> [a]rbitrarily ranking the woman as inferior to the man by directing that the probate court take no account of the respective qualifications of the individuals involved, lacks a fair and substantial relation to a permissible legislative purpose. The judgment that "in general men are better qualified to act as an administrator than are women" rests on totally unfounded assumptions of differences in mental capacity or experience relevant to the office of administrator. To eliminate a woman who shares an eligibility category with a man when there is no basis in fact to assume that women are less competent to administer than are men, is patently unreasonable and constitutionally impermissible.[390]

Here, Sally's counsel identified the faulty assumption, or premise, on which the statute rested, arguing that a classification based on sex, without accounting for the applicants' individual qualifications, stems from unfair views of the inherent capabilities of men and women for such a position, both in terms of

386. *E.g.*, Brief for Appellant at 8, *Reed*, 404 U.S. 71 (No. 70-4).
387. PERELMAN, *supra* note 75, at 26.
388. Brief for Appellant, *supra* note 386, at 5.
389. *Id.*
390. *Id.* at 7.

capacity and life experience. This argument flagged for the Court the narrative underlying the provision's simple statement that a man is to be preferred over a woman. Specifically, Sally's counsel asserted, the sex line drawn in the statute (1) created a suspect classification with no compelling justification; and, alternatively, (2) without regard for the suspect classification, lacked a reasonable relation to any legitimate state interest.[391]

Sally's counsel used an analogy to race to support her argument that the statute was based on a faulty premise.[392] Counsel directed this analogy toward the Court as the audience because the Court had considered race cases in recent years.[393] Therefore, counsel used the analogy as a means to gain the Court's adherence by connecting the current argument to an argument that had been previously successful before the Court. Counsel argued that it is impermissible to "distinguish on the basis of congenital and unalterable biological traits of birth over which the individual has no control and for which he or she should not be penalized."[394] Specifically, such legislative discrimination, "for purposes unrelated to any biological difference between the sexes, ranks with legislative discrimination based on race, another condition of birth, and merits no greater judicial deference."[395]

Sally's counsel continued the analogy by comparing other minority groups "that have been assisted toward full equality before the law via the 'suspect classification' doctrine."[396] Noting that the road to equal opportunity in the face of the "pervasive social, cultural and legal roots of sex-based discrimination" is long,[397] counsel asserted that women lacked political or legislative power to alter the discriminatory practices that they must endure under the law and in society.[398] The authors warned that without "firm" constitutional protection, "women seeking to be judged on their individual merits" will continue to face discrimination sanctioned under the law.[399]

In the appellant brief, Sally's counsel sought to obtain the Court's consent through a meeting of the minds, as described by Perelman, by arguing that

391. *Id.* at 10.
392. *Id.* at 15.
393. *See* Love Koenig, Oseid & Vorenberg, *supra* note 177, at 1289.
394. Brief for Appellant, *supra* note 386, at 15.
395. *Id.* at 24.
396. *Id.* at 6, 24–25.
397. *Id.* at 6.
398. *Id.* at 6, 26–32.
399. *Id.* at 6.

the time was right to recognize Sally's rights. To achieve a meeting of the minds, the Court would need to recognize a shift in value judgments about gender equality under the law. Sally's counsel asserted that the Court's own decisions had contributed to women's "separate and unequal status" but that the "national conscience has been awakened" to what is the dominant male culture's "sometimes subtle" treatment of women as inferior.[400] They asserted that, increasingly, federal and state courts had criticized sex lines drawn in the law and that those lines had not survived judicial scrutiny.[401] Therefore, they argued, "the time is ripe for *this* Court to repudiate the premise that, with minimal justification, the legislature may draw 'a sharp line between the sexes,' just as this Court has repudiated once settled law that differential treatment of the races is constitutionally permissible."[402] Extrapolating from other courts' conclusions about sex lines, they pointed out that biological differences are not relevant to the duties of an estate administrator[403]—and that a state's interest in avoiding a hearing on the capacity of the candidates for administrator should not justify discrimination on the basis of sex.[404]

This discussion of a change in value judgments carries through the reply brief. Responding to Cecil's counsel, Sally's counsel stressed in the reply brief that the issue before the Court was vital and "at least as substantial as any this Court has heard: the constitutional right of a person, who is a woman, to be judged on the basis of her individual qualifications, rather than pre-judged by a male legislature's assignment of second rank status to all members of the female sex."[405] Again employing argument by example, counsel noted that another, similar male-preference law in the District of Columbia had been eliminated by Congress as "outmoded and discriminatory."[406] However, laws like those in Idaho were "still flourishing" because the Court had not yet stated a "principle of equality before the law without regard to sex."[407]

Sally's counsel concluded by employing Perelman's technique of incitement to action. The unacceptable "myth" that women are not as capable as men (based on assumptions that women are less educated or have less practical

400. *Id.*
401. *Id.*
402. *Id.* (emphasis added).
403. *Id.* at 7.
404. *Id.*
405. Reply Brief for Appellant at 2, Reed v. Reed, 404 U.S. 71 (1971) (No. 70-4).
406. *Id.* (quoting H.R. Rep. No. 92-178, at 1, 3, 6 (1971)).
407. *Id.*

knowledge about financial matters), Sally's counsel stated, was perpetuated through the Court's silence in not correcting these notions:

> The time to break the vicious cycle which sex discriminatory laws create is overdue. If a legislature can bar a woman from service as a fiduciary on the basis of once popular, but never proved, assumptions that women are less qualified than men are to perform such services, then the myth becomes insulated from attack, because the law deprives women of the opportunity to prove it false.
>
> Sally Reed awaits a day in Court on her application to be appointed administrator; all women await this Court's affirmation that the Constitution guarantees to them, together with men, equal justice under the law.[408]

Here is a call to action, premised on the value judgments that Perelman found critical in argumentation: if the Court doesn't stay silent, if it does the right thing by calling out a violation of women's rights under the Equal Protection Clause, then the Court can correct the injustices in society.

4.1.3. U.S. Supreme Court decision

The U.S. Supreme Court's decision reflects consideration of these arguments, illustrating the success of Sally's counsel in using Perelman's theories of gaining audience adherence and eliciting incitement to action.

In its decision, the Court embraced the points made by Sally's counsel. The Court, recognizing the irrationality of the sex line drawn in the case, first noted that in Idaho a woman could be an administrator and would be given preference over male relatives if her spouse died intestate.[409] The Court also took notice that because women live longer, a large number of estates are administered by women.[410] The Court established that the statute at issue, section 15-314, was subject to scrutiny under the Equal Protection Clause because it accorded different treatment to applicants based on their sex.[411] It also recognized that although the states may treat different classes in different ways under the Fourteenth Amendment, the states may not legislate different treatment of classes of people "on the basis of criteria wholly unrelated to the objective of

408. *Id.* at 3.
409. *Reed*, 404 U.S. at 75.
410. *Id.*
411. *Id.*

that statute."[412] Therefore, the Court characterized the issue before it as whether the different treatment of the parents based on their sex bears a rational relationship to the state objective that the two Idaho statutes sought to advance.[413]

The Court accepted Sally's counsel's call to action and reasoned that men and women, when similarly situated, must be treated equally. The Court noted the Idaho Supreme Court's conclusion that section 15-312 eliminated controversy when multiple applicants who were equally entitled sought to become the administrator of an estate:[414] in other words, the section was meant to reduce the probate courts' workload, which the U.S. Supreme Court understood to have "some legitimacy."[415] However, the Court stated, the "crucial question" is whether the provision advances "that objective in a manner consistent with the command of the Equal Protection Clause."[416] The Court said no.[417] To answer otherwise would be to "make the very kind of arbitrary legislative choice" prohibited under the Constitution.[418] The Court concluded that the dissimilar treatment of men and women, who are otherwise similarly situated under the statute, violated the Equal Protection Clause.[419]

In sum, the Court's reasoning demonstrates that the arguments Sally's counsel presented were appropriately tailored to the Court as the audience—ultimately achieving a meeting of the minds. The way the Court's decision mirrors the arguments made in Sally's briefs suggests that the Court accepted Sally's thesis. Underlying Sally's arguments are strong value statements about the way women and other minorities should be treated under U.S. law. The concrete examples that Ginsburg and her cocounsel used to place their arguments about legislative sex discrimination in a historical context carefully focused the Court's attention on why it was important to rule in Sally's favor. The use of the techniques described by Perelman elevated the argument from an issue of administrative efficiency in the probate court to one about equal protection.

412. *Id.* at 75–76.
413. *Id.* at 76.
414. *Id.*
415. *Id.*
416. *Id.*
417. *Id.*
418. *Id.*
419. *Id.*

4.2. Practical reasoning: Arguments for a warrant in *Weinberger v. Wiesenfeld*

> *A sound argument, a well-grounded or firmly-backed claim, is one which will stand up to criticism, one for which a case can be presented coming up to the standard required if it is to deserve a favourable verdict.*
>
> —Stephen Toulmin[420]

In 1975, Ginsburg represented Stephen Wiesenfeld, a widower who sought to receive Social Security survivors' benefits after his wife passed away.[421] *Weinberger v. Wiesenfeld* was an opportunity for Ginsburg to represent a male, part of her plan as an advocate for equality to uphold the constitutional rights of both men and women.

On appeal in this case, the parties—Wiesenfeld, the widower who had sued the government to receive his benefits, and Weinberger, the Secretary of Health, Education, and Welfare seeking to justify the government's refusal to pay the benefits—put forth arguments to support their position on what the warrant, as Toulmin defined a rule, should be. At the trial court level, arguments use established and accepted warrants, which are typically referred to as the "rules" in law school textbooks and classrooms. On appeal, however, the warrant is up for debate: What should the rule of law, or the warrant, be? At the appellate level, a warrant is whatever a court says is the rule of law, and the backing is whatever the court uses to support its ruling. This is consistent with Toulmin's reference to warrants as hypothetical constructs: they are hypothetical in the law until the appellate court announces their existence in a decision. Importantly, although courts may phrase a warrant consistently, warrants can change in our precedential system in the United States as subsequent courts add to a warrant or modify it slightly over time.

In *Wiesenfeld*, the U.S. Supreme Court considered the constitutionality of a statute that made a deceased man's Social Security benefits based on his earnings payable to his widow and children but did not provide those same benefits to a widower; only the minor children of the deceased female employee and the widower would receive benefits.[422] Ginsburg, on behalf of Wiesenfeld, argued

---

420. TOULMIN, *supra* note 113, at 8 (introduction).
421. Weinberger v. Wiesenfeld, 420 U.S. 636, 639 (1975).
422. *Id.* at 637–38.

that the gender distinction in the statute discriminated against female employees, as well as their surviving spouses and children, constituting a denial of equal protection under the Due Process Clause of the Fifth Amendment.[423] This argument formed a warrant that the Constitution protects individuals, as a matter of equal protection under the Fifth Amendment, from gender discrimination premised on assumptions about dependency. Weinberger's counsel argued as a warrant that the statutory decision "to grant benefits to widows caring for children and to deny benefits to widowers does not deny equal protection" under either a rational basis standard or strict scrutiny standard.[424] In this case, the interplay between the arguments that each side presented forms a discourse about the warrant—what level of constitutional review to apply. The case also demonstrates a discourse about the backing for the warrant—what presumptions about wage earners and the effect of their gender on their dependents' needs should the Court consider and find persuasive.

The Court ultimately was more swayed by Ginsburg's arguments than by those of her opposing counsel, even though both sides presented strong arguments. The Court concluded that "the Constitution forbids the gender-based differentiation that results in the efforts of female workers required to pay social security taxes producing less protection for their families than is produced by the efforts of men."[425] Moreover, the Court's backing for this conclusion was that the Constitution forbids a statute from differentiating on the basis of gender using outdated, overgeneralized assumptions about dependency.[426]

4.2.1. Background of the case

At issue was a statute in the Social Security Act, 42 U.S.C. § 402(g), which allowed a widow to receive survivors' benefits based on her deceased husband's earnings, benefiting both the widow and the children in her care.[427] Stephen Wiesenfeld's wife, Paula, who was a teacher and the primary source of financial support in the family, died in childbirth.[428] After his wife died, Wiesenfeld and the couple's infant son received benefits under other Code provisions, but Wiesenfeld was told that he was ineligible for benefits under § 402(g) because

423. Brief for Appellee at i, *Wiesenfeld*, 420 U.S. 636 (No. 73-1892).

424. Brief for Appellant at I, *Wiesenfeld*, 420 U.S. 636 (No. 73-1892).

425. *Wiesenfeld*, 420 U.S. at 645.

426. *Id.* at 643–45 (quoting and relying on the Court's previous decision in *Frontiero v. Richardson*, 411 U.S. 677 (1973)).

427. *Id.* at 640–41.

428. *Id.* at 639.

those funds were for women (widows), not men (widowers).[429] Wiesenfeld sought a declaration that the statute was unconstitutional because it treated men and women as wage earners differently.[430]

4.2.2. Arguments before the Court

Wiesenfeld's counsel, Ginsburg and Melvin L. Wulf, a lawyer with the American Civil Liberties Union, based their arguments for a warrant on a legal theory that the child of a deceased person is the one who is disadvantaged by a gender line.[431] In contrast, Weinberger, on behalf of the appellant, argued that the statute was designed to help female widows stay at home with their children.[432] Because Wiesenfeld won at the district court level,[433] on direct appeal to the U.S. Supreme Court, Wiesenfeld's position was that of appellee.

First, Weinberger argued that a rational basis standard of review should be used on the basis that gender classifications are not suspect classifications warranting strict scrutiny review.[434] Second, Weinberger argued that the statute was valid under the application of the rational basis test.[435] Asserting that the statute was "compassionate," Weinberger backed up this argument with an assertion that women in the past and at the time of the briefing were not able to earn incomes commensurate with men.[436] Weinberger's counsel attempted to sidestep the Court's decision in *Frontiero v. Richardson*, where the Court had applied rational basis to the military benefits due a servicewoman and held that the benefits scheme failed an equal protection analysis.[437] Weinberger attempted to distinguish *Frontiero* by arguing that the benefits in *Frontiero* were automatically tied to compensation, whereas in the Social Security death benefit context, they are not solely tied to compensation because those benefits are allocated by Congress's judgment when it determines the needs of the beneficiaries upon death.[438] Finally, Weinberger argued, the statute served a compelling government interest and did not discriminate against female

429. *Id.* at 639–40.
430. *Id.* at 641.
431. Brief for Appellee, *supra* note 423, at 6.
432. Brief for Appellant *supra* note 424, at 11–12.
433. *Wiesenfeld*, 420 U.S. at 638.
434. *Id.* at 8.
435. *Id.* at 11.
436. *Id.* at 11–12.
437. *Id.* at 17.
438. *Id.*

employees.[439] Here, Weinberger focused on the needs of the surviving beneficiaries.[440]

Wiesenfeld first argued in response that § 402(g) violated the constitutional guarantee of equal protection because it discriminated against female wage earners and their spouses and children.[441] "A social insurance benefit, which is designed to facilitate close parent-child association, is not constitutionally allocated when it includes children with dead fathers, but excludes children with dead mothers," counsel asserted.[442] Section 402(g) perpetuated a "familiar stereotype" of women breadwinners:

> The female insured individual, who is treated equally for Social Security contribution purposes, is ranked as a secondary breadwinner for purposes of determining family benefits due under her account. Just as the female insured individual's status as a breadwinner is denigrated, the parental status of her surviving spouse is discounted. For the sole reason that appellee is a father, not a mother, he is denied benefits that would permit him to attend personally to the care of his infant son, a child who has no other parent to provide that care.[443]

Relying on the Court's decision in *Frontiero v. Richardson*,[444] Wiesenfeld's counsel argued that the statute discriminated against not only employed women who contribute to Social Security but also their spouses and their children.[445] They asserted that a father, who should similarly be allowed to stay at home with his children, is being deprived of the opportunity to do so.[446] The ultimate loser in this equation is the child, who—by losing a breadwinning mother and not a father—is deprived of the surviving parent's ability to care for that child under the Social Security scheme.[447] In their brief, Ginsburg and Wulf also continued to explore the themes evident in the briefing in *Reed*: a female breadwinner must contribute equally to the Social Security system, they said, but is treated as secondary for the benefits due.[448]

---

439. *Id.* at 18–21.
440. *Id.* at 20–21.
441. Brief for Appellee, *supra* note 423, at 10–13.
442. *Id.* at 6.
443. *Id.* at 5.
444. 411 U.S. 677 (1973).
445. Brief for Appellee, *supra* note 423, at 10–13.
446. *Id.* at 11–12.
447. *Id.* at 12.
448. *Id.* at 11–12.

Wiesenfeld's counsel accordingly argued that the statute failed to meet rational basis review and, correspondingly, strict scrutiny.[449] First, no legitimate governmental interest was fostered:[450] excluding a deceased female worker's spouse is not fairly related to Congress's aim to provide for deceased workers' families.[451] As in *Reed*, here, too, Wiesenfeld's counsel referred to drawing a sex line that "impermissibly distinguishes between men and women without regard to individual or family need, ability, preference or life situation."[452] The gender line might be convenient, but it is not permissible "when the effect is invidious discrimination against the families of women workers."[453] Moreover, such line drawing creates gross stereotyping as the basis for legislative distinction[454]—and excluding a man from Social Security benefits "does not operate to remedy the effects of past discrimination against women," they argued.[455] Nor could governmental cost savings be a valid reason for the line drawing.[456] Benefits must be allocated without using gender as a basis for such allocation, for "classification based on gender per se is impermissible in employment-related regulation."[457] Finally, in keeping with *Frontiero*, Wiesenfeld urged the Court to "declare the benefit equally applicable to mothers and fathers."[458]

4.2.3. U.S. Supreme Court decision

The Court held that the statute was unconstitutional under the Equal Protection Clause.[459] The Court looked to its 1973 decision in *Frontiero*, which held that a gender-based distinction in the statutes providing dependents' benefits to the wife of a serviceman but not to the husband of a servicewoman, unless she proved that she provided more than half of the husband's support, violated the constitutional guarantee of equal protection under the Fifth Amendment.[460] In *Wiesenfeld*, the Court determined that the gender-based distinction in § 402(g) of the Social Security Act was indistinguishable from

449. *Id.* at 14–15.
450. *Id.* at 14.
451. *Id.* at 15.
452. *Id.* at 16.
453. *Id.*
454. *Id.*
455. *Id.* at 23.
456. *Id.* at 26–27.
457. *Id.* at 30–31.
458. *Id.* at 45–49.
459. Weinberger v. Wiesenfeld, 420 U.S. 636, 646–48 (1975).
460. *Id.* at 642–43 (citing Frontiero v. Richardson, 411 U.S. 677 (1973)).

the distinction invalidated in *Frontiero*.[461] After acknowledging the legislative history of § 402(g)—that is, the provision was designed in 1939 to supplement the wife of a man who would have been the person financially supporting his spouse and children in life[462]—the Court observed that men are likely to be the primary breadwinners for their spouse and children.[463] Even so, the Court stated, such a "generalization cannot suffice to justify the denigration of the efforts of women who do work and whose earnings contribute significantly to their families' support."[464] The Court explained that the Social Security provision operated in the same way that the benefits provisions did in *Frontiero*, but it was even more problematic because (1) Wiesenfeld was not even given the chance to show his dependency, and (2) Social Security was deducted from the decedent's paycheck.[465]

Incidentally, Ginsburg was on the team that argued *Frontiero*, and she even presented an oral argument in that case (her first Supreme Court oral argument).[466] Therefore, she was quite familiar with the arguments made in *Frontiero* and could point out an internal inconsistency in the arguments made by the government in that case and in the present case. In fact, her analogy to *Frontiero* won the day for Wiesenfeld: the Court agreed that the analogy to the benefits in *Frontiero* was not only favorable but, in fact, identical.[467] Thus, because the benefits scheme in *Frontiero* was deemed to violate the Equal Protection Clause, it must necessarily follow, using rational basis as the standard of choice, that the scheme in *Wiesenfeld* violated the Equal Protection Clause, too.[468]

Accordingly, the Court agreed with Wiesenfeld's warrant and devoted the rest of the decision to answering Weinberger's arguments in support of his warrant. The Court addressed two points.

First, the Court addressed Weinberger's argument that Congress is not required to provide female employees the same benefits as male employees because Social Security is not necessarily correlated to compensation for work

461. *Id.* at 643.
462. *Id.* at 644.
463. *See id.* (not without empirical support).
464. *Id.* at 645.
465. *Id.*
466. Love Koenig, Oseid & Vorenberg, *supra* note 177, at 1292–93.
467. *Wiesenfeld*, 420 U.S. at 645.
468. *Id.*

done.[469] In response, the Court stated that the benefits are related to years worked and amount earned, not directly to the beneficiaries' need.[470] Therefore, because only covered employees are required to pay into Social Security and the benefits depend on the participation of covered employees, the classifications cannot be divided along sex lines.[471]

Second, the Court addressed Weinberger's characterization of the statute as compensating women who struggle economically to support themselves and their children.[472] The Court reasoned that because the provision was linked to providing women with the ability to care for minor children instead of working, it was not "premised upon any special disadvantages of women" and accordingly could not "serve to justify a gender-based distinction which diminishes the protection afforded to women who do work."[473] The Court supported this reasoning with cites to the legislative history: it observed that in light of the statute's purpose to enable a surviving parent to stay home with children, the gender-based distinction is irrational because it discriminates among children based on the sex of their surviving parent.[474]

Ginsburg and Wulf recognized that in arguing before the Court, they needed to use backing that would support the warrant that they sought. Here, the request for a warrant was twofold: (1) identifying the standard of review to use, and (2) demonstrating that the statute violated the constitutional guarantee of equal protection under the standard of review. The backing that Ginsburg and Wulf chose—that the case fit squarely with the reasoning of *Frontiero* and that the statute rested on constitutionally impermissible assumptions about the family breadwinner—moved gender equality forward in the United States on behalf of not only women but also men and children.

469. *Id.* at 646.
470. *Id.* at 647.
471. *Id.*
472. *Id.* at 648.
473. *Id.*
474. *Id.* at 649–51.

4.3. Methods of interpretation: The importance of a word in *Yates v. United States*

> *[S]table laws require a stable vocabulary, for a principal part of every judicial process is definition, or decision about the correct name of an action.*
>
> —Richard M. Weaver[475]

Yates v. United States illustrates Justice Ginsburg's argumentation at work in her statutory construction.[476] Justice Ginsburg's opinion presents a traditional statutory interpretation, and that methodology follows Weaver's methods of interpreting a subject using definition, comparison, cause and effect, and authority.[477] This case also exemplifies the power of language, as Weaver described it. In the Court's opinion, one phrase, *tangible object*, acts as a "great storehouse of universal memory"[478] and embodies the community of language.

4.3.1. Background of the case

In *Yates*, the Court considered whether a fisherman, who knowingly disposed of undersized red grouper fish to prevent the government from taking lawful custody and control of them, violated the Sarbanes-Oxley Act.[479] A person violates 18 U.S.C. § 1519 of the act by destroying, concealing, or covering up a tangible object with the intent to impede, obstruct, or influence government investigation.[480] Specifically, the section states that a person who "knowingly alters, destroys, mutilates, conceals, covers up, falsifies, or makes a false entry in any record, document, or tangible object with the intent to impede, obstruct, or influence" a federal investigation may be fined or imprisoned for up to twenty years.[481]

Yates was a fisherman on a commercial fishing boat, the *Miss Katie*, in the Gulf of Mexico.[482] An officer of the Florida Fish and Wildlife Conservation

---

475. WEAVER, *supra* note 153, at 33, 54.
476. 574 U.S. 528 (2015).
477. WEAVER, *Language Is Sermonic*, *supra* note 58, at 201, 209.
478. WEAVER, *supra* note 153, at 33, 44.
479. 574 U.S. at 531–32.
480. *Id.* at 531.
481. *Id.*
482. *Id.* at 532.

Commission boarded the vessel and saw three undersized red grouper hanging from a hook.[483] On that basis, the officer decided to investigate further and found seventy-two undersized fish.[484] After the *Miss Katie* docked, another crew member admitted under questioning that Yates had instructed him to throw the undersized fish overboard and to replace them with other, longer fish.[485] Yates was indicted for destroying property to prevent federal seizure under 18 U.S.C. § 2232(a); and for destroying, concealing, and covering up undersized fish to impede a federal investigation under § 1519 of the Sarbanes-Oxley Act.[486]

Yates argued at the district court that in the context of the Sarbanes-Oxley Act, which was enacted after the Enron debacle and was designed to protect investors, the term *tangible object* refers to items used to store information such as "computer hard drives, logbooks, [and] things of that nature" and should not be more broadly applied to fish in the ocean.[487] The government's position was that § 1519 encompasses things "other than a document or record."[488]

The district court determined that *tangible object* could mean things other than a record or document, and, ultimately, Yates was convicted of violating § 1519.[489] The U.S. Court of Appeals for the Eleventh Circuit upheld the conviction because, under a plain text reading of § 1519, fish fall within the dictionary definition of *tangible object* as "[h]aving or possessing physical form."[490]

4.3.2. U.S. Supreme Court decision

The U.S. Supreme Court, however, reversed the judgment, holding that a "tangible object" is one used "to record or preserve information."[491] Employing Weaver's four topics of invention—definition, comparison, cause and effect, and authority—to interpret the statute, the Court, in a plurality decision

483. *Id.* at 532–33.

484. *Id.* at 533.

485. *Id.* at 534.

486. *Id.*

487. *Id.* (quoting App. at 91–92).

488. *Id.* (quoting App. at 93).

489. *Id.* at 535.

490. *Id.* (quoting *Tangible Object*, Black's Law Dictionary 1592 (9th ed. 2009)).

491. *Id.* at 535–36. Justice Kagan's dissent in this case has become rather famous and is worth exploring, both as a matter of statutory interpretation and for its clever fish puns and allusions. *Yates*, 574 U.S. at 552–70 (Kagan, J., dissenting, joined by Scalia, Kennedy, Thomas, JJ.). Justice Kagan determined that a fish is a tangible object under the meaning of § 1519. *Id.* at 553–54.

authored by Justice Ginsburg, rejected the government's argument that the term *tangible object* creates a "general ban on spoliation of evidence, covering all physical items that might be relevant to any matter under federal investigation."[492] The Court was persuaded by Yates's argument that the Court should use a "contextual reading" to examine *tangible object* in the context of (1) the surrounding words of the statute, (2) its placement within the Sarbanes-Oxley Act, and (3) related provisions enacted at the same time.[493] Such a reading would show, Yates argued, that a *tangible object* in § 1519 must refer to "records, documents, and tangible objects used to preserve them, *e.g.*, computers, servers, and other media on which the information is stored."[494]

Definition. In this case, language flexes its rhetorical muscle as the power of a term is on display. The arguments on either side, as well as the Court's own reasoning, all focus on properly defining the term *tangible object*, both the starting point of Weaver's sources of interpretation and the proper place to begin a statutory interpretation. The definition here impacted the potential prosecution of a man, who could have faced a felony conviction and up to twenty years in prison. More broadly, the definition of *tangible object* affected the government's ability to pursue people based on their actions in handling items that could be considered evidence: this case impacted future investigations and prosecutions, especially because the Court did not rule in the government's favor. Therefore, in interpreting the meaning of the phrase *tangible object*, the Court created a covenant in the legal community, encompassing all of the statute's users, to follow this definition as a matter of stare decisis.

The Court first observed that a statutory term is unambiguous based not only on its dictionary definition but also on the specific context in which the term is used and the statute's broader context as a whole.[495] The Court further noted that "the same words, placed in different contexts, sometimes mean different things."[496] Additionally, the same language can convey different things in different statutes, or in different provisions in the same statute.[497] Therefore, the dictionary definitions of *tangible* and *object* were insufficient to answer the question before the Court.[498]

492. *Id.* at 536.
493. *Id.*
494. *Id.*
495. *Id.* at 537 (quoting Robinson v. Shell Oil Co., 519 U.S. 337, 341 (1997)).
496. *Id.*
497. *Id.*
498. *Id.* at 538.

The Court looked to § 1519's caption and position within chapter 73 of title 18 for a signal that § 1519 was not a blanket spoliation ban.[499] In doing so, the Court began with the premise that words in the law do not exist in a vacuum: words must be placed in context within the statute and surrounding Code provisions and language. The Court then examined the words surrounding the term *tangible object* in § 1519—that is, *falsifies, or makes a false entry in any record [or] document*[500]—and concluded that those words constricted the term.[501] Specifically, in identifying the genus of the term *tangible object*, the Court defined the actions that would render someone guilty under the statute—and in excluding fish from the definition of tangible object, the Court engaged in the process of defining "the nature of the thing," as Weaver described the process of definition.

Comparison. In this case, the Court did not directly compare or analogize the facts of another case, but comparison did come into play as the Court rejected the government's attempt to analogize the language of the older Model Penal Code of 1962 with § 1519.[502] Both the government and the Court engaged in what Weaver described as comparing the nature of two things.

That language from the Model Penal Code imposed liability more broadly on anyone altering, destroying, or concealing physical evidence.[503] The Court, which had started with the narrowest assessment of the heading of the statute, now broadened the scope of its analysis to include analogous language in the Model Penal Code—ultimately finding the analogy to be not on point.

The Court noted that the government tried to transfer the thrust of the Model Penal Code's language—which broadly prohibited and prevented destruction of evidence—to the context of § 1519.[504] However, the Court disagreed. The Court asserted that the Model Penal Code, unlike § 1519, did not specifically relate to records and the like "used to record or preserve information."[505] It therefore distinguished the Model Penal Code provision by establishing that it did not have the limiting language of § 1519. Therefore, using Weaver's reference to comparing "the nature of two things," the

499. *Id.* at 539–40.
500. *Id.* at 543.
501. *Id.*
502. *Id.* at 546.
503. *Id.*
504. *Id.*
505. *Id.* at 546–47.

two provisions could not be analogized because they did not both relate to records or the preservation of records.

Cause and effect. Weaver's cause-and-effect source of interpretation can be seen in the Court's use of legislative history to respond to another argument presented by the government and asserted by the dissent.[506] The government argued that "§ 1512(c)(1)'s reference to 'other object' includes any and every physical object."[507] The Court observed that § 1512(c)(1) of the Sarbanes-Oxley Act was drafted and proposed after § 1519.[508] Under the government's interpretation, the Court noted, a violation of one provision would be a violation of the other.[509] The Court refused to read the two statutes in a way that would "render superfluous an entire provision passed in proximity as part of the same Act."[510] The use of legislative history in this case therefore can be seen as a form of cause-and-effect argumentation: the drafting process (cause) provided clues as to the meaning of the statute, both in the text of the provision and in its relationship to other statutes (effect). Legislative history as a source of interpretation can be considered an internal source, consistent with Weaver's description of a cause-and-effect framework, because it is part of the legislative record.

Authority. Weaver's fourth source of interpretation, authority, is an external source. In *Yates*, the Court applied canons of construction as extrinsic interpretative tools to aid its reading of the statute.[511] Canons of construction are interpretative maxims or principles that guide statutory construction. These principles or maxims are known to legislators and others aiding in the statutory drafting process. Because a statute's language must comport with the canons, the effect is to read the statute in a way consistent with the canons.

First, the Court applied *noscitur a sociis*, a canon of construction that means "a word is known by the company it keeps," to construe that the language of falsification surrounding *tangible object* limited it.[512] Here, the canon of construction provides authority to back up the argument by establishing a standardized test to apply to § 1519's language. The Court stated that applying the *noscitur a sociis* canon leads to the conclusion that "'[t]angible object' is the last in a list of terms that begins 'any record [or] document.' The term is

506. *Id.* at 542.
507. *Id.*
508. *Id.*
509. *Id.*
510. *Id.* at 543.
511. *Id.* at 543–46.
512. *Id.* at 543–44.

therefore appropriately read to refer, not to any tangible object, but specifically to the subset of tangible objects involving records and documents, *i.e.*, objects used to record or preserve information."[513]

The Court backed up its interpretation with another canon of construction, *ejusdem generis*, which provides that general words following specific words are construed to "embrace only objects similar in nature to those objects enumerated by the preceding specific words."[514] Here, the Court applied the standard to reason that Congress would not have used the terms *record* or *document* if it had intended to refer to disparate items such as fish and documents.[515]

The Court did not simply apply these canons but also took time to define and describe them, lending further credence to their use. Ultimately the Court was satisfied, in applying these methods of statutory interpretation, that Congress did not intend a general spoliation statute covering all manner of items in its catch.[516]

Finally, the Court applied the rule of lenity, a substantive canon of construction,[517] providing that ambiguity in a criminal statute should be resolved in favor of a defendant—in favor of Yates, in this case.[518] This standard is a well-settled maxim supported by numerous past decisions—and is an easy example of authority in interpretation.

****

Weaver's sources of argument or interpretation line up well with the process of statutory construction in defining text, comparing the text to other statutes, reviewing the legislative history, and using external interpretive tools such as canons of construction.

---

513. *Id.*

514. *Id.* at 545 (quoting Wash. State Dep't of Soc. & Health Servs. v. Guardianship Est. of Keffeler, 537 U.S. 371, 384 (2003)).

515. *Id.* at 546.

516. *Id.*

517. Amy Coney Barrett, *Substantive Canons and Faithful Agency*, 90 B.U. L. Rev. 109 128 (2010) (noting that the rule of lenity provides that criminal statutes should be narrowly construed).

518. 574 U.S. at 547–49.

5. Conclusion

My father always used to say, 'Don't raise your voice. Improve your argument.'

—Desmond Tutu[519]

The law is best regarded not so much as a set of rules and doctrines or as a bureaucratic system or as an instrument for social control but as a culture, for the most part a culture of argument. It is a way of making a world with a life and a value of its own. The conversation that it creates is at once its method and its point, and its object is to give to the world it creates the kind of intelligibility that results from the simultaneous recognition of contrasting positions.[520]

The conversation at the heart of an argument, as identified by White, emanates at its core from a conflict, but lawyers are problem solvers whose main goal is to resolve conflict through zealous advocacy of their clients.[521] This process starts with an advocate identifying, as White noted, the positions on each side of the conflict. The process continues with employment of rhetorical theories—such as those of Perelman, Toulmin, and Weaver—which empower the advocate to interpret and organize arguments, recognizing the contrasting positions on both sides.

An advocate must consider the power of each word, for, as Weaver said, words create a covenant with an audience, and that bond will persuade. White said that argument, as a process, "makes our choice of language conscious rather than habitual and creates a moment at which controlled change of language and culture becomes possible."[522] An advocate can draw upon the "great storehouse of universal memory," as described by Weaver; in doing so, an advocate builds a sense of community with an audience.

Moreover, Perelman's theory of audience adherence emphasizes an audience-centered approach. The conversation central to the development and presentation of an argument demands that the advocate consider the audi-

519. *Desmond Tutu Quotes*, GOODREADS QUOTES, https://www.goodreads.com/quotes/132841-my-father-always-used-to-say-don-t-raise-your-voice (last visited Jan. 23, 2023).

520. James Boyd White, *The Conversational Process of the Law*, 29 L. QUADRANGLE (formerly L. QUAD NOTES) 26, 28 (1985).

521. *See* MODEL RULES OF PROF'L CONDUCT r. 1.3 cmt. 1 (AM. BAR ASS'N 1983).

522. White, *supra* note 520, at 31.

ence and bring the audience into that conversation. An advocate, according to White, "must always operate within strict limits imposed by time and the interest of his audience."[523] If an advocate has captivated the audience, if the advocate has locked in the audience members, a meeting of the minds will be achieved, motivating the audience to act in favor of the client.

Developing an argument requires an advocate to understand the logical steps that explain how and why the thesis is correct. Toulmin's grounds-warrant-claim methodology for practical reasoning guides advocates to reason through the messiness of human problems. And Weaver's sources of interpretation create a systematic approach to inventing arguments. Finally, Perelman's techniques for arrangement structure complex legal ideas and facts in a way that highlights an argument's strengths.

Knowledge of statutes and other sources of law is but one aspect of practicing law. To be an effective advocate on behalf of clients—for justice—an advocate must take that knowledge and use it to shape the way that others think about legal issues. Doing so demands knowledge of rhetorical theories of argumentation—shaped in modern times but steeped in traditions dating back to Aristotle. This chapter has touched on a few contemporary rhetoricians and their theories about and insights into argumentation and has examined some examples of such argumentation in action. Beyond this chapter, to develop argumentation skills, an attorney should carefully study the arguments presented in briefs and oral arguments, as well as the way in which courts frame the rationale supporting their decisions. These persuasive documents are excellent sources for inspiration and present an opportunity to evaluate the efficacy of the parties' and the courts' argumentation strategies.

Dale Carnegie once said that "[t]he only way to get the best of an argument is to avoid it."[524] Not true…in the legal profession, in any event. In law, you should not only not avoid arguments, you should craft them. In law, the only way to get the best of a case is to argue it—and the best way to argue it is to employ rhetorical theories of argumentation.

---

523. *Id.* at 29.

524. *Dale Carnegie Quotes*, BRAINYQUOTE, https://www.brainyquote.com/quotes/dale_carnegie_126129 (last visited Jan. 27, 2023).

Summing It Up

- Argumentation is the process of creating and delivering an argument.
- Rhetoric is central to argumentation.
- Contemporary rhetorical theories of argumentation rest, in part, on the canons of classical rhetoric—in particular, the canons of invention and arrangement.
- Chaïm Perelman, Stephen Toulmin, and Richard M. Weaver were three contemporary rhetoricians whose ideas focused on practical argumentation.
- Weaver's assessment of the power of language and Perelman's consideration of audience constitute part of the foundation that a legal advocate uses to prime an argument—the first considerations of how to shape an argument and the thematic narrative that will drive the argument.
- In preparing to prime an audience, advocates consider language and word choice, as well as the audience to which the argument is presented.
- Language is power, so word choice and definitions matter in argumentation.
- Words build a community of discourse in the law. Words used in the law, such as in case precedent, create a collective memory of the law. A word's meaning can change in the law, representing shifts in the legal community's thinking.
- Lawyers should recognize the power of words to move an audience, such as a judge, a jury, or an opposing party.
- Rhetoric is the art of creating presence in an argument; by creating presence, an advocate will maintain an audience's attention.
- An advocate should aim to create a meeting of the minds with an audience. When an advocate and an audience have a meeting of the minds, the audience is going to consent to the advocate's thesis.
- An advocate should seek not only to elicit audience adherence to arguments but also to incite action from the audience. Therefore, an advocate needs to think carefully about who the audience is so that the advocate can present arguments to which the audience will be

receptive. An advocate should consider the thesis, presumptions, and values associated with the argument.

- An audience needs to see how the facts relate favorably to the argument, as will be discussed in more detail in chapter 4.
- Weaver's sources of an argument and Toulmin's layout of an argument aid an advocate in considering how to invent and structure an argument, as well as how to critique an argument.
- An advocate must invent an argument—in other words, an advocate must create or develop an argument. An advocate can develop an argument using these four sources to interpret a subject: (1) definition, (2) comparison or analogy, (3) cause and effect, and (4) testimony or authority. Argument by circumstance is a specific subset of cause.
- An advocate can use practical reasoning to determine how to move from grounds (the data or facts) to a claim (the conclusion). A warrant—a bridge between the grounds and the claim—answers the question "How did you get there?" A warrant legitimizes the claim and justifies the steps in the advocate's reasoning.
- Perelman's guidance on the arrangement of an argument encapsulates how the structure and order of an argument are important to draw in an audience and to focus on what is most beneficial to persuade that audience.
- The value of a persuasive introduction cannot be overstated. A good introduction will create goodwill with an audience.
- An argument can be ordered to place the strongest argument first, the strongest argument last, or the strongest arguments at the beginning and at the end.
- An advocate must assess an argument's strength—that is, an argument's efficacy and validity.
- Attorneys should study court decisions and other lawyers' case briefings to develop their own ability to effectively use rhetoric for argumentation.

Suggestions for Further Reading

Ruggero J. Aldisert, Logic for Lawyers: A Guide to Clear Legal Thinking (3d ed. 1997).

Linda L. Berger & Kathyrn M. Stanchi, Legal Persuasion: A Rhetorical Approach to the Science (2018) (Law, Language & Communication Series).

Linda H. Edwards, Readings in Persuasion: Briefs That Changed the World (2012).

Sonja K. Foss, Rhetorical Criticism: Exploration and Practice (4th ed. 2009).

Sonja K. Foss, Karen A. Foss & Robert Trapp, Contemporary Perspectives on Rhetoric (1985).

Michael H. Frost, Introduction to Classical Rhetoric: A Lost Heritage (2005).

Wilson Huhn, The Five Types of Legal Argument (2002).

Chaïm Perelman, The Realm of Rhetoric (William Kluback trans., Univ. of Notre Dame Press 1982) (1977).

Chaïm Perelman & Lucie Olbrechts-Tyteca, The New Rhetoric: A Treatise on Argumentation (John Wilkinson & Purcell Weaver trans., Univ. of Notre Dame Press 1969) (1958).

The Rhetorical Tradition: Readings from Classical Times to the Present (Patricia Bizzell & Bruce Herzberg eds., 2d ed. 2001).

Kristen Konrad Robbins-Tiscione, Rhetoric for Legal Writers: The Theory and Practice of Analysis and Persuasion (2009).

Stephen Toulmin, The Uses of Argument (8th prtg. 2008).

Stephen Toulmin, Richard Rieke & Allan Janik, An Introduction to Reasoning (2d ed. 1984).

Richard M. Weaver, A Rhetoric and Composition Handbook (reprt. 1974) (1967).

Richard M. Weaver, The Ethics of Rhetoric (1985).

Richard M. Weaver, Language Is Sermonic (Richard L. Johannesen, Rennard Strickland & Ralph T. Eubanks eds., 1970).

Chapter Four

Narrative

JULIE A. OSEID

1. Introduction

Let's start with a story:

> Snowcapped peaks rising from verdant forests. The quick glimpse of a grizzly mother shepherding her cub. A rancher riding the range. The riffle of a mountain stream with a hand-tied fly riding the current. Prairie grasses undulating beneath an enormous sky. Montana is all of that and more.

> But we cannot take these things for granted. The world is changing at a dizzying pace. Climate change and unbridled development are threatening the natural bounty that feeds both our souls and our economy. We must seize this window of opportunity to make a difference for the fate of Montana's lands and waters and the people and wildlife that depend on them.
>
> More Montana is our commitment to conserving Montana's true nature, and we invite you to join us.[1]

Maybe this story persuades you to act by making a contribution to the Nature Conservancy. Perhaps it is because you can picture yourself in the scene. Or maybe you are influenced by the moral imperative to help make a difference. Maybe you aren't persuaded. Perhaps it is because you can't identify with the people and wildlife in Montana. Or perhaps you don't think the story rings true because, in your experience, climate change is not happening at a "dizzying pace." Rhetorical theories about how and why stories persuade underpin all possible reactions to this story. A lawyer's job is to persuade, and the rich tradition of rhetoric can help lawyers understand why telling stories makes persuasion easier.

Storytelling is a crucial point of intersection between law and rhetoric because both disciplines are in the business of persuasion. Of course, pointing out that intersection is not particularly insightful because story is critical for all human understanding of the world—thus, it is at the intersection of everything. We humans experience our own lives and the lives of others in terms of stories. We understand life "as a series of ongoing narratives, as conflicts, characters, beginnings, middles, and ends."[2] Narrative is essential because humans understand conflict in terms of stories, including the conflicts at the heart of legal disputes.

At times, though, lawyers are reluctant to embrace storytelling. This reluctance likely results from "a mistaken belief that stories are incompatible with the rigorous, logical demands of legal reasoning."[3] Lawyers may think there

---

1. *More Montana: Conserving Montana's True Nature*, NATURE CONSERVANCY (Aug. 30, 2021), https://www.nature.org/en-us/about-us/where-we-work/united-states/montana/stories-in-montana/more-montana-campaign.

2. WALTER R. FISHER, HUMAN COMMUNICATION AS NARRATION: TOWARD A PHILOSOPHY OF REASON, VALUE, AND ACTION 24 (1987).

3. RUTH ANNE ROBBINS, STEVE JOHANSEN & KEN CHESTEK, YOUR CLIENT'S STORY: PERSUASIVE LEGAL WRITING 54 (2d ed. 2019).

is a dichotomy between logic and emotion. But that is false line drawing; in fact, "[s]torytelling does not conflict with rigorous logic-based reasoning, but rather enhances it."[4]

Rhetoricians concur. Walter Fisher's narrative paradigm decries the privileged status of logic, what he called the "rational-world paradigm," because it necessarily denigrates the power of emotions and values in reasoning.[5] Fisher pointed out that narrative is better than logic alone because it intertwines logic and emotion:

> The narrative paradigm can be considered a dialectical synthesis of two traditional strands that recur in the history of rhetoric: the argumentative, persuasive theme and the literary, aesthetic theme.... The [narrative] paradigm I offer does not disregard the roles of reason and rationality; it expands their meanings, recognizing their potential presence in all forms of human communication.[6]

Jerome Bruner pointed out that we have two major modes of cognition: scientific and narrative.[7] The scientific mode uses a "formal, mathematical system" to describe and categorize things and events.[8] Science is driven by a hypothesis and "seeks to transcend the particular."[9] In contrast, the narrative mode values the particular and our ability to explain and understand events through stories:

> Narrative, moreover, differs from purely logical argument in that it takes for granted that the puzzling problems with which it deals do not have a single "right" solution—one and only one answer that is logically permissible. It takes for granted, too, that a set of contested events may be organized into alternative narratives and that a choice between them can depend upon perspective, circumstances, interpretative frameworks.[10]

This description of narrative is consistent with how lawyers approach problems because lawyers recognize there is not just one answer to a legal problem and

---

4. *Id.*
5. *See* Fisher, *supra* note 2, at 59–62.
6. *Id.* at 58.
7. Jerome Bruner, Actual Minds, Possible Worlds 11–12 (1986).
8. *Id.* at 12.
9. *Id.* at 13.
10. Anthony G. Amsterdam & Jerome Bruner, Minding the Law 141 (2000).

solutions depend on the circumstances. The role of the lawyer depends on this conflict between alternative narratives and multiple solutions to a problem.

Bruner also recognized that stories can seem like manipulations and thus inferior to logic: "We sense, for example, that too good a story is somehow not to be trusted. It implies too much rhetoric, something fake. Stories, presumably in contrast to logic or science, seem too susceptible to ulteriority—to special pleading and particularly to malice."[11] Yet lawyers don't have to pick between the two. One fascinating way to think of logic and narrative is that they are intertwined strands working together, reminiscent of the double helix model for DNA.[12] Robert Burns noted that persuasion at the trial level "relies on two strands—one strand of narrative and one of logical argument—related to each other like a twisting double helix that forms a lawyer's theory of the case."[13]

Lawyers instinctively know that an emotional appeal combined with a logical appeal can help a judge or jury make the best decision possible. Science is now backing up that instinct. New developments in neuroscience suggest that making a complex decision based on reason alone results in poor decisions.[14] Instead, the best decisions are made when "the rational parts of our brain, i.e., the frontal cortex, work in concert with the emotional parts of our brain."[15] In addition to this scientific knowledge, literary analysis also offers ideas about why stories in the law matter. Plus, those literary theories present very particular storytelling techniques that can help make a story persuasive. For example, the theories explain the critical importance of character development and how to identify what type of conflict is at issue.[16] In other words, neuroscience and literary theories both offer insights into stories as persuasive tools.

But understanding the long, nuanced tradition of rhetoric offers additional insights about stories as persuasive tools, including in the realm of law. Rhet-

---

11. Jerome Bruner, Making Stories 5 (2002).

12. *Double Helix*, Nat'l Hum. Genome Rsch. Inst., https://www.genome.gov/genetics-glossary/Double-Helix (last visited Mar. 2, 2022) ("Double helix is the description of the structure of a DNA molecule. A DNA molecule consists of two strands that wind around each other like a twisted ladder.").

13. J. Christopher Rideout, *Storytelling, Narrative Rationality, and Legal Persuasion*, 14 Legal Writing 53, 60 (2008) (citing Robert Burns, A Theory of the Trial 164–66 (1999)).

14. Steven J. Johansen, *Was Colonel Sanders a Terrorist? An Essay on the Ethical Limits of Applied Legal Storytelling*, 7 J. Ass'n Legal Writing Dirs. 63, 81 (2010).

15. *Id.*

16. Robbins, Johansen & Chestek, *supra* note 3, at 121, 136.

oric helps explain how a combination of logic and emotion persuades. Judges make decisions based on both logic and narrative, despite an expectation that judges "make decisions based solely on reason."[17] A lawyer's best persuasive argument made to a judge should give the judge both motivating (emotional) and justifying (legal) reasons to rule in the client's favor.[18] Because rhetoricians know how and why narratives persuade, this chapter examines legal storytelling under a rhetorical lens.

The chapter begins by exploring the deep connection between rhetoric and narrative. Then the components of a story are defined. Stories proceed in a sequence, which has a special appeal to lawyers because lawyers value order. Narratives also reflect the values of a culture in the same way that the law reflects cultural values.

A set of rules or accepted standards govern stories told to persuade, so the next section of this chapter examines the unique aspects of storytelling in the law. For one thing, the law is a culture of argument, so competing stories are told. In addition, the rules of civil procedure, evidence, and professional responsibility regulate how and when a story can be told and even who can tell a story. Furthermore, stories permeate the law. Lawyers tell stories about clients, precedent cases, and why the law developed in a certain way. Even "the law [itself] has stories."[19] Since the late 1990s, legal scholars increasingly have been interested in narrative because they have realized that some stories were not being told, the law was stagnant but change might happen through storytelling, and stories could help explain the law to nonlawyers.[20] An explosion of interest and attention to narrative in the law has happened in the past twenty-five years; that interest shows no signs of stopping.

---

17. Johansen, *supra* note 14, at 81 (citing ANTONIN SCALIA & BRYAN A. GARNER, MAKING YOUR CASE: THE ART OF PERSUADING JUDGES 32 (2008) ("Good judges pride themselves on the rationality of their rulings and the suppression of their personal proclivities, including most especially their emotions.")).

18. RICHARD K. NEUMANN, JR., ELLIE MARGOLIS & KATHRYN M. STANCHI, LEGAL REASONING AND LEGAL WRITING 261–62 (9th ed. 2021).

19. Linda H. Edwards, *Once Upon a Time in Law: Myth, Metaphor, and Authority*, 77 TENN. L. REV. 883, 883–84 (2010) (citing Robert M. Cover, Foreword, *Nomos and Narrative*, 97 HARV. L. REV. 4, 4–5 (1983); JAMES B. WHITE, THE LEGAL IMAGINATION: STUDIES IN THE NATURE OF LEGAL THOUGHT AND EXPRESSION (1973) (early texts discussing how lawyers and judges tell stories about the law itself)).

20. Paul Gewirtz, *Introduction*, *in* LAW'S STORIES: NARRATIVE AND RHETORIC IN THE LAW 12–13 (Peter Brooks & Paul Gewirtz eds., 1996).

This chapter then turns to some of the leading modern rhetorical theories about persuasion that can help lawyers understand the power of narrative. Kenneth Burke, the foremost rhetorician in the twentieth century,[21] left a legacy of key terms and theories about rhetoric. Fisher, a speech communication theorist, built on Burke's work and made original contributions about narrative probability and fidelity. Bruner, the go-to expert for those writing about legal storytelling, was a psychologist whose work on language development and the narrative construction of reality was groundbreaking.[22] Luckily for lawyers, he spent the last years of his academic career at New York University School of Law teaching lawyers about the power of narrative and coauthoring books and articles with civil rights litigator Anthony G. Amsterdam.[23] This section of the chapter includes examples of storytelling to illustrate the rhetorical theories. All of these examples show skilled legal storytellers at work. Many of these legal storytellers may not have known it, but they relied on rhetorical theories to persuade through narrative.

Note that I follow the lead of most lawyers and use the words *narrative* and *story* interchangeably, but I tend to use *narrative* when referring to theory and *story* when referring to the application of theory to practice. Obviously, a narrative need not be written. The law is awash in written documents, but oral storytelling is also common, such as when a client initially tells a story to the lawyer, when a lawyer makes opening and closing arguments at trial, and when a lawyer answers questions at oral argument. Most of the examples in this chapter are from judicial opinions, with the notable exception of the closing arguments from the *State v. Chauvin* trial.[24]

---

21. James L. Golden, Goodwin F. Berquist & William E. Coleman, The Rhetoric of Western Thought 179 (6th ed. 1997).

22. Benedict Carey, *Jerome S. Bruner, Who Shaped Understanding of the Young Mind, Dies at 100*, N.Y. Times, June 9, 2016, at B14.

23. *Id.* ("He finished his career at N.Y.U. as a law professor, using his ideas about thinking, culture, and storytelling to analyze legal reasoning and punishment.").

24. *See* 955 N.W.2d 684 (Minn. Ct. App. 2021) (court remanded to district court to reconsider the third-degree murder charge after noting that a previous opinion was binding).

2. The deep connection between rhetoric and narrative

No matter how strictly a case is argued—scientifically, philosophically, or legally—it will always be a story.

—Walter Fisher[25]

Rhetoric is a challenging term to define; rhetoricians themselves give different definitions.[26] The classical understanding of "rhetoric" was "the use of language for persuasive purposes."[27] The principles of classical rhetoric originally focused on the spoken word, but the principles were extended to the written word in the fifteenth century.[28] The contemporary understanding of *rhetoric* is that it means persuasion, usually in an argumentative setting, and applies to both the written and spoken word.

The connection between rhetoric and narrative is both long-standing and deeply ingrained. The rhetorical power of story was immediately recognized by classical rhetoricians, and it continues to be recognized by modern rhetoricians.

Burke famously pointed out that humans are unique from other animals because humans are symbol-making animals:

Man is
the symbol-using (symbol-making, symbol-misusing) animal
inventor of the negative (or moralized by the negative)
separated from his natural condition by instruments of his own making
goaded by the spirit of hierarchy (or moved by the sense of order)
and rotten with perfection.[29]

---

25. FISHER, *supra* note 2, at 49.

26. Aristotle described the principles of rhetoric 2,500 years ago. ROBBINS, JOHANSEN & CHESTEK, *supra* note 3, at 27.

27. MICHAEL R. SMITH, ADVANCED LEGAL WRITING: THEORIES AND STRATEGIES IN PERSUASIVE WRITING 11 n.1 (3d ed. 2013) (citing EDWARD P. J. CORBETT & ROBERT J. CONNORS, CLASSICAL RHETORIC FOR THE MODERN STUDENT 15 (4th ed. 1999)).

28. *Id.* at 12.

29. KENNETH BURKE, LANGUAGE AS SYMBOLIC ACTION 16 (1966) (emphasis and formatting in original).

Burke believed that the essential role of rhetoric is the use of words by human agents to form attitudes or to induce actions in other human agents. Humans communicate via symbols, which dictate how we persuade other humans. These symbols are often used to tell a story. Burke saw rhetoric as broad and all-encompassing: "Wherever there is persuasion, there is rhetoric."[30]

Story is also a challenging term to define. Yet both Burke's theory of dramatism based on a pentad and Amsterdam and Bruner's definition of *story* are instructive. Five common elements emerge: act, agent, scene, means, and purpose. Burke viewed human conduct as a play, so he used drama terms for his pentad.[31] His pentad explains why people act in the ways they do. Burke defined the five parts of the pentad:

> Dramatism centers in observations of this sort: For there to be an *act*, there must be an *agent*. Similarly, there must be a *scene* in which the agent acts. To act in a scene, the agent must employ some means, or *agency*. And it can be called an act in the full sense of the term only if it involves a *purpose*.[32]

The five parts of the pentad are strikingly similar to the elements identified in Amsterdam and Bruner's popular definition of *story*: "The essential elements of narrative are Agents who Act to achieve Goals in a recognizable Setting by the use of certain Means and who run into Trouble."[33]

The following table offers a side-by-side comparison of the two definitions:

30. Kenneth Burke, A Rhetoric of Motives 172 (1969).

31. Kenneth Burke, Permanence and Change 274 (2d ed. 1954). Burke's use of the term *motives* was his "principal contribution to ... what might be called a 'new rhetoric.'" Golden, Berquist & Coleman, *supra* note 21, at 179.

32. Kenneth Burke, *Dramatism, in* International Encyclopedia of the Social Sciences 446 (1968) (emphasis in original). Burke, in a later edition of *A Grammar of Motives*, added a sixth element—the term *attitude*—to his pentad, transforming it into a hexad. J. Clarke Rountree III, *Coming to Terms with Kenneth Burke's Pentad*, 1 Am. Commc'n J. 1., no. 3 (Spring 1998). He defined *attitude* as a specific form of "incipient" action, meaning "in what manner" or "how." *Id.* Still, most scholars continue to refer to Burke's theory as a pentad.

33. Amsterdam & Bruner, *supra* note 10, at 46.

TABLE 1. Comparison of terms used by Burke and Amsterdam/Bruner to define story

Burke	Amsterdam & Bruner
Act	Act
Agent	Agent
Scene	Setting
Means (Agency)	Means
Purpose	Goals

Amsterdam and Bruner added *trouble* to their list. They explained that the story typically moves from a steady state to a disruption, which is resolved by a return to a steady state or to a new steady state.[34]

Stories also have a sequence. Aristotle described the "whole" of a story as containing a beginning, a middle, and an end.[35] Fisher noted, "The various modes of communication—all forms of symbolic action—then may be seen as stories, interpretations of things in sequence."[36] Adding another layer, Burke noted that the ability to talk about the past, the present, and the future distinguishes us from all other animals.[37]

Sequencing and order are critical in legal storytelling. Lawyers must consider all the facts and then organize them into a coherent, easy-to-read story. A legal reader expects a story to identify the five elements of the pentad/story definition: what happened that led to a legal problem (the act), the important people (the agents), where and when those events happened (the scene), how the event happened (means/agency), and what the important people hope to accomplish (purpose/goals). Every element of the pentad/story is significant to a lawyer. For example, the exact date and location of the event will determine what law governs. A lawyer will also be interested in the "trouble"—why the

---

34. *Id.*

35. Robbins, Johansen & Chestek, *supra* note 3, at 52 n.1 (citing Aristotle, The Poetics 31 (W. Hamilton Fyfe trans., 1973)).

36. Fisher, *supra* note 2, at 24.

37. Burke also pointed out that language is created collaboratively: "[L]anguage is a *collective* product and the capacity of complex symbolic action is distinctive of the human race." Kenneth Burke, A Grammar of Motives 300 (1945) (emphasis in original).

important people are unable to resolve the legal issue. A lawyer does what Burke said makes us different from all other animals because lawyers are steeped in the past, the present, and the future. Lawyers tell stories about the past event; the present status of the legal dispute; and the future, long-term resolution.

One final note: Stories convey morals and values. That is why public speakers and advocates of all kinds use stories to persuade. After listing the elements of a story, Bruner and Amsterdam pointed out that "the story concludes by drawing the then-and-there of the tale that has been told into the here-and-now of the telling through some *coda*—say, for example, Aesop's characteristic *moral of the story*."[38] Lawyers, too, know that stories are not morally neutral. All stories, including those told in the law, are told from one point of view.

3. The unique aspects of storytelling in the law

> *Every lawsuit is a story. I don't care if it is about a dry contract interpretation; you've got two people who want to accomplish something, and they're coming together—that's a story.*
>
> —Chief Justice John Roberts[39]

Rhetoricians consider the persuasive power of story in all rhetorical contexts. Storytelling in the law shares much with storytelling in any context. Storytelling is always an attempt to persuade a listener to adopt the speaker's worldview, but a few aspects of storytelling in the law are unique.

3.1. Storytelling within a culture of argument

Listeners and readers constantly weigh whether a story makes sense and whether a story rings true.[40] But most storytellers do not have another com-

38. AMSTERDAM & BRUNER, *supra* note 10, at 114 (emphasis in original).

39. Bryan A. Garner, *Interview with Chief Justice John G. Roberts Jr.*, 13 SCRIBES J. LEGAL WRITING 5, 16 (2010).

40. *See infra* Section 4.4 (discussing Fisher's work on narrative probability and narrative fidelity).

peting story told at every stage of the process like a lawyer does, starting with the competing story told in the answer and continuing all the way through to the final appeal. Legal storytelling is distinct because "[s]torytelling in law is narrative within a culture of argument."[41] That culture of argument means that law is "all about competing stories."[42]

Legal scholars often demonstrate how every legal case presents at least two different narratives by comparing the majority and dissenting opinions from United States Supreme Court cases.[43] An even more striking variation occurs when the same judge tells two completely different stories about the same event to support two different legal decisions. Justice Potter Stewart did just that when addressing the legality of the April 12, 1963, civil rights marches in Birmingham, Alabama.[44]

Justice Stewart authored the Supreme Court's first decision in the case when it held that protesters who deliberately violate an injunction without first asking to modify the injunction cannot challenge the injunction's constitutionality during a trial for violating the order. Justice Stewart wrote the facts this way to support that decision:

> A group of about 50 or 60 proceeded to parade along the sidewalk while a crowd of 1,000 to 1,500 onlookers stood by, "clapping, and hollering, and [w]hooping." Some of the crowd followed the marchers and spilled out into the street. At least three of the petitioners participated in this march.... [A crowd] occupied the entire width of the street and overflowed onto the sidewalks. Violence occurred. Members of the crowd threw rocks that injured a newspaperman and damaged a police motorcycle.[45]

---

41. Gewirtz, *supra* note 20, at 5.

42. Peter Brooks, *The Law as Narrative and Rhetoric, in* LAW'S STORIES: NARRATIVE AND RHETORIC IN THE LAW 14, 16 (Peter Brooks & Paul Gewirtz eds., 1996).

43. *See, e.g.*, Rideout, *supra* note 13, at 78–86 (discussing the opinions in *Parents Involved in Community Schools v. Seattle School District No. 1*, 552 U.S. 701 (2007)); Thomas Ross, *The Richmond Narratives*, 68 TEX. L. REV. 381 (1989) (author criticizing Scalia for not including more narrative).

44. Thanks to several authors for the idea to compare how authors describe the facts in the Birmingham civil rights cases. *See* Julie M. Spanbauer, *Teaching First-Semester Students that Objective Analysis Persuades*, 5 LEGAL WRITING 167 (1999); Ken Swift, *Teaching Students to Utilize the Facts Section*, 16 THE SECOND DRAFT: BULL. LEGAL WRITING INST. 11–12 (Dec. 2001); Shaun B. Spencer, *Dr. King, Bull Connor, and Persuasive Narratives*, 2 J. ASS'N LEGAL WRITING DIRS. 209 (2004).

45. Walker v. City of Birmingham, 388 U.S. 307, 310–11 (1967).

In stark contrast, when Justice Stewart also wrote the majority opinion holding that the Birmingham ordinance that prohibited public demonstrations without a permit was an unconstitutional prior restraint on free speech, he wrote:

> On the afternoon of April 12, Good Friday, 1963, 52 people, all Negroes, were led out of a Birmingham church by three Negro ministers, one of whom was the petitioner, Fred L. Shuttlesworth. They walked in orderly fashion, two abreast for the most part, for four blocks. The purpose of their march was to protest the alleged denial of civil rights to Negroes in the city of Birmingham. The marchers stayed on the sidewalks except at street intersections, and they did not interfere with other pedestrians. No automobiles were obstructed, nor were traffic signals disobeyed. The petitioner was with the group for at least part of this time, walking alongside the others, and once moving from the front to the rear. As the marchers moved along, a crowd of spectators fell in behind them at a distance. The spectators at some points spilled out into the street, but the street was not blocked and vehicles were not obstructed.[46]

Justice Stewart's two fact summaries suggest contrasting events even though he was describing the exact same civil rights march. The first version depicts a riot; the second, a peaceful protest. The first portrays a large crowd; the second omits the number of spectators. The first sounds violent; the second sounds calm. But both stories fit with the controlling precedent and ultimately supported the legal decisions made in each case. Amsterdam and Bruner pointed out, "This [telling a competing story] is what is usually afoot in the process that lawyers call (with a confident simplicity that is truly astounding when one considers the mysteriousness of the process) 'applying the law to the facts.'"[47] Justice Stewart told these competing stories to support both of the Court's decisions: the injunction's constitutionality must be challenged at the right time, and Birmingham's ordinance prohibiting public demonstrations was unconstitutional. The lawyer's special challenge is convincing an audience while knowing that the audience is also weighing the lawyer's story against another story. A lawyer's job is, "in a word, to persuade, to persuade that your story is the right one."[48]

---

46. Shuttlesworth v. City of Birmingham, 394 U.S. 147, 148–49 (1969).
47. Amsterdam & Bruner, *supra* note 10, at 12.
48. Karl N. Llewellyn, The Bramble Bush 32 (1930) (reprinted 2012).

3.2. Rules of storytelling

All storywriters follow rules. A short-story writer is constrained by length.[49] A sonnet writer must comply with the form of the poem.[50] Most writers, if they want readers, have to "capture the reader immediately and force him to keep reading."[51]

Lawyers, too, are constrained by rules, but the rules are enforceable laws. Lawyers don't have the option, like other writers might, of breaking the rules. For example, the Federal Rules of Civil Procedure tell a lawyer how to write a complaint:

> Under Fed. R. Civ. P. 8(a)(2), a complaint must include a "short and plain statement of the claim showing that the pleader is entitled to relief...." The words "short and plain" are themselves short and plain, and they mean what they say: A complaint must be concise, and it must be clear. Rule 8 was not promulgated to provide helpful advice; it has the force of law, and it must be followed.[52]

A lawyer is, of course, also bound by the applicable rules of professional responsibilities. When telling a story, a lawyer should remember all ethical duties, such as "the duty to keep client confidences, the duty of candor to the tribunal, and the duty to be truthful to third parties."[53] And a lawyer should

---

49. Edgar Allan Poe was very specific in defining the parameters of a short story:

> We allude to the short prose narrative, requiring from a half-hour to one or two hours in its perusal. The ordinary novel is objectionable, from its length.... As it cannot be read at one sitting, it deprives itself, of course, of the immense force derivable from *totality*. Worldly interests intervening during the pauses of perusal, modify, annul, or counteract, in a greater or less degree, the impressions of the book. But simple cessation in reading, would, of itself, be sufficient to destroy the true unity. In the brief tale, however the author is enabled to carry out the fullness of his intention, be it what it may.

Edgar Allan Poe, *Critique of Nathaniel Hawthorne's* Twice-Told Tales (1842), *reprinted in* GREAT AMERICAN SHORT STORIES: FROM HAWTHORNE TO HEMINGWAY 523, 525 (Corrine Demas ed., 2004) (emphasis in original).

50. *Sonnet*, POETS.ORG, https://poets.org/glossary/sonnet (last visited Aug. 11, 2021) ("Traditionally, the sonnet is a fourteen-line poem written in iambic pentameter, employing one of several rhyme schemes, and adhering to a tightly structured thematic organization.").

51. WILLIAM ZINSSER, ON WRITING WELL: THE CLASSIC GUIDE TO WRITING NONFICTION 55 (7th ed. 2016).

52. Gurman v. Metro Hous. & Redev. Auth., 842 F. Supp. 2d 1151, 1152 (D. Minn. 2011) (Schiltz, J.).

53. Johansen, *supra* note 14, at 85.

not lie or fail to remember that a "story may enhance, but not replace, legal analysis."[54]

The Federal Rules of Evidence limit trial testimony, including whether a given witness can testify at all, what parts of a story a witness can tell, and how a witness can tell the story. Lay witnesses can testify only if they can provide relevant evidence—testimony that a reasonable person would find helpful in deciding the probability of a contested fact.[55] Historically, when relevance was tied to logical probability, stories "fell out of the picture."[56] Witnesses were no longer allowed to naturally tell their stories. Instead, lawyers examined witnesses through precise questions.[57] The practice of a lawyer guiding the way a witness tells a story continues today. If allowed to testify, lay witnesses can testify about their firsthand, nonexpert knowledge that is helpful to the fact finder.[58]

An expert can testify only after meeting strict criteria showing the expert is qualified "by knowledge, skill, experience, training, or education" and the expert testimony will help the factfinder.[59] The expert can rely on "facts or data in the case that the expert has been made aware of or personally observed."[60] In a civil case, an expert's opinion on an ultimate issue is not automatically objec-

---

54. *Id.*

55. "Evidence is relevant if: (a) it has any tendency to make a fact more or less probable than it would be without the evidence; and (b) the fact is of consequence in determining the action." FED. R. EVID. 401. Stefan Krieger and Jonathan Krieger support replacing the probabilistic paradigm with an explanatory paradigm which "examines whether particular explanations, if true, would be better or worse at explaining the evidence and the underlying events than alternative explanations." Stefan H. Krieger & Jonathan D. Krieger, *Storytelling and Relevancy*, 99 OR. L. REV. 163, 181 (2020) (citing Michael Pardo, *The Nature and Purpose of Evidence Theory*, 66 VAND. L. REV. 547, 596–97 (2013)).

56. *Id.* at 170.

57. *Id.* at 170–71. This change in witness testimony resulted from a fear that nonrelevant evidence could taint the record. *Id.* at 171.

58. The rule states:

If a witness is not testifying as an expert, testimony in the form of an opinion is limited to one that is:

> (a) rationally based on the witness's perception;
> (b) helpful to clearly understanding the witness's testimony or to determining a fact in issue; and
> (c) not based on scientific, technical, or other specialized knowledge within the scope of Rule 702.

FED. R. EVID. 701.

59. FED. R. EVID. 702.

60. FED. R. EVID. 703.

tionable, but in a criminal case, an expert cannot testify about the defendant's mental state because that is an issue for the fact finder.[61]

Other evidence rules are designed with an emphasis on truthful testimony. For instance, the hearsay rule limits what things a witness can say. A witness cannot rely on hearsay—a statement made out of court used to prove the truth of the matter asserted[62]—unless an exception applies.[63] Hearsay is seen as dangerous because of the risks of "faulty perception, faulty memory, accidental miscommunication, and insincerity."[64] Further, all witnesses must swear or affirm that they will tell the truth.[65]

3.3. Client stories throughout litigation

Litigators have always known that client stories are essential throughout litigation.[66] Lawyers have also woken up to the potency of stories in nonlitigation contexts, such as storytelling in transactional legal work[67] and in articles

---

61. Rule 704 states:

> (a) In General—Not Automatically Objectionable. An opinion is not objectionable just because it embraces an ultimate issue.
>
> (b) Exception. In a criminal case, an expert witness must not state an opinion about whether the defendant did or did not have a mental state or condition that constitutes an element of the crime charged or of a defense. Those matters are for the trier of fact alone.

FED. R. EVID. 704.

62. Rule 801(c) states:

> *Hearsay* means a statement that:
>
> (1) the declarant does not make while testifying at the current trial or hearing; and
>
> (2) a party offers in evidence to prove the truth of the matter asserted in the statement.

FED. R. EVID. 801(c).

63. FED. R. EVID. 802, 803, 804.

64. Olin Guy Wellborn III, *The Definition of Hearsay in the Federal Rules of Evidence*, 61 TEX. L. REV. 49, 53 (1982).

65. "Before testifying, a witness must give an oath or affirmation to testify truthfully. It must be in a form designed to impress that duty on the witness's conscience." FED. R. EVID. 603.

66. Edwards, *supra* note 19, at 883–84.

67. *See, e.g.*, Susan M. Chesler & Karen J. Sneddon, *Telling Tales: The Transactional Lawyer as Storyteller*, 15 LEGAL COMMC'N & RHETORIC: J. ASS'N LEGAL WRITING DIRS. 119 (2018) (asserting that transactional lawyers are also storytellers); Susan M. Chesler & Karen J. Sneddon, *Once Upon a Transaction: Narrative Techniques and Drafting*, 68 OKLA. L. REV. 263 (2016) (discussing the applicability of narrative techniques to transactional drafting); Karen J. Sneddon, *The Will as Personal Narrative*, 20 ELDER L.J. 355 (2013)

authored by legal academics.[68] The focus here, however, is on storytelling throughout litigation.

During litigation, lawyers tell narratives about a human client facing a conflict and how the client hopes to resolve the conflict. Many lawyers will concede that there is a place for storytelling at trial, but not many have consciously considered how storytelling is important at all stages during a lawsuit. In simple terms, the "life of a civil lawsuit" can be explained in a timeline, moving from left to right, with these occurrences: an event, investigation, complaint, answer, discovery, pretrial motions, trial, posttrial motions, and appeal.[69] This simplified version of what happens in a civil case shows how a client's case progresses. The client's story is told "over time, often in pieces"[70]—starting with the pleadings and ending with the final appeal.[71]

The complaint is the plaintiffs' first formal chance to tell their story.[72] Of course, it is most often the lawyer who is actually telling the story on behalf of the client. Regardless, Professors Elizabeth Fajans and Mary R. Falk pointed out that the complaint contains "the central narrative of a civil action."[73] Fajans

(classifying testamentary instruments as narratives); Susan M. Chesler & Karen J. Sneddon, *Tales from a Form Book: Stock Stories and Transactional Documents*, 78 Mont. L. Rev. 237 (2017) (stories not just about the individuals but also stock stories).

68. *See* Richard A. Matasar, *Storytelling and Legal Scholarship*, 68 Chi.-Kent L. Rev. 353, 353 (1992) ("I end with a call for including narratives, both one's own and those of others, to make legal scholarship more interesting, relevant, and valuable to students of the law.").

69. Special thanks to Lisa Montpetit Brabbit, associate dean for External Relations and Programs at the University of St. Thomas School of Law, for this idea. She used a similar timeline during an alternative dispute resolution presentation to first-year students during my first years of teaching.

70. Robbins, Johansen & Chestek, *supra* note 3, at 52.

71. *Id.* at 52–53 (noting that each of these steps can be considered a chapter of the overall story). Storytelling is important in pleadings and through to final appeals. Herbert A. Eastman, *Speaking Truth to Power: The Language of Civil Rights Litigators*, 104 Yale L.J. 763, 792 (1995) (pleadings); Brooks, *supra* note 42, at 16 (appeals).

72. The complaint is the official start of a legal proceeding. The complaint must contain "a short and plain statement of the claim showing that the pleader is entitled to relief." Fed. R. Civ. P. 8(a)(2). Thus, the plaintiff lists relevant facts and asserts that the plaintiff is entitled to relief in a way that gives the defendant fair notice of the claim and the ground upon which it rests.

73. Elizabeth Fajans & Mary R. Falk, *Untold Stories: Restoring Narrative to Pleading Practice*, 15 Legal Writing 3, 3 n.1 (2009). The article focuses on the complaint, but the authors noted that there are places for stories in other pleadings, such as answers (including affirmative defenses) and third-party complaints. *Id.*

and Falk reminded us that the complaint itself is a story: "[T]he plaintiff complains of ill-treatment at the defendant's hands and pleads for relief. Indeed, in medieval English courts, plaintiffs were required to plead their case (pro se or through a 'pleader') by way of a detailed oral statement called 'narratio' in Latin, translated as 'tale' in English."[74] The complaint is perhaps the most crucial pleading in litigation because a misstep in a complaint can end the lawsuit. For example, a mistaken assertion of jurisdiction or failure to provide the appropriate notice to the defendant will stop the lawsuit almost as soon as it starts.[75] With so many boxes to check when drafting a complaint, lawyers may forget that complaints have always been the principal way for clients to tell their story.

Clients seek help from lawyers because they believe that they are entitled to redress and they want someone in the justice system to hear their story. Because so many cases settle, the complaint may be the only chance to tell the client's full story.[76] That story needs to be heard "so that justice can be done, but also out of simple respect."[77]

Storytelling does not stop at the complaint. Stories can be told during discovery—certainly, discovery can be used to help a lawyer flesh out a narrative.[78] Even at the very end of the line, during the appellate process, a brief including a client story is more likely to persuade a judge than a brief without a client story.[79]

Every recommendation about good storytelling applies with equal force to telling a story in the complaint and during discovery, motion practice, trial, and appeal. The plot needs a beginning, a middle, and an end. The plot should include an initial steady state, a disruption, an effort to redress so that the

---

74. *Id.* at 3.

75. *See id.* (noting that complaints have many functions, including "invoking the court's jurisdiction, providing notice to the defendant, narrowing the issues, uncovering facts").

76. Data from 2004 shows that 97 percent of civil cases in the United States are settled or dismissed without a trial. *Government Survey Shows 97 Percent of Civil Cases Settled*, PHOENIX BUS. J. (May 30, 2004, 12:00 PM), https://www.bizjournals.com/phoenix/stories/2004/05/31/newscolumn5.html.

77. Fajans & Falk, *supra* note 73, at 8–9.

78. *See* Anne E. Ralph, *Narrative-Erasing Procedure*, 18 NEV. L.J. 574, 615 (2018) (noting that the new proportional discovery rule can be harmful because "[r]obust discovery enables narrative development, while restrictions on discovery limit the kinds of stories that can be told in a case").

79. *See* Kenneth D. Chestek, *The Plot Thickens: The Appellate Brief as Story*, 14 J. LEGAL WRITING 127 (2008); Ken Chestek, *Judging by the Numbers: An Empirical Study of the Power of Story*, 7 J. ASS'N LEGAL WRITING DIRS. 1, 32 (2010).

steady state is restored or a new steady state emerges, and a conclusion.[80] Furthermore, other "narrative techniques such as sequence, character development, point of view, and detail" help the reader believe powerful narratives.[81]

3.4. Stories about the law itself

Stories in the law are not limited to stories about clients. Lawyers tell other stories all the time—when describing precedent cases and making analogies or distinctions to the present case, when discussing the legislative history of a statute and whether the legislature considered this situation, when explaining why a constitutional provision does or does not allow certain behavior, and on and on. This ever-present aspect of stories is simply how lawyers reason, remember, understand, and decide.

Storytelling is such an essential part of the law that Linda Edwards suggested that "we may not be able to talk about these sources of law [cases, statutes, and constitutional provisions] without telling stories about them."[82] These discussions "do not sound like stories, of course," but "when we talk about legal authority, using the logical forms of rules and their bedfellows of analogy, policy, and principle, we are actually swimming in a sea of narrative."[83]

A very common practice in legal writing is to set out the rule and then illustrate that rule by telling the reader the story from the precedent case. Narrative helps humans process information quickly. Abstract rules can be hard to understand, but a story can make the rule clear.[84] These mini-stories can also be told in a parenthetical illustration.[85] These illustrations, whether in the text or in a parenthetical, can show how the rule operated in the prior case, eliminate misinterpretation of the rule, make the rule more meaningful by "explaining it in familiar terms," or emphasize how the rule operates beyond the precedent case.[86]

---

80. Anne E. Ralph, *Not the Same Old Story: Using Narrative Theory to Understand and Overcome the Plausibility Pleading Standard*, 26 Yale J.L. & Humans. 1, 31 (2014).

81. *Id.* at 32.

82. Edwards, *supra* note 19, at 884. Edwards further pointed out that "[i]n discussions of cases, statutes, and constitutional provisions, there are stories of birth, death, battle, betrayal, tricksters, and champions." *Id.*

83. *Id.*

84. *See* Smith, *supra* note 27, at 38.

85. *Id.* at 40.

86. *Id.* at 41–47.

Many of these illustrative stories are built on stock structures ("stock stories") that help the reader quickly envision a complete narrative.[87] Michael Smith uses the stock story examples of a "patient's hospital room" and "burglary" to show that when we hear those words, we have a mental image of a place or event.[88] Stock stories are shortcuts based on a reader's own knowledge and experience; thus, the stock story can be misinterpreted.[89] An even bigger danger is that stock stories can bolster implicit bias: stock stories reinforce historical, cultural, and social values; and listeners react to those values instead of what happened in the unique current situation.[90] For example, "[t]he stories that have surrounded the fatal shootings of unarmed, African American males often bring to mind a number of familiar narratives that invoke prevalent racial stereotypes."[91] Stock stories cannot take the place of the full story about what happened. Full stories are vital; those whose voices have been silenced, such as people of color, women, and those with disabilities, need a chance to tell their stories and have their stories be heard.[92]

Hypothetical questions at oral argument are stories, too. A questioning judge is asking the lawyer to consider a different set of facts and then determine how the law would apply to the new story before the court. In opinions, judges also use stories to explain the parameters of the rule.[93] Judges also tell

---

87. *Id.* at 48.

88. *Id.* at 49–50; *see also* ROBBINS, JOHANSEN & CHESTEK, *supra* note 3, at 44.

89. ROBBINS, JOHANSEN & CHESTEK, *supra* note 3, at 45.

90. Jennifer Sheppard, *Once Upon a Time, Happily Ever After, and in a Galaxy Far, Far Away: Using Narrative to Fill the Cognitive Gap Left by Overreliance on Pure Logic in Appellate Briefs and Motion Memorandum*, 46 WILLAMETTE L. REV. 255, 262–63 (2009).

91. Sherri Lee Keene, *Victim or Thug? Examining the Relevance of Stories in Cases Involving Shootings of Unarmed Black Males*, 58 HOW. L.J. 845, 852 (2015) [hereinafter Keene, *Victim or Thug?*]; *see also* Sherri Lee Keene, *Stories That Swim Upstream: Uncovering the Influence of Stereotypes and Stock Stories in Fourth Amendment Reasonable Suspicion Analysis*, 76 MD. L. REV. 747 (2017) (analyzing the challenge of cognitive shortcuts like stock stories that can mask implicit racial bias).

92. Keene, *Victim or Thug*, *supra* note 91, at 855–56; *see also* Pamela A. Wilkins, *Confronting the Invisible Witness: The Use of Narrative to Neutralize Capital Jurors' Implicit Racial Bias*, 115 W. VA. L. REV. 305 (2012) (focusing on narratives that can reduce jurors' racial bias in the sentencing phase of capital trials).

93. *See infra* Section 4.3 (Justice Elena Kagan using a story to explain the rule adopted in the case).

stories as cautionary tales to set moral and ethical standards for every lawyer's behavior.[94]

4. Rhetorical theories explained and applied to stories in the law

> *The law, focused on putting facts in the world into coherent form and presenting them persuasively—to make a 'case'—must always be intimately intertwined with rhetoric and narrative.*
>
> —Peter Brooks[95]

This section describes rhetorical theories about how and why stories persuade. These rhetorical insights are then illustrated with legal stories. Note that each legal example begins with the full story, followed by specific points showing how the story illustrates the rhetorical theory.

4.1. The pentad and terministic analysis: *Florida v. Jardines*

The power of the pentad rests not in naming the five elements of act, agent, scene, agency, and purpose. Even Burke acknowledged that the foundation of his pentad was not unique because Aristotle and others also listed those five elements.[96] But Burke's pentad makes two critical contributions: it emphasizes the relationships between the five elements,[97] and it focuses on act as the key or "god-term":

> Dramatism is... designed to show that the most direct route to the study of human relations and human motives is via a methodical inquiry into cycles or clusters of terms and their functions.

94. *See infra* Section 4.6 (discussing how stories about lawyer behavior solidify the morals and values of the legal profession).

95. Brooks, *supra* note 42, at 14.

96. Kenneth Burke, Dramatism and Development 22 (1972).

97. Ten such ratios are possible: scene-act, scene-agent, scene-agency, scene-purpose, act-purpose, act-agent, act-agency, agent-purpose, agent-agency, and agency-purpose. Burke, *supra* note 37, at 15.

> The dramatistic approach is implicit in the key term "act." "Act" is thus a terministic center from which many related considerations can be shown to "radiate," as though it were a "god-term" from which a whole universe of terms is derived.[98]

Burke distinguished action from motion by noting that the mere motion of falling over an obstruction is not an act unless the person willed his fall.[99] In a similar way, lawyers distinguish action from intent. For example, a criminal defendant is not punished for thoughts alone. Instead, nearly all crimes require proof that the defendant acted, for example, by firing a gun or by selling drugs.[100]

Even with act at the terministic center, the other elements of the pentad can influence how the act is judged. Using scene as one example, Burke pointed out, "In brief, whatever terms are chosen to define the scene, matters of policy will necessarily be debated *in terms* of them. In the selection of terms for *describing* the scene, one automatically *pre*scribes the range of *acts* that will seem 'reasonable,' 'implicit,' or 'necessary.'"[101] For a lawyer, scene matters because it raises questions of jurisdiction and authority. Scene is also an element in specific legal decisions. A crisis, for example, expands the range of acceptable legal actions because one may trespass to save a life. In addition, scene implicates context. The law is based on precedent and thus cannot be understood apart from its historical, societal, and political scene. And Burke's point that scene impacts policy helps lawyers because policy undergirds all law.

Burke's pentad can be used to discover how "the persuader has attempted to achieve the restructuring of the audience's view of reality."[102] A speaker can

---

98. Burke, *supra* note 32, at 445.

99. Burke, *supra* note 37, at 14.

100. Mark Osler, Contemporary Criminal Law 11 (2018). A smaller subset of crimes requires proof of a failure to act, such as the failure to report a crime. *Id.* Note that the prosecutor in *State v. Chauvin* (discussed below) emphasized intent by pointing out that Derek Chauvin "did not trip and fall and find himself upon George Floyd's head and neck.... [H]e didn't, again, trip and fall and find himself there." *Prosecution Closing Argument Full Transcript: Derek Chauvin Trial for Murder of George Floyd*, Rev, at 19:47 (Apr. 19, 2021) [hereinafter *Prosecution Closing Argument*], https://www.rev.com/blog/transcripts/prosecution-closing-argument-full-transcript-derek-chauvin-trial-for-murder-of-george-floyd; *see infra* Section 4.4.1.

101. Burke, *supra* note 32, at 341 (emphasis in original).

102. David A. Ling, *A Pentadic Analysis of Senator Edward Kennedy's Address to the People of Massachusetts, July 25, 1969*, 21 Cent. States Speech J. 81, 83 (Summer 1970),

emphasize one part of the pentad and deflect attention away from the other parts to convince an audience to accept a certain view of the world.[103]

David Ling famously used Burke's pentad to evaluate Edward Kennedy's speech after Mary Jo Kopechne's death at Chappaquiddick. Ling noted that Kennedy's speech identified the five pentad elements:

The scene (the events surrounding the death of Miss Kopechne)

The agent (Kennedy)

The act (Kennedy's failure to report the accident immediately)

The agency (whatever methods were available to make such a report)

The purpose (to fulfill his legal and moral responsibilities)[104]

Kennedy ordered the pentad elements "in such a way that the scene became controlling" and "minimize[d] his role as agent."[105] Kennedy said, "Little over a mile away the car that I was driving on an *unlit* road went off a *narrow bridge* which had *no guard rails* and was built on a *left angle* to the road. The car overturned into a *deep pond* and immediately filled with water."[106] Kennedy also said the tide was "strong" and "murky" and he "made repeated efforts to save Mary Jo."[107] Kennedy was attempting to convince his listeners that he, the agent, had no control in these unusual circumstances. Kennedy said that "some awful curse did actually hang over the Kennedys," suggesting that *he* was the victim.[108] In any legal situation, a lawyer can emphasize any one of the elements of the pentad, like Kennedy did, to persuade.

Burke's pentad, with act serving as a terministic center, is a rhetorical way to explain the majority, concurrence, and dissent in *Florida v. Jardines*.[109] The fact sections in all three opinions are short but paint very different pictures because each justice focused on a separate element of the pentad when analyzing the

---

reprinted in SONJA K. FOSS, RHETORICAL CRITICISM: EXPLORATION AND PRACTICE 366–71 (4th ed. 2009).

103. BURKE, *supra* note 37, at 17.

104. Ling, *supra* note 102, at 83.

105. *Id.*

106. *Id.* at 84 (emphasis in original).

107. *Id.* Kennedy also pointed out that he had a concussion after the accident. *Id.*

108. *Id.* Ling also evaluated the second part of the speech, where Kennedy focused on the agents—the people of Massachusetts—and whether they would believe rumors and lose confidence in Kennedy as their senator. *Id.* at 84–85.

109. 569 U.S. 1 (2013).

actions of the police. Each unique focus, in turn, was used to persuade the reader that the justice was correctly interpreting the law.

All three justices agreed on the five parts of Burke's pentad:

The scene: the front porch of Jardines's home

The agent: the police officer and his trained police dog

The act: entering the porch without a warrant to conduct a dog sniff

The agency: bringing a trained police dog to the porch

The purpose: to check on a tip that marijuana was being grown in the home

The legal issue was "whether using a drug-sniffing dog on a homeowner's porch to investigate the contents of the home is a 'search' within the meaning of the Fourth Amendment."[110] This framing conclusively demonstrated that the act was a god-term because the particular act—using a drug-sniffing dog on a porch—formed the precise statement of the ultimate legal issue in the case.

Similar to when Edward Kennedy focused on the scene to detract from the agent, all three justices highlighted a different part of the pentad to either emphasize or detract from the act of police entering the porch using a trained police dog without a warrant. The act implicated Fourth Amendment law because the law prohibits the police from intruding, without a warrant, into private homes or places where citizens have an expectation of privacy.

Justice Antonin Scalia authored the 5–4 majority opinion holding that this "use of trained police dogs to investigate the home and its immediate surroundings" was a search.[111] Justice Scalia highlighted the scene when describing the situation:

> Detective Pedraja [and other members of a joint surveillance team] watched the home for fifteen minutes and saw no vehicles in the driveway or activity around the home, and could not see inside because the blinds were drawn. Detective Pedraja then approached Jardines' home accompanied by Detective Douglas Bartelt, a trained canine handler who had just arrived at the scene with his drug-sniffing dog. The dog was trained to detect the scent of [drugs].

110. *Id.* at 3 (citations omitted).

111. *Id.* at 11–12.

> Detective Bartelt had the dog on a six-foot leash, owing in part to the dog's "wild" nature and tendency to dart around erratically while searching. As the dog approached Jardines' front porch, he apparently sensed one of the odors he had been trained to detect, and began energetically exploring the area for the strongest point source of that odor. As Detective Bartelt explained, the dog "began tracking that airborne odor by... tracking back and forth," engaging in what is called "bracketing," "back and forth, back and forth." Detective Bartelt gave the dog "the full six feet of the leash plus whatever safe distance [he could] give him" to do this—he testified that he needed to give the dog "as much distance as I can." And Detective Pedraja stood back while this was occurring, so that he would not "get knocked over" when the dog was "spinning around trying to find" the source.
>
> After sniffing the base of the front door, the dog sat, which is the trained behavior upon discovering the odor's strongest point.[112]

Justice Scalia centered the reader's attention on the scene: the police did not see anything unusual about Jardines's home, the dog was wildly tracking back and forth on the front porch, and the police officer had to move back to avoid being knocked over by the dog. The Court reasoned that the porch was part of the home's curtilage and that a police intrusion there violated Jardines's property rights.

Justice Samuel Alito, joined by Chief Justice John Roberts, Justice Anthony Kennedy, and Justice Stephen Breyer, authored the dissent. The four dissenting justices believed the police activity was not a search under either property or privacy grounds because the law of trespass allows a visitor to approach the front door of a home and a reasonable person does not expect privacy when knowing that odors can emanate from a house and be detected from public locations.[113] Justice Alito focused on the agents, Detective Bartelt and the trained police dog, Franky:

> The opinion of the Court may leave a reader with the mistaken impression that Detective Bartelt and Franky remained on respondent's property for a prolonged period of time and conducted a far-flung exploration of the front yard ("trawl for evidence with impunity"), ("marching his bloodhound into the garden"). But that is not what happened.

---

112. *Id.* at 4–5 (citations omitted).
113. *Id.* at 16–17 (Alito, J., dissenting).

> Detective Bartelt and Franky approached the front door via the driveway and a paved path—the route that any visitor would customarily use—and Franky was on the kind of leash that any dog owner might employ. As Franky approached the door, he started to track an airborne odor. He held his head high and began "bracketing" the area (pacing back and forth) in order to determine the strongest source of the smell. Detective Bartelt knew "the minute [he] observed" this behavior that Franky had detected drugs. Upon locating the odor's strongest source, Franky sat at the base of the front door, and at this point, Detective Bartelt and Franky immediately returned to their patrol car.
>
> A critical fact that the Court omits is that, as respondent's counsel explained at oral argument, this entire process—walking down the driveway and front path to the front door, waiting for Franky to find the strongest source of the odor, and walking back to the car—took approximately a minute or two. Thus, the amount of time that Franky and the detective remained at the front porch was even less. The Court also fails to mention that, while Detective Bartelt apparently did not personally smell the odor of marijuana coming from the house, another officer who subsequently stood on the front porch, Detective Pedraja, did notice that smell and was able to identify it.[114]

Justice Alito focused on the agents, which minimized the agents' acts. The police detective and his harmlessly named dog Franky simply went up to the front porch in the way that any person would go to the door. Franky immediately detected the scent of drugs. The entire incident was over in one or two minutes.

Justice Elena Kagan, joined by Justice Ruth Bader Ginsburg and Justice Sonia Sotomayor, wrote the concurrence.[115] The concurring justices believed that the use of the dog violated both the defendant's property and privacy rights and thus was an unreasonable search. Justice Kagan focused on the agency, or means, used by the actors. She likened the use of a trained police dog to the use of a sense-enhancing device. The Supreme Court has long held the Fourth Amendment is violated when police use sense-enhancing devices to discover things inside a home. Justice Kagan wrote:

> For me, a simple analogy clinches this case—and does so on privacy as well as property grounds. A stranger comes to the front door of your

114. *Id.* at 17–18 (citations omitted).
115. *Id.* at 12 (Kagan, J., concurring).

> home carrying super-high-powered binoculars. He doesn't knock or say hello. Instead, he stands on the porch and uses the binoculars to peer through your windows, into your home's furthest corners. It doesn't take long (the binoculars are really very fine): In just a couple of minutes, his uncommon behavior allows him to learn details of your life you disclose to no one. Has your "visitor" trespassed on your property, exceeding the license you have granted to members of the public to, say, drop off the mail or distribute campaign flyers? Yes, he has. And has he also invaded your "reasonable expectation of privacy," by nosing into intimacies you sensibly thought protected from disclosure? Yes, of course, he has done that too.
>
> That case is this case in every way that matters. Here, police officers came to Joelis Jardines' door with a super-sensitive instrument, which they deployed to detect things inside that they could not perceive unassisted. The equipment they used was animal, not mineral. But contra the dissent (noting the ubiquity of dogs in American households), that is of no significance in determining whether a search occurred. Detective Bartelt's dog was not your neighbor's pet, come to your porch on a leisurely stroll. As this Court discussed earlier this Term, drug-detection dogs are highly trained tools of law enforcement, geared to respond in distinctive ways to specific scents so as to convey clear and reliable information to their human partners. They are to the poodle down the street as high-powered binoculars are to a piece of plain glass. Like the binoculars, a drug-detection dog is a specialized device for discovering objects not in plain view (or plain smell). And as in the hypothetical above, that device was aimed here at a home—the most private and inviolate (or so we expect) of all the places and things the Fourth Amendment protects. Was this activity a trespass? Yes, as the Court holds today. Was it also an invasion of privacy? Yes, that as well.[116]

By focusing on the agency used by the police, Justice Kagan painted another vivid picture. The police could only discover drugs by using this unnamed, highly trained, super-sensitive tool, a police dog. And this police dog was not like other dogs. To make her point, Justice Kagan never named the police dog.

The pentad and terministic analysis help explain how a lawyer can persuade by focusing on one element of the story and its relationship to the act—the

116. *Id.* at 12–13 (citations omitted).

element that is at the center of legal conflict. For example, a focus on the scene puts emphasis on the scene and deemphasizes the actor. This emphasis on one element takes the audience's attention away from the other elements—an effective use of storytelling to convince the audience to believe a certain viewpoint.

4.2. Identification: *Fry v. Napoleon School District*

Burke also proposed the rhetorical concept of identification. He noted that persuasion is needed because people are divided—physically, ideologically, and experientially—from one another.[117] Thus, anyone attempting to persuade is seeking connection with that distinct other person. Persuasion entails the whole being in that "[y]ou persuade a man only insofar as you can talk his language by speech, gesture, tonality, order, image, attitude, idea, *identifying* your ways with his."[118] Burke's famous example of identification: the politician who begins a speech to a group of farmers with the words, "I am a farm boy myself."[119]

Fry v. Napoleon School District[120] shows the rhetorical concept of identification in action. The crucial storytelling is in the complaint, showing the importance of crafting a narrative at the earliest stage of litigation. Even more than that, though, the case is a great example of Burke's theory that identification is the most important part of persuasion—the speaker must identify with the reader. In *Fry*, Justice Kagan used Ehlena Fry's story to help readers identify with Ehlena's plight of navigating school as a child with cerebral palsy.

United States Supreme Court Justices do not often cite to the plaintiff's complaint. Yet Justice Kagan cited the complaint multiple times in this case about the scope of the exhaustion requirement under the Individuals with Disabilities Education Act (IDEA). Justice Kagan did not make the reader wait for the decision; she ended the first paragraph of the opinion with the Court's holding: "We hold that exhaustion is not necessary when the gravamen of the plaintiff's

---

117. Burke, *supra* note 30, at 22. To understand the psychology of persuasion, one must understand the nature of human souls—as Burke wrote, "the arousing and fulfillment of desires." Kenneth Burke, Counter-Statement 124 (1968).

118. Burke, *supra* note 30, at 55 (emphasis in original).

119. *Id.* at xiv.

120. 137 S. Ct. 743 (2017). Thanks to Ross Guberman for flagging this case by using it to show five specific writing techniques that make Justice Kagan such a good writer. Ross Guberman, *Five Ways to Write Like Justice Kagan*, Legal Writing Pro (Mar. 20, 2018), https://www.legalwritingpro.com/blog/five-ways-write-like-justice-kagan.

suit is something other than the denial of the IDEA's core guarantee—what the Act calls a 'free appropriate public education.' § 1412(a)(1)(A)."[121]

It is quickly apparent that Justice Kagan cited to the complaint partly because the controlling legal test required the Court to look to the "substance, or gravamen, of the plaintiff's complaint."[122] Obviously, it would be hard to determine the "crux" of the case[123] without taking a very close look at the complaint.

But something else grabs the reader's attention: the complaint is a masterful example of storytelling. Justice Kagan, one of the best writers on the Court, described the facts by seamlessly fusing statements from the complaint, indicated with quotation marks, with her own words:

> Petitioner E.F.[124] is a child with a severe form of cerebral palsy, which "significantly limits her motor skills and mobility." When E.F. was five years old, her parents—petitioners Stacy and Brent Fry—obtained a trained service dog for her, as recommended by her pediatrician. The dog, a goldendoodle named Wonder, "help[s E.F.] to live as independently as possible" by assisting her with various life activities. In particular, Wonder aids E.F. by "retrieving dropped items, helping her balance when she uses her walker, opening and closing doors, turning on and off lights, helping her take off her coat, [and] helping her transfer to and from the toilet."
>
> But when the Frys sought permission for Wonder to join E.F. in kindergarten, officials at Ezra Eby Elementary School refused the request. Under E.F.'s existing IEP [Individualized Education Plan], a human aide provided E.F. with one-on-one support throughout the day; that two-legged assistance, the school officials thought, rendered Wonder superfluous. In the words of one administrator, Wonder should be barred from Ezra Eby because all of E.F.'s "physical and academic needs [were] being met through the services/programs/accommodations" that the school had already agreed to. Later that year, the school

---

121. Fry, 137 S. Ct. at 748.

122. *Id.* at 752. The Court described the full test: "We next conclude that in determining whether a suit indeed 'seeks' relief for such a denial, a court should look to the substance, or gravamen, of the plaintiff's complaint." *Id.*

123. *Id.* at 755. Justice Kagan explained, "What matters is the crux—or, in legal-speak, the gravamen—of the plaintiff's complaint, setting aside any attempts at artful pleading." *Id.*

124. Ehlena Fry is referred to as "E.F." throughout the Court's opinion, presumably because Ehlena was a minor when her claim arose.

> officials briefly allowed Wonder to accompany E.F. to school on a trial basis; but even then, "the dog was required to remain in the back of the room during classes, and was forbidden from assisting [E.F.] with many tasks he had been specifically trained to do." And when the trial period concluded, the administrators again informed the Frys that Wonder was not welcome. As a result, the Frys removed E.F. from Ezra Eby and began homeschooling her.
>
> In response to OCR's [U.S. Department of Education's Office for Civil Rights'] decision [that Ezra Eby's exclusion of the service animal discriminated against children with disabilities], school officials at last agreed that E.F. could come to school with Wonder. But after meeting with Ezra Eby's principal, the Frys became concerned that the school administration "would resent [E.F.] and make her return to school difficult." Accordingly, the Frys found a different public school, in a different district, where administrators and teachers enthusiastically received both E.F. and Wonder.[125]

The narrative here begins with the choices the lawyers made in drafting the complaint. Ehlena's lawyers told her story but avoided the trap of belaboring the facts. One particularly effective decision was to start the complaint with a nine-paragraph "Introduction" that laid out all the important facts, ending with Ehlena's parents suing the school district and its principal. Another smart choice was to avoid interrupting the story with the phrase *incorporated by reference* in later sections.[126] Instead, the lawyers simply restated the facts from the Introduction, sometimes word for word, when the reader needed a reminder about a pertinent fact.

Justice Kagan used several techniques to describe the experience of Ehlena and Wonder. And her decisions comported with Burke's insistence that a writer can best persuade by appealing to the whole reader and by finding a way to help the reader identify with the plight of the writer's client.

First, Justice Kagan used detail to make the story come to life and to help readers identify with Ehlena and her dog, Wonder. Justice Kagan told us the dog was a goldendoodle so that we could picture this specific dog. Justice

---

125. Fry, 137 S. Ct. at 750–51 (footnotes and citations omitted). Justice Kagan, before writing these facts, started the opinion with a story about the precedent surrounding the IDEA. *Id.* at 748–50.

126. *See* Antonio Gidi, *Incorporation by Reference: Requiem for a Useless Tradition*, 70 Hastings L.J. 989 (2019).

Kagan included the name of the dog, "Wonder," subtly suggesting that the dog was a wonder in giving Ehlena her independence. Plus, providing the dog's given name, in contrast to Justice Kagan's decision to omit the name of the dog in her *Jardines* concurrence, was a way to help the reader see and identify with this particular, helpful dog.

Justice Kagan was not satisfied with the broad term *independence*. Instead, she told the reader exactly what kinds of things Wonder did for Ehlena. The reader can picture Wonder helping Ehlena turn lights on and off, close and open doors, and take off her coat. Many of us will remember that these were the same kinds of tasks with which we struggled in our own early school days. We might remember the sense of accomplishment and independence we felt when we mastered those tasks. If we don't remember our own school experience, we might recall our children going through these daily school tasks. In short, we are identifying with Ehlena.

Second, Justice Kagan provided the counter facts and counterarguments. Legal readers always know there is another way of explaining the law, so Justice Kagan noted that the school district did not completely ignore Ehlena's needs in that all of the tasks with which Wonder helped Ehlena were handled by the accommodations the school was willing to provide. As Justice Kagan described it, "two-legged assistance, the school officials thought, rendered Wonder superfluous."[127] However, Justice Kagan pointed out that the OCR, in its early decision, had "analogized the school's [offer of human assistance] to 'requir[ing] a student who uses a wheelchair to be carried' by an aide or 'requir[ing] a blind student to be led [around by a] teacher' instead of permitting him to use a guide dog or cane."[128] Justice Kagan wanted the reader to know that she carefully considered the school's point of view, but it did not persuade her.

Finally, Justice Kagan ended with examples showing the heartlessness of the school. This decision helped her tap into her audience's own experiences with injustice. The school allowed Wonder to attend school with Ehlena, but Wonder had to stay in the back of the room. A reader can relate to Wonder's frustration when he was prevented from doing his job to help Ehlena. After the trial period, the school affirmed its earlier position and "informed the Frys that Wonder was not welcome." The words *not welcome* give the reader a visceral response. The school finally reversed its position, but only after the OCR

127. Fry, 137 S. Ct. at 751.

128. *Id.*

found that the school had violated Ehlena's rights. Justice Kagan told us that the Frys were worried the school administrators would make Ehlena's return to school difficult. Justice Kagan ended with the zinger that the Frys found a new school, "where administrators and teachers enthusiastically received both E.F. and Wonder." There is no better way to help a reader identify with Ehlena than to end with this picture of the school staff at the new school welcoming Ehlena and Wonder with open arms.

The rhetorical theory of identification helps explain how a lawyer can persuade by helping the audience identify with a client. A legal reader who recognizes, relates to, and becomes invested in another person will be less divided from that other person. Ultimately, the legal reader who feels connected to the lawyer's client will want the best possible result for that client.

4.3. The negative: *Fry v. Napoleon School District*

According to Burke, "man is an inventor of the negative."[129] In other words, man defines things according to what they are not: God is immortal (not mortal); freedom can only be explained by describing that it means not being restrained.[130] The law also relies on the negative. Burke explained that the law is premised on the negative because "[l]aws are essentially negative; 'mine' equals 'not thine'; insofar as property is not protected by the thou-shalt-not's of either moral or civil law, it is not protected at all."[131]

Justice Kagan did not limit her storytelling in *Fry v. Napoleon School District* to the facts that would help a reader identify with Ehlena and Wonder. She used two hypotheticals—complemented with two mini-stories—to explain the rule about the exhaustion requirement under the IDEA. In these two stories, she demonstrated Burke's point that the law depends on the negative.

Justice Kagan wrote:

> One clue to whether the gravamen of a complaint against a school concerns the denial of a FAPE [free appropriate public education],[132] or instead addresses disability-based discrimination, can come from asking a pair of hypothetical questions. First, could the plaintiff have brought essentially the same claim if the alleged conduct had occurred at a public fa-

129. *See* Golden, Berquist & Coleman, *supra* note 21, at 191.
130. *Id.*
131. Burke, *supra* note 29, at 11.
132. Justice Kagan defined FAPE early in the opinion. Fry, 137 S. Ct. at 748.

cility that was *not* a school—say, a public theater or library? And second, could an *adult* at the school—say, an employee or visitor—have pressed essentially the same grievance? When the answer to those questions is yes, a complaint that does not expressly allege the denial of a FAPE is also unlikely to be truly about that subject; after all, in those other situations there is no FAPE obligation and yet the same basic suit could go forward. But when the answer is no, then the complaint probably does concern a FAPE, even if it does not explicitly say so; for the FAPE requirement is all that explains why only a child in the school setting (not an adult in that setting or a child in some other) has a viable claim.

Take two contrasting examples. Suppose first that a wheelchair-bound child sues his school for discrimination under Title II (again, without mentioning the denial of a FAPE) because the building lacks access ramps. In some sense, that architectural feature has educational consequences, and a different lawsuit might have alleged that it violates the IDEA: After all, if the child cannot get inside the school, he cannot receive instruction there; and if he must be carried inside, he may not achieve the sense of independence conducive to academic (or later to real-world) success. But is the denial of a FAPE really the gravamen of the plaintiff's Title II complaint? Consider that the child could file the same basic complaint if a municipal library or theater had no ramps. And similarly, an employee or visitor could bring a mostly identical complaint against the school. That the claim can stay the same in those alternative scenarios suggests that its essence is equality of access to public facilities, not adequacy of special education. And so § 1415(*l*) does not require exhaustion.

But suppose next that a student with a learning disability sues his school under Title II for failing to provide remedial tutoring in mathematics. That suit, too, might be cast as one for disability-based discrimination, grounded on the school's refusal to make a reasonable accommodation; the complaint might make no reference at all to a FAPE or an IEP. But can anyone imagine the student making the same claim against a public theater or library? Or, similarly, imagine an adult visitor or employee suing the school to obtain a math tutorial? The difficulty of transplanting the complaint to those other contexts suggests that its essence—even though not its wording—is the provision of a FAPE, thus bringing § 1415(*l*) into play.[133]

---

133. *Id.* at 756–57 (emphasis in original) (footnotes and citations omitted).

Hypotheticals, on their own, are often tiny stories. Justice Kagan used these two contrasting stories to show the boundaries of the law. First, she wanted her readers to picture the disabled child unable to enter school because there is no ramp, plus the disabled adult who can't enter the building for the same reason. Justice Kagan then contrasted that story with the story of a student (notice that she uses *student* instead of *child* for this story) with a learning disability asking for remedial tutoring. The two contrasting stories show that one scenario is like Ehlena's situation, but the other is not. This "not" story shows how the negative sets the legal parameters for when a plaintiff claiming discrimination must exhaust administrative remedies.

Not everyone on the court agreed that Kagan's stories were helpful. Justice Alito and Justice Clarence Thomas concurred in part and concurred in the judgment. Justice Alito wrote:

> I join all of the opinion of the Court with the exception of its discussion... in which the Court provides several misleading "clue[s]" for the lower courts.
>
> The Court first instructs the lower courts to inquire whether the plaintiff could have brought "essentially the same claim if the alleged conduct had occurred at a public facility that was *not* a school—say, a public theater or library." Next, the Court says, a court should ask whether "an *adult* at the school—say, an employee or visitor—[could] have pressed essentially the same grievance." These clues make sense only if there is no overlap between the relief available under the following two sets of claims: (1) the relief provided by the Individuals with Disabilities Education Act (IDEA), and (2) the relief provided by other federal laws (including the Constitution, the Americans with Disabilities Act of 1990 (ADA), and the Rehabilitation Act of 1973). The Court does not show or even claim that there is no such overlap—to the contrary, it observes that "[t]he same conduct might violate" the ADA, the Rehabilitation Act and the IDEA. And since these clues work only in the absence of overlap, I would not suggest them....
>
> Although the Court provides these clues for the purpose of assisting the lower courts, I am afraid that they may have the opposite effect. They are likely to confuse and lead courts astray.[134]

---

134. *Id.* at 759 (Alito, J. concurring) (emphasis in original) (citations omitted).

Justice Alito did not contest that the negative is part of determining legal rights. Instead, he suggested that Justice Kagan's hypotheticals did not help draw the line between what the gravamen of the complaint was and what it was not. His criticism was also grounded in Burke's central theory that although every utterance is an invitation to persuade, this assertion is tempered by the fact that every word is but a selection of reality.[135] Justice Alito criticized Justice Kagan for not including the reality that the same conduct can violate multiple federal laws.

The structure of the law is in sync with the rhetorical theory of the negative. Humans understand what can be done by first understanding what cannot be done. A lawyer can use this idea of the negative to help persuade a legal audience that a client's behavior is well within the confines of legality.

4.4. Narrative probability and fidelity: *State v. Chauvin*

Fisher agreed that man is fundamentally a storyteller, building on Burke's premise that man is a symbol-using animal.[136] Fisher called this the "narrative paradigm" and explained, "The narrative paradigm proposes that human beings are inherently storytellers who have a natural capacity to recognize the probability and fidelity of stories they tell and experience."[137] He contributed two major ideas—narrative probability and narrative fidelity—to explain how people both construct and determine the worth of stories.[138]

Narrative probability[139] tests "whether a story hangs together" and makes sense.[140] Narrative probability depends on three types of coherence: (1) structural coherence, meaning internal consistency within the story itself; (2)

135. Burke noted, "Men seek for vocabularies that will be faithful *reflections* of reality. To this end, they must develop vocabularies that are *selections* of reality. And any selection of reality must, in certain circumstances, function as a *deflection* of reality." BURKE, *supra* note 37, at 59 (emphasis in original).

136. Fisher wrote, "The *Homo narrans* metaphor is thus an incorporation and extension of Burke's definition of 'man' as the 'symbol-using (symbol-making, symbol-misusing) animal.'" FISHER, *supra* note 2, at 63. In contrast to Burke's approach where people are passive, that is, "actors performing roles constrained or determined by scripts provided by existing institutions," Fisher emphasized that people are active, that is, "full participants in the making of messages, whether they are agents (authors) or audience members (co-authors)." *Id.* at 18.

137. *Id.* at 24.

138. *Id.* at 19.

139. Fisher often used the terms *narrative probability* and *narrative coherence* interchangeably.

140. FISHER, *supra* note 2, at 47.

material coherence, meaning the story fits with other stories; and (3) characterological coherence, meaning the "characters behave characteristically."[141] In short, the first two kinds of coherence look at internal consistency (whether the parts of the story are consistent with each other) and completeness (whether all important facts, arguments, and issues are included).[142] Internal consistency and completeness are expected in pure logical arguments, too. It is the third type of coherence—and its focus on character—that distinguishes narrative probability from traditional logic.[143] Fisher stated, "Whether a story is believable depends on the reliability of characters, both as narrators and as actors."[144] The audience's values and expectations help it interpret a character's actions and words.[145] The audience will test a character's motives and only trust a character if the character behaves consistently.[146]

Narrative fidelity tests the "truthfulness" of a story. Narrative fidelity depends on whether a story not only fits with experiences that the audience knows are true but also has a "logic of good reasons" to motivate action.[147] In short, the story is evaluated "by looking to whether the substantive features of the story match up with what we think about how the world works."[148] The "good reasons" are based on values, but good reasons go beyond abstract ideals like "truth" or "justice" to motivate an audience to believe the story and then act.[149] Narrative fidelity "relies on social values as much as it relies on reasoning."[150] Thus, the audience can go further than where logic alone can take it. J. Christopher Rideout explained:

---

141. *Id.* For an excellent and detailed discussion of narrative probability and narrative fidelity, see Rideout, *supra* note 13, at 60–65, 69–72.

142. Rideout, *supra* note 13, at 64–65.

143. Fisher, *supra* note 2, at 47.

144. *Id.*

145. *Id.*

146. *Id.*

147. *Id.*

148. Linda L Berger, *The Color-Blind Constitution: Choosing a Story to Live By*, 2015 Mich. St. L. Rev. 1397, 1405 (2015).

149. Fisher, *supra* note 2, at 47–48. "These are questions about *fact, relevance, consequence, consistency*, and *transcendental* issues." *Id.* at 48 (emphasis in original). Fisher defined *good reasons* as "*those elements that provide warrants for accepting or adhering to the advice fostered by any form of communication that can be considered rhetorical.*" *Id.* at 107 (emphasis in original).

150. Jennifer Sheppard, *What If the Big Bad Wolf in All Those Fairy Tales Was Just Misunderstood?: Techniques for Maintaining Narrative Rationality While Altering Stock Stories That Are Harmful to Your Client's Case*, 34 Hastings Commc'ns & Ent. L.J. 187, 202 (2012).

> That audience is, in a sense, implied by the text of the story, but because the story itself is situated historically and socially, then in that respect the universal audience—universal in its willingness to appeal to the highest ideals for justice—is also an audience of the moment, also situated in an historical and social setting.[151]

Narrative fidelity translates to a normative understanding that fits neatly with legal narrative because the law is constantly evaluating what is and is not permissible.[152] Common sense is another way of saying that all people have the ability to judge the narrative fidelity of a story.[153] That is why using jurors to make decisions is reasonable and valuable.[154]

The narrative paradigm also refutes three troubling ideas: values are not important, logic is separate from everyday discourse, and expert knowledge and discourse should be privileged.[155] Fisher offered a more expansive view. He pointed out that "values" are more persuasive than any "individual form of argument."[156] Thus, argument can be effective, but narrative rationality is better because it focuses on "all forms of human communication."[157] And humans take into account much more than just logic.[158] Fisher stated, "*Humans as rhetorical beings are as much valuing as they are reasoning animals.*"[159]

Fisher openly confronted the idea that expert knowledge is better than lay experience. He had full confidence in a lay audience. Sure, an expert can be helpful in the role of a counselor whose "contribution to public dialogue is to impart knowledge, like a teacher, or wisdom, like a sage. It is not to pronounce a story that ends all storytelling."[160] A lay audience is perfectly capable of judging the worth of a story by considering narrative probability:

---

151. Rideout, *supra* note 13, at 72.

152. *Id.*

153. FISHER, *supra* note 2, at 68; *see also* Sheppard, *supra* note 150, at 202 ("In sum, a story possesses narrative fidelity when it comports with the audience's common sense.").

154. FISHER, *supra* note 2, at 68.

155. *Id.* at 9.

156. *Id.* at 48.

157. *Id.* at 48–49.

158. *Id.* at 49.

159. *Id.* at 105 (emphasis in original).

160. *Id.* at 73. Fisher did not discount the contributions that experts can make but said that the public should be the ultimate decision maker:

> [S]ome discourse is more veracious, reliable, and trustworthy in respect to knowledge, truth, and reality than some other discourse, but no *form* or *genre* has final claim to these virtues. Some persons know more than others, are wiser, and are

> [T]he experts' stories are not at all beyond analysis of the layperson. The lay audience can test the stories for coherence and fidelity. The lay audience [members are] active, irrepressible participants in the meaning-formation of the stories that any and all storytellers tell... [on any issue] that impinges on how people are to be conceived and treated in their ordinary lives.[161]

The narrative paradigm does not deny a hierarchy of stories. What it denies is the assumption that only those formally schooled in reason and argument can make legitimate judgments:

> [T]he narrative paradigm does not deny that the "people" can be wrong. But, then, so can elites, especially when a decision is social or political.... The sort of hierarchy to which the narrative paradigm is inimical is hierarchy based on the assumption that some people are qualified to be rational and others are not.[162]

We humans simply can't pay attention to everything.[163] Even experts are limited because their field of expertise will define the nature of their human perception: doctors see pathology, entomologists see the life cycle of an insect, typographers see fonts, and lawyers see potential lawsuits.[164] Relatedly, Burke warned that experts should avoid using expert terminology and instead speak in plain terms to explain what happened.[165]

> more to be heeded than others. But no one knows all there is to know about his or her own area of specialization. I contend further that human communication in all of its forms is imbued with mythos—ideas that cannot be verified or proved in any absolute way.

Id. at 19 (emphasis in original).

161. *Id.* at 72.

162. *Id.* at 67.

163. *See* ALEXANDRA HOROWITZ, ON LOOKING: ELEVEN WALKS WITH EXPERT EYES (2013) (noting that even as you read this text, you are not paying attention to every sound, every variation in light, or even every sensation in your body).

164. *Id.* (providing a fascinating window into what different experts pay attention to). Horowitz, a cognitive psychologist, took a walk with eleven different experts and asked each to describe what the expert saw.

165. Burke added, "Insofar as any science has a nomenclature especially adapted to its particular field of study, the extension of its *special* terms to provide a definition of man *in general* would necessarily oversociologize, overbiologize, overpsychologize, or overphysicize, etc., its subject." Kenneth Burke, *Dramatism*, *in* GOLDEN, BERQUIST & COLEMAN, *supra* note 21, at 200 (emphasis in original).

The narrative paradigm, not logic alone, best supports the role of the jury in the American legal process. The jury is a full-fledged participant in the trial process, fully capable of deciding the merits of a case because morals and values are inextricably connected to decisions in all realms of life. Jurors can make decisions between the two narratives presented by opposing sides because stories are not equal in their worth: "Obviously some stories are better stories than others, more coherent, more 'true' to the way people and the world are—in perceived fact and value. In other words, some stories better satisfy the criteria of the logic of good reasons, which is attentive to reason *and* values."[166]

The Story Model, a widely adopted theory about how juries make decisions, gives further support to the narrative paradigm because it suggests that the first thing a juror does is create a coherent narrative.[167] Nancy Pennington and Reid Hastie, the two psychologists who developed and tested the theory, emphasized that "one central claim of the model is that the story the juror constructs determines the juror's decision."[168] The jurors can use the story to make sense of what happened and use logic to justify their decision based on legal arguments.[169]

Coming full circle, Fisher tied his ideas of narrative probability and narrative fidelity to Burke's point that identification is the fundamental concept in persuasion: "The operative principle of narrative rationality is *identification* rather than deliberation."[170] Fisher ended his book by noting that he could not deny the usefulness of traditional logic, but he offered a more expansive view of rhetorical logic. Fisher further explained:

> The two major principles of such logic are, I believe, *coherence* and *fidelity*. We naturally and without formal instruction ask about any account of any sort whatever whether or not it "holds together" and adds up to a reliable claim to reality. We ask whether or not an account is faithful to related accounts we already know and believe. On these terms we *identify*

166. FISHER, *supra* note 2, at 68.

167. Nancy Pennington & Reid Hastie, *A Cognitive Theory of Juror Decision Making: The Story Model*, 13 CARDOZO L. REV. 519, 521 (1991). Note that the authors pointed out that although the Story Model was developed and tested in the context of a criminal case, the principles likely extend to civil trials. *Id.* at 521 n.9. Pennington and Hastie explained that "a central cognitive process in juror decision making is *story construction*." *Id.* at 520 (emphasis in original).

168. *Id.* at 521. Pennington and Hastie described three processing stages: "(1) evidence evaluation through story construction, (2) representation of the decision alternatives by learning verdict category attributes, and (3) reaching a decision through the classification of the story into the best fitting verdict category." *Id.*

169. *See* Rideout, *supra* note 13, at 60.

170. FISHER, *supra* note 2, at 66 (emphasis in original).

> with an account (and its author) or we treat it as mistaken. We identify with stories or accounts when we find that they offer "good reasons" for being accepted.[171]

The prosecutor's closing argument in *State v. Chauvin* demonstrates how narrative probability and narrative fidelity work in a legal case. The killing of George Floyd and the subsequent trial and guilty verdict against Derek Chauvin gripped both the nation and the world. Chauvin, a former Minneapolis officer, was charged with second-degree unintentional murder, third-degree murder, and second-degree manslaughter in the killing of George Floyd on May 25, 2020, in Minneapolis.[172] A video recorded at the scene showed "Floyd was handcuffed and lying face down on the pavement during the agonizing period that Chauvin's knee was on his neck."[173] The trial lasted 14 days.[174] The focus here is on the closing argument because, as the only time when the lawyer has a "chance to put the pieces together and to present a flowing, uninterrupted narrative to the decisionmaker,"[175] it is perhaps the best example of storytelling in the law. The prosecutor's closing argument in *State v. Chauvin* featured Fisher's two critical components of narrative rationality: narrative probability and narrative fidelity.

4.4.1. Narrative probability

Listeners evaluate a story to determine how well it hangs together. In this instance, the state's case—that Chauvin used excessive force and murdered Floyd—was internally coherent, complete, and consistent. It added up to a reliable claim of reality.

Prosecutor Steve Schleicher referenced the length of time that Chauvin knelt on Floyd's neck—nine minutes and twenty-nine seconds—twenty-two times in his closing argument.[176] The continual reference to nine minutes and

---

171. *Id.* at 194 (emphasis in original).

172. Paul Walsh, Aby Simons & Hannah Sayle, *What Happened Each Day in the Derek Chauvin Trial*, STAR TRIB. (Apr. 20, 2021, 5:15 PM), https://www.startribune.com/what-happened-today-in-the-derek-chauvin-trial/600031856.

173. Jeannie Suk Gersen, *The Simple Facts of Derek Chauvin's Trial*, NEW YORKER (Apr. 10, 2021). Professor Gersen also pointed out, "The killing of George Floyd... set off worldwide protests of the deadly and pervasive subordination of Black Americans by the police." *Id.*

174. Walsh, Simons & Sayle, *supra* note 172.

175. Gewirtz, *supra* note 20, at 8.

176. *See* Shaila Dewan, Tim Arango, Nicholas Bogel-Burroughs & John Eligon, *Focus Is on Video as Chauvin Trial Goes to the Jury*, N.Y. TIMES, Apr. 20, 2021, at A1 ("The pros-

twenty-nine seconds supported the state's case that the force was excessive and the cause of Floyd's death.

Schleicher built a story around his repeated time references, showing that the state's case was probable because:

1. Floyd was not a threat to the police or the public, so the force was excessive;
2. Chauvin had intent; and
3. the justifications that the defendant raised did not cause Floyd's death.

The following excerpts, organized under these three categories, are taken from Schleicher's one-hour-and-forty-three-minute closing.[177]

1. Floyd was not a threat to the police or the public, so the force was excessive:

    He was trapped with the unyielding pavement underneath him, as unyielding as the men who held him down, pushing him, a knee to the neck, a knee to the back, twisting his fingers, holding his legs for nine minutes and 29 seconds. The defendant's weight on him....[178]

    ...They took him from this position, handcuffed on his knees, they pushed him down onto the ground. Didn't need to. Not at all. For what? He's handcuffed....[179]

    ...He wasn't resisting. He just wasn't able to comply.... [T]hey had four officers, they had a fifth one off in the distance. He was handcuffed behind his back. He wasn't going anywhere. He wasn't doing anything. He didn't need to be put in the prone position, that's a temporary position to facilitate handcuffing....[180]

    ...Now, the greatest skeptic of this case among you, how can you justify the continued force on this man when he has no pulse?[181]

---

ecution focused on the 9 minutes 29 seconds that Derek Chauvin...kept his knee on the neck of Mr. Floyd.").

177. *Prosecution Closing Argument*, *supra* note 100.

178. *Id.* at 2:47.

179. *Id.* at 35:48.

180. *Id.* at 1:27:07.

181. *Id.* at 1:36:30.

2. Chauvin had intent:

   The medical examiner ruled the death a homicide, death at the hands of another. What the defendant did to George Floyd killed him....[182]

   No question. This was not an accident. He did not trip and fall and find himself upon George Floyd's knee and neck. He did what he did on purpose, and it killed George Floyd. That force for nine minutes and 29 seconds, that killed George Floyd....[183]

   ...It's pretty simple. If you're doing something that hurts somebody, and you know it, and you keep doing it, you're doing it on purpose.[184]

3. The justifications that the defendant raised did not cause Floyd's death:

   His two justifications were that George Floyd was big and that he might be on something. Well, you know the standards, you've heard the standards many times, you know the difference between a risk and a threat. Officers are authorized to use force to respond to a threat. They're not authorized to use force to respond to a risk.[185]

Note that Schleicher also contested the defendant's justifications for his actions. Those statements are included in the next section on narrative fidelity.

4.4.2. Narrative fidelity

Listeners also evaluate a story to determine if it rings true with other stories the jurors know to be true and if the story's values accord with their experiences. Schleicher repeatedly told the jurors to use their common sense, another word for narrative fidelity. He also told them to believe their own eyes. He emphasized that even a nine-year-old witness to Floyd's killing knew how wrong it was.

Again, the following excerpts are taken from Schleicher's closing:

---

182. *Id.* at 11:48, 12:24.
183. *Id.* at 19:47.
184. *Id.* at 1:06:54.
185. *Id.* at 1:24:56.

> Was it drugs? He just miraculously died of a drug overdose in that time? Maybe it was the tailpipe. Maybe it was his enlarged heart. Maybe not. Use your common sense. Use your common sense. Believe your eyes. What you saw, you saw....[186]
>
> ...You as jurors are not required, nor should you leave your common sense at the courthouse steps. As jurors, you must rely on your common sense....[187]
>
> ...You can see this with your own eyes. You could see what happened, that he couldn't breathe. He said he couldn't breathe. The defendant was on top of him, on his back, on his neck with his knees, pressing down. Of course! You saw how his body just deflated into the ground, past the point of consciousness....[188]
>
> ...He could have listened to the bystanders. He could have listened to fellow officers. He could have listened to his own training. He knew better, he just didn't do better. He knew that kneeling on somebody's neck, in addition to the positional asphyxia, just the pressure, is dangerous. Anyone can tell you that. A nine-year-old can tell you that, did tell you that.[189]

4.4.3. The dynamic duo of narrative probability and narrative fidelity

Schleicher made several statements combining aspects of narrative probability and narrative fidelity. He pointed out that the jurors could trust the state's story because it was reliable, accounted for all the evidence, and fit with their own life experiences:

> The motto of the Minneapolis Police Department is to "Protect with courage and to serve with compassion." But George Floyd was not a threat to anyone. He wasn't trying to hurt anyone. He wasn't trying to do anything to anyone. Facing George Floyd that day, that did not require one ounce of courage, and none was shown on that day. No courage was

---

186. *Id.* at 37:55.
187. *Id.* at 39:44.
188. *Id.* at 1:02:05.
189. *Id.* at 1:13:37.

> required. All that was required was a little compassion and none was shown on that day....[190]
>
> This case is exactly what you thought when you saw it first, when you saw that video. It is exactly that. You can believe your eyes. It's exactly what you believed. It's exactly what you saw with your eyes. It's exactly what you knew. It's what you felt in your gut. It's what you now know in your heart. This wasn't policing. This was murder. The Defendant is guilty of all three counts. All of them. And there's no excuse. Thank you.[191]

The jury found Chauvin guilty of on all charges for the death of George Floyd.[192] The guilty verdicts show that the jury believed both the narrative probability and the narrative fidelity of the prosecutor's story.

Understanding the rhetorical concept of narrative probability (does this story seem likely?) and narrative fidelity (does this story seem true?) will help lawyers persuade an audience. The audience will be persuaded only if the story is both likely and true. Lawyers thus must test their stories to make sure that the events comport with typical human experiences and common sense.

4.5. Trouble: *United States v. Curry*

As noted, Bruner and Amsterdam added a critical term to Burke's definition of *story*: trouble.[193] The concept of trouble, or some disruption in a story, is also present in Burke's theories because he focused on the misalignment between the five elements of his pentad.[194] Trouble is what makes a story interesting. And trouble is at the very heart of the law—law gives society "continuity in value judgments across time and changing conditions."[195] The law gives general rules, and those rules are tested and applied to specific cases.

Sometimes, lawyers disagree about what the precise trouble is. Judges sometimes disagree, too. Chief Judge Roger L. Gregory disagreed with Judge James

---

190. *Id.* at 7:51.

191. *Id.* at 1:42:51.

192. Laurel Wamsley, *Derek Chauvin Found Guilty of George Floyd's Murder*, NPR (Apr. 20, 2021), https://www.npr.org/sections/trial-over-killing-of-george-floyd/2021/04/20/987777911/court-says-jury-has-reached-verdict-in-derek-chauvins-murder-trial.

193. *See supra* notes 33–34 and accompanying text.

194. Amsterdam & Bruner, *supra* note 10, at 130.

195. *Id.* at 140.

Harvie Wilkinson III's summary of the trouble in *United States v. Curry*.[196] All fifteen judges on the United States Court of Appeals for the Fourth Circuit reheard the case en banc. The issue was "whether the Fourth Amendment's exigent circumstances doctrine justified the suspicionless seizure of Defendant-Appellee Billy Curry, Jr."[197] The police had responded to gunshots fired near an apartment complex less than a minute earlier. The police saw several men, including Curry, walking in a public area behind the complex, away from "where the officers believed the shots originated."[198] The police stopped Curry, who complied with a request to put his hands in the air and then pointed toward where the shots were coming from.[199] The police eventually patted down Curry and found a pistol on the ground nearby.[200] The court affirmed the district court's holding that exigent circumstances did not justify the suspicionless, investigatory stop of Curry and suppressed the firearm.[201]

Chief Judge Gregory challenged the characterization of the trouble as the risk that police would be driven from some communities.[202] Chief Judge Gregory wrote:

> When I read the first line of Judge Wilkinson's dissent I was heartened by the thought: well, at least he acknowledges that there are "two Americas." But this glint of enlightenment was to serve as a "soap box" for his charge against the majority's decision.... More to the point, his recognition of a divided America is merely a preamble to the fallacy-laden exegesis of "predictive policing" that follows. Through his opinion, my colleague contributes to the volumes of work gifted by others who felt obliged to bear their burden to save minority or disadvantaged communities from themselves.
>
> ...There's a long history of black and brown communities feeling unsafe in police presence.... This increased protection, however, led to what has been described as "a central paradox of the African American experience: the simultaneous over- and under-policing of crime."

196. 965 F.3d 313, 331 (4th Cir. 2020).
197. *Id.* at 315.
198. *Id.*
199. *Id.* at 317.
200. *Id.*
201. *Id.* at 316, 331.
202. *Id.* at 331 (Gregory, C.J., concurring) (responding to Judge Wilkinson's dissent).

> Judge Wilkinson chooses to focus largely on one dimension of this paradox, ignoring the details of the familiar perils of over-policing. . . . Judge Wilkinson mitigates the concerns of some that any encounter with an officer could turn fatal. . . . In so doing, my dissenting colleague in turn presents a sordid view of under-policing, suggesting that our decision today will lead to "an America where gated communities will be safe enough and dispossessed communities will be left to fend increasingly for themselves."
>
> But we know that many of our fellow citizens already feel insecure regardless of their location. In a society where some are considered dangerous even when they are in their living rooms eating ice cream, asleep in their beds, playing in the park, standing in the pulpit of their church, birdwatching, exercising in public, or walking home from a trip to the store to purchase a bag of Skittles, it is still within their own communities—even those deemed "dispossessed" or "disadvantaged"—that they feel the most secure.[203]

Chief Judge Gregory then explained his view of the actual fundamental trouble in the case:

> Permitting unconstitutional governmental intrusions into these communities in the name of protecting them presents a false dichotomy. My colleague insists on a Hobson's choice for these communities: decide between their constitutional rights against unwarranted searches and seizures or forgo governmental protection that is readily afforded to other communities.[204]

Plus, Chief Judge Gregory feared that predictive policing might "enable, or even justify, a high-tech version of racial profiling."[205]

A precise and careful description of exactly what the trouble is will help a lawyer convince the legal audience that this really is the underlying problem. Only then can the lawyer convince the legal audience that a proposed solution will actually fix the true problem.

---

203. *Id.* at 331–32 (citations omitted).

204. *Id.* at 332–33.

205. *Id.* at 334 (quoting Andrew Guthrie Ferguson, *Policing Predictive Policing*, 94 WASH. U. L. REV. 113, 1149 (2017)).

4.6. Morality: *Welk v. GMAC Mortgage, LLC*

Culture, and the values inherent in culture, are critical to Bruner's description of narrative. He and Amsterdam acknowledged, "[L]ife in the law is not lived in a vacuum. It is part of a pervasive world of *culture*. If law is to work for the people in a society, it must be (and must be seen to be) an extension or reflection of their culture."[206] That culture, in turn, depends on "values, faiths, and beliefs about the way in which human beings should be treated."[207] Burke also emphasized that morals are important to his theory of dramatism—that is, the theory focuses on the "moralistic" negative ("Thou shalt not . . .").[208] Burke posited that this desire for order and a just society is implicit in the nature of man as a symbol-using animal.

Welk v. GMAC Mortgage, LLC[209] reinforces the point that a story concludes with a coda, or moral of the story.[210] That coda is often used to persuade another that a lawyer's client is acting morally and not breaking any moral rules of the culture. Lawyers, too, should be reminded of ethical and moral obligations.

William B. Butler, a lawyer representing "a couple hundred plaintiffs . . . made a cottage industry out of filing frivolous show-me-the-note actions."[211] Butler's argument was that "because the entity that holds her mortgage (say, MERS) is not the same as the entity that holds her note (say, U.S. Bank), the mortgage on her home or the foreclosure of that mortgage is invalid."[212] But the problem with Butler's legal theory was that every court in Minnesota rejected it. Judge Schiltz explained, "All of these courts have held—clearly, repeatedly, and recently—that, under Minnesota law, the entity that holds the mortgage can foreclose on the mortgage even if that entity does not also hold the note."[213]

The defendants moved for sanctions. The court "sua sponte issued a short order pursuant to Fed. R. Civ. P. 11(c) requiring Butler to show cause why he should not be sanctioned."[214]

---

206. Amsterdam & Bruner, *supra* note 10, at 2 (emphasis in original).

207. *Id.* at 6.

208. Burke, *supra* note 32, at 450. Burke spun out the complications of this moralistic conception of the negative, which is an idea focused on order: "'[O]rder,' being a polar term, implies a corresponding idea of 'disorder,' while these terms in turn involve ideas of 'obedience' or 'disobedience' to the 'authority' implicit in 'order.'" *Id.*

209. 850 F. Supp. 2d 976 (D. Minn. 2012).

210. Amsterdam & Bruner, *supra* note 10, at 114.

211. Welk, 850 F. Supp. 2d at 981.

212. *Id.* at 980.

213. *Id.* at 980–81.

214. *Id.* at 999.

Judge Schiltz wrote:

> This order—and defendants' motion for sanctions—were prompted by more than just Butler's conduct in this case. As noted, Butler has made a cottage industry of filing frivolous show-me-the-note claims. As also noted, Butler has not only filed (at last count) nearly 30 frivolous lawsuits, but he has engaged in brazen delay tactics and judge-shopping by voluntarily dismissing actions only to turn around and refile them again immediately afterwards....
>
> In short, Butler has been abusing, not using, the judicial system, and his conduct appears to violate multiple provisions of the Minnesota Rules of Professional Conduct....
>
> At the end of the day, then, most of what Butler offers is smoke and mirrors.... Butler's repeated attempts to cloak this claim in new garb are an expensive and time-consuming burden on both the courts and his opponents. And Butler's litigation conduct—his repeated dismissals and refilings; his delay tactics; his judge shopping; his misrepresentations; his constantly shifting and contradictory arguments; his strategic packaging of large numbers of unrelated plaintiffs into unwieldy cases whose sheer size overwhelms the court and the defendants—all of this is powerful evidence of Butler's bad faith.[215]

The court held that Butler violated Rule 11(b). In an unusual move, Judge Schiltz imposed a monetary sanction on Butler because "Butler knows exactly what he is doing; he has deliberately chosen to bring hundreds of frivolous claims in the most burdensome manner possible, and he has repeatedly used deceptive and misleading tactics to delay their ultimate resolution."[216] This was not a case of lawyer negligence, so the usual warnings and sanctions were not sufficient. Judge Schiltz concluded, "Only a significant monetary sanction [$50,000] will deter Butler from further misconduct of this kind."[217] A legal reader will be convinced, after reading Judge Schiltz's opinion, that a serious monetary sanction was justified by Butler's continued, persistent, order-defying conduct.

Burke pointed out that the law is built on the negative—what people must not do.[218] So, too, are the professional and ethical rules that govern a lawyer's actions. The *Welk* opinion affirms this: a lawyer cannot ignore binding

215. *Id.* at 999–1000, 1003.

216. *Id.* at 1004.

217. *Id.*

218. *See supra* note 131 and accompanying text.

precedent, a lawyer cannot bring a frivolous claim, a lawyer cannot abuse the judicial system, and a lawyer cannot act in bad faith. In other words, the moral takeaway of *Welk* is that lawyers can tell stories, but those stories must be true and grounded in a viable legal theory. (An aside: Hearing stories about how lawyers practice law beefs up the coda of morality and shared values in our largely self-policed legal profession.)

Morality underpins all the earlier examples in this chapter, too. In simple terms, the moral lesson of all of the prior legal cases is that this is not the way that we should treat people. We shouldn't use highly trained drug-detection dogs to snoop into someone's home. We shouldn't take independence away from a child with cerebral palsy by prohibiting her service dog from helping her at school. We shouldn't kneel on and choke a person who is no threat to others. We shouldn't stop a suspicionless person in the aftermath of gunshots.

Audiences look at stories through a cultural lens, seeking and then testing the moral of the story. A lawyer can persuade the legal reader by tapping into the legal reader's desire to know what values and norms are reflected in the story. The goal is to convince the legal reader to believe that the right and just moral emerges from the events in the story.

5. Conclusion

When you read a legal brief or a judicial opinion, maybe you are persuaded to view the legal problem and its suggested result in the way that the legal writer has framed it. Perhaps it is because you can picture yourself in the scene described. Or maybe you are influenced by the values and morals at the heart of the story's resolution. Or maybe you are not persuaded. Perhaps it is because you can't identify with the people described in the legal story. Or maybe the story doesn't ring true because it conflicts with your life experience. Rhetorical theories about how and why stories persuade underpin all those potential reactions.

Lawyers know that stories can persuade. They know it by instinct, from scientific studies showing that humans are hardwired to pay attention to stories, or from personal experiences of being persuaded by oral and written stories. This chapter highlights the power of story in one more way—through the use of rhetoric. Rhetorical theories, developed by rhetoricians like Burke, Fisher, and Bruner, help lawyers understand why telling stories makes persuasion easier. Rhetoric can help lawyers tell effective stories to aid clients and shine a light on those who haven't been seen or protected by the law—and, in this way, narrative can help change the justice system.

Summing It Up

- Rhetoric is one way to explain how and why stories persuade. Lawyers who understand rhetorical theories will be better able to persuade through stories.
- We see our lives and the lives of others as stories. A story has several consistent elements: act, agent, scene, agency, and purpose.
- Legal audiences will be persuaded more easily when responding to an emotional appeal combined with logic. Stories combine logic and emotion because they are told sequentially from a point of view.
- Storytelling in the legal context is restricted. First, the law operates in a culture of argument, so competing stories are told. Second, rules dictate how a story can be told. Finally, stories are told throughout the legal process, including stories about the law itself.
- The relationship between the elements of a story creates tension and drama. Lawyers should focus on one of these relationships, such as why the actor performed that act, to impact how the audience views the story.
- The best stories help the audience identify with the actors and their plight. Lawyers should use detail and context to help an audience relate to and identify with a client's story.
- Law is grounded in the negative because what is allowed is in large part determined by what is not allowed. Lawyers should use this negative when telling stories to help the audience understand the boundaries of the law.
- An audience tests a story for its narrative probability (does this story seem likely?) and narrative fidelity (does this story seem true?). Lawyers should test their stories for coherence and truthfulness.
- The trouble, or conflict, at the heart of a story can be described in different ways depending on who tells the story. Lawyers should recognize that their culture and experiences can impact how they identify the trouble in a story.
- An audience's response to a story depends on the framing of the trouble, or disruptive event, in the story. Lawyers should carefully decide how to describe the precise legal trouble at the heart of a client's story.
- An audience looks for the moral of the story. Lawyers should include that moral, either explicitly or implicitly, when telling stories.

Suggestions for Further Reading

ANTHONY G. AMSTERDAM & JEROME BRUNER, MINDING THE LAW (2000).

PETER BROOKS & PAUL GEWIRTZ, EDS., LAW'S STORIES: NARRATIVE AND RHETORIC IN THE LAW (1996).

JEROME BRUNER, ACTUAL MINDS, POSSIBLE WORLDS (1986).

KENNETH BURKE, COUNTER-STATEMENT (1968).

Kenneth Burke, *Dramatism*, *in* INTERNATIONAL ENCYCLOPEDIA OF THE SOCIAL SCIENCES (1968).

KENNETH BURKE, A GRAMMAR OF MOTIVES (1969).

KENNETH BURKE, LANGUAGE AS SYMBOLIC ACTION (1966).

KENNETH BURKE, PERMANENCE AND CHANGE (2d ed. 1954).

KENNETH BURKE, A RHETORIC OF MOTIVES (1969).

WALTER FISHER, HUMAN COMMUNICATION AS NARRATION: TOWARD A PHILOSOPHY OF REASON, VALUE, AND ACTION (1987).

JAMES L. GOLDEN, GOODWIN F. BERQUIST & WILLIAM E. COLEMAN, THE RHETORIC OF WESTERN THOUGHT (6th ed. 1997).

RUTH ANNE ROBBINS, STEVE JOHANSEN & KEN CHESTEK, YOUR CLIENT'S STORY: PERSUASIVE LEGAL WRITING (2d ed. 2019).

MICHAEL R. SMITH, ADVANCED LEGAL WRITING: THEORIES AND STRATEGIES IN PERSUASIVE WRITING (4th ed. 2013).

WILLIAM ZINSSER, ON WRITING WELL: THE CLASSIC GUIDE TO WRITING NONFICTION (7th ed. 2016).

Chapter Five

Metaphor & Analogy

LINDA L. BERGER

---

1. Introduction

During the first year of the coronavirus pandemic, health officials sometimes referred to Covid-19 as the "invisible enemy" and declared that Covid-19 was "winning," while politicians declared on different occasions that the "battle had been won" or that we were "turning the corner in our fight." Of course, a virus is neither a person nor an entity, and so a virus is literally incapable of being an enemy, engaging in battle, or winning or losing a fight. But the ease with which we understood those metaphorical characterizations (we are *at war* with the virus) and implicit analogies (the virus is *like an enemy*)[1] demonstrates how prevalent metaphor and analogy are in our everyday conversation and how little inclined we are to question their use.

This chapter focuses on metaphor and analogy in the law, and especially on their use as framing devices that guide lawyers and judges into particular ways of thinking and talking about a legal issue. The chapter takes an explicitly rhetorical view of metaphor and analogy, using rhetorical analysis as a window to explore how the use of language and symbols affects an audience. Or to put it another way, how might speakers and writers use metaphor and analogy to persuade their listeners and readers, to help them understand unfamiliar situations, and on some occasions, to lead them down a garden path?[2]

When speakers and writers use metaphor and analogy to frame the background context of a legal question, the images (metaphors) and examples (analogies) they choose will highlight some aspects of the background and underplay others, sometimes with far-reaching effects. By their nature, both images and examples fail to capture the whole of the situation. When, for example, the metaphor of war is applied to drugs or crime, it may reorient the reader's perspective in two directions. The first effect is to subtly incline the reader negatively, against efforts to advance individual healthcare or promote social welfare, while the second is to gently influence the reader positively, in

---

1. Traditionally, metaphors were differentiated from analogies by their phrasing. When we first learned about figures of speech, we were taught that a metaphor directly states that one thing "is" another unlike thing, anticipating that the listener would infer implicit relationships or likenesses: the metaphor that time *is* money may imply to the listener that both concepts are valuable and limited. Similarly, and in contrast, the wording of an analogy makes the comparison between the two unlike things more explicit: life is *like a* box of chocolates. Still, the listener must make inferential leaps—does the analogy imply that both life and boxes of chocolates are full of sweet and sour surprises?—and the speaker cannot count on the listener to understand the analogy in the way it was intended.

2. This lovely phrase apparently can be phrased as either "up" or "down" a garden path and means you have deceived someone. *Lead (someone) down/up the garden path Definition*, MERRIAM-WEBSTER DICTIONARY, https://www.merriam-webster.com/dictionary/lead%20%28someone%29%20down%2Fup %20the%20garden%20path (last visited March 1, 2022).

favor of arguments to carry out the kinds of policing actions that mimic military endeavors.[3]

This effect echoes one essential message of this chapter. Metaphor and analogy provide meaningful frames for the legal issues we argue about, influencing the audience's perception and understanding, but the resulting argument frames are incomplete, partial, and ideologically weighted. Thus, for example, when we approach free speech questions as if they existed in a marketplace of ideas, freedom of religion issues as if the Constitution had erected a wall between church and state, and the right of privacy as if a penumbra emanated from the stated rights of the Constitution, we are being influenced not only by those images but also by all the cultural and social associations that cling to them.

Because it is less often mentioned, a more important message of the chapter may be that metaphor and analogy are as significant for the invention of arguments as they are for the persuasive presentation of arguments.[4] Whenever we try to understand or explain something—the foundation of a persuasive argument—we are seeking a metaphor, an analogy, or a story that will illuminate the issue in a favorable way. When there are no roadmaps, or when the course has not been charted, the writer or the speaker must imagine and test a range of potentially effective approaches.

To illustrate more concretely, let's imagine that you are the school board attorney trying to justify the punishment of a high school student who used vulgar language when she referred to school activities, teachers, and coaches in a social media posting.[5] After not being selected for her preferred positions on the softball team and varsity cheerleading team, the student posted on Snapchat an image showing her and a friend with raised middle fingers and a caption reading: "Fuck school fuck softball fuck cheer fuck everything." The

3. For support that such metaphors shift the reader's perspective in this way, see Paul H. Thibodeau & Lera Boroditsky, *Metaphors We Think with: The Role of Metaphor in Reasoning*, PLOS ONE 6(2) (2011); Paul H. Thibodeau & Lera Boroditsky, *Natural Language Metaphors Covertly Influence Reasoning*, PLOS ONE 8(1) (2013); Sarah Higinbotham, *The Law as Violence: Essay: Bloodletting and Beasts: Metaphors of Legal Violence*, 49 WAKE FOREST L. REV. 727, 742 (2014).

4. In classical rhetoric, the canons were identified as invention, arrangement, style, memory, and delivery. [CICERO,] RHETORICA AD HERENNIUM 7 (Harry Caplan trans., 1954).

5. The example is based on *Mahanoy Area Sch. Dist. v. B.L.*, 141 S. Ct. 2038, 2046 (2021). The Court held that punishing the student's expression violated the First Amendment. The ACLU, which represented the plaintiff, later sold T-shirts bearing the phrase.

principal suspended the student from after-school activities for two weeks, but the student argued that the First Amendment protected her social media posting: it was written at home, not at school, and it was available to readers for less than a day. You know that First Amendment protection for high school students' speech is more limited than for adults and that in the past, students have been protected when their "speech" took the form of wearing armbands protesting the Vietnam war (*Tinker*)[6] but not when they carried a sign advocating drug use (*Bong Hits 4 Jesus*).[7] The essential arguments to be made by both the school board attorney and the student's attorney would follow the standard script for presenting arguments based on diverging case law precedents interpreting the constitutional protection.

But at least as important as the development of these analogous case arguments is to create the rhetorical setting that best frames the arguments your client needs to win. In this illustration, for example, the school board attorney might choose a well-known metaphor or image as the background setting. That choice would take advantage of the audience's tacit knowledge and acceptance by tapping into their shared understanding. For example, if the attorney were to refer to the student's social media posting as "shouting fire" within the school community, the attorney would be asking the audience to accept the implications of comparing something clearly dangerous (fire) to something much less obviously harmful (posting a vulgar message). If successful, this acceptance would come about because the audience does not question the long-established metaphor that *speech is fire* or the well-known, if outdated, analogy between harmful speech and *shouting fire in a crowded theater*.[8]

As will be discussed later, depending on the circumstances, the attorney could choose other alternatives, such as using a less well-known metaphor or a factual analogy not tied to existing case law. But first, the chapter will go into detail about how metaphor and analogy work, tracing the development of rhetorical and cognitive theory on both subjects. Applying a backward-and-forward-looking lens to *Cohen v. California*, 403 U.S. 15 (1971),

6. Tinker v. Des Moines Ind. Cmty. Sch. Dist., 393 U.S. 503, 504 (1969) (conduct of wearing black armbands to protest Vietnam war was analogous to pure speech which was entitled to comprehensive protection under the First Amendment, absent facts that might reasonably have led school officials to forecast substantial disruption of or material interference with school activities).

7. Morse v. Frederick, 551 U.S. 393, 396 (2007) (schools may take steps to safeguard those entrusted to their care from speech that can reasonably be regarded as encouraging illegal drug use, here a banner carrying the phrase Bong Hits 4 Jesus).

8. See Schenck v. United States, 249 U.S. 47 (1919), discussed as part of the development of the *speech as fire* metaphor later in this chapter.

the Supreme Court opinion often referred to as the "fuck the draft" case, the chapter will then explore the interaction of metaphor and analogy with the law's development.

2. Metaphor and analogy in theory and research

Everyone who uses language becomes a better communicator when they understand how metaphor and analogy work. This understanding is essential for lawyers and judges because their arguments and decisions center on the meaning of legal language. In turn, legal language is shot through with metaphor, and its interpretation often is determined by analogy. The popular notion that legal reasoning relies primarily on logical arguments based on syllogisms (major premise, minor premise, conclusion) or common law reasoning glosses over the importance of stories, metaphors, and fact analogies.

Because metaphor and analogy pervade our writing and thinking about the law, metaphor and analogy are persuasive. And they are persuasive both when they are used directly, in propositions that support arguments, and when they are used indirectly, as more subtle suggestions that change the minds of audience members by influencing their perception and understanding. For example, when lawyers insist that a corporation should be viewed *as a person competing in the marketplace of ideas* or that intellectual property should be treated *like real property*, they are using metaphor and analogy as propositions supporting an argument.[9] But when lawyers suggest that a *tsunami of corporate money has swept away small contributions*, that a criminal defendant's *violence has ripped apart* his family, or that an unemployed family member has acted *like a parasite* on the rest of the family, the images are designed to bring about "changes in the associations and comparisons" the listener makes, "differences in the vivid or 'felt' appreciation" of things the listener already knows about, or changes in the listener's "habits of attention and sense of the important and the trifling."[10] Such changes pave the way for the listener to come around and more willingly accept the lawyer's argument when it is later stated explicitly.

---

9. Unlike the propositional arguments made in the form of complete syllogisms, the mapping supported by metaphor and analogy goes unstated.

10. Richard Moran, *Seeing and Believing: Metaphor, Image, and Force*, 16 Critical Inquiry 87, 100 (Autumn 1989). For more discussion, see Elisabeth Camp, *Metaphor in the Mind: The Cognition of Metaphor*, 1 Phil. Compass 154 (2006); Elisabeth Camp, *Saying*

2.1. A brief sketch of *is* and *like*

Metaphor and analogy rely on our capacity to see one thing as another. This capacity is the root of imagination. It enables us to make the leap from Juliet to the sun (the Shakespearean metaphor) or from the automobile to the skateboard (the legal analogy based on the prototypical rule, "no vehicles in the park"). By helping us see one thing as another, metaphor and analogy leverage our propensity to make connections and to find similarities across difference. This propensity underlies all our thinking and decision making.[11] Like stories, but in patterns rather than plot-driven paths, metaphor and analogy reassure us that things hang together, providing a sense of coherence to the frameworks we employ for perception and expression.[12] Although categorizing a particular example as metaphor or analogy is difficult, it is usually true that when you deliberately select a metaphor, your listener understands it as a more subtle and less literal comparison.[13] You have more room to stretch, but there is more leeway for misunderstanding. In contrast, when you explicitly propound an analogy, your listener will be more prone to question and test the comparison. Once accepted, however, the listener may be more willing to let you extend your analogy through an expanded series of ramifications.

---

and Seeing-as: The Linguistic Uses and Cognitive Effects of Metaphor (2003) (Dissertation, University of California Berkeley).

11. Despite the close relationship of metaphor and analogy, proponents differ about which is the more powerful. Linguist George Lakoff and philosopher Mark Johnson claim that all human thought and expression revolve around metaphor. *See, e.g.*, George Lakoff, *The Contemporary Theory of Metaphor*, *in* METAPHOR AND THOUGHT 202 (Andrew Ortony ed., 2d ed. 1993); GEORGE LAKOFF, WOMEN, FIRE, AND DANGEROUS THINGS: WHAT CATEGORIES REVEAL ABOUT THE MIND (1987); GEORGE LAKOFF & MARK JOHNSON, METAPHORS WE LIVE BY (1980). Although he does not claim that analogy is like the sun, Douglas Hofstadter uses a related metaphor: "[A]nalogy is anything but a bitty blip [in the broad blue sky of cognition]—rather, it's the very blue that fills the whole sky of cognition—analogy is *everything*, or very nearly so, in my view." Douglas R. Hofstadter, *Epilogue: Analogy as the Core of Cognition*, *in* THE ANALOGICAL MIND: PERSPECTIVES FROM COGNITIVE SCIENCE 499, 499 (Dedre Gentner et al. eds., 2001). *See also* Linda L. Berger, *Metaphor and Analogy: The Sun and Moon of Legal Persuasion*, 22 J. L. & POL'Y 147 (2013).

12. Linda L. Berger, *The Lady or the Tiger: A Field Guide to Metaphor and Narrative*, 50 WASHBURN L.J. 275 (2011).

13. Dan Hunter distinguished between the two on the ground that analogy has an explicit predictive or explanatory effect while metaphor nudges the reader toward reaching inferences and conclusions on her own. Dan Hunter, *Teaching and Using Analogy in Law*, 2 J. ALWD 151 (2004).

The leading rhetorical view of metaphor highlights another quality. In addition to allowing us to see one thing as another, metaphor helps us see things in a *new* way. I.A. Richards's foundational description covers all situations where we speak of one thing as though it were another thing, but also of metaphoric "processes in which we perceive or think or feel about one thing in terms of another—as when looking at a building it seems to have a face and to confront us with a peculiar expression."[14] In the same vein, Kenneth Burke pointed out that metaphor brings out the "thisness of a that, or the thatness of a this."[15] These descriptions emphasize that metaphor, by enhancing our ability to "see one thing as another," encourages the listener or reader to see resemblances and relationships and to make inferences about patterns where they might not otherwise be revealed. As Donald Davidson wrote, the point is not so much the content of the metaphor but what the metaphor makes us notice.[16]

When it comes to analogy, the rhetorical focus adjusts. From the rhetorical view, analogy helps us understand new experiences and make decisions about them. When we are confronted with a new situation, we might feel "helpless unless and until [we] can see some resemblance between that and some other already familiar situation."[17] Our ability to analogize helps us (1) classify new experiences into categories and find frameworks into which they can be slotted, (2) assign symbols or labels to those categories and frameworks, and (3) suggest hypotheses about how things will work out for those categories and frameworks. These functions interact. When we form categories and subcategories, we do so based on perceived analogies or similarities. The labels we give to each new category usually are analogically consistent with the labels of existing categories. All this is part of the process of creating symbols and expanding available language resources. For example, "the 'space age' carries an inherent comparison to 'ice age' and the 'iron age,' 'the atomic revolution' implicitly compares with the 'agricultural revolution' and the 'industrial revolution.'"[18] Finally, analogy helps us generate hypotheses about the nature and characteristics of the new experience. The analogy does not only present one

---

14. I. A. RICHARDS, THE PHILOSOPHY OF RHETORIC 116–17 (1936).

15. Kenneth Burke, *Four Master Tropes*, 3 THE KENYON REV. 421–38 (1941).

16. Donald Davidson, *What Metaphors Mean*, CRITICAL INQUIRY 31, 46 (Autumn 1978). Davidson's view that there was no independent cognitive content to metaphor was criticized by Max Black, among others.

17. James R. Wilcox & H.L. Ewbank, *Analogy for Rhetors*, 12 PHIL. & RHETORIC 1, 10–11 (1979).

18. *Id.* at 12.

thing as another, it presents the unfamiliar item "filtered by the qualities of the second domain." This leads to broader implied conclusions about the unfamiliar item.[19]

Although we were taught to view metaphor and analogy as linguistically different (metaphor being stated as "Juliet is the sun," and analogy as "Juliet is like the sun"), for rhetorical purposes, their similarities outweigh their differences. Whether "reasoning" through metaphor or analogy, we depend on a process of mapping characteristics and relationships from the source domain (the domain from which relevant concepts are being pulled) to the target domain (the domain being explained). In both instances, A (Juliet) is the target domain, and B (the sun) is the source domain. When the purpose of using an analogy or a metaphor is to explain, the target (A) typically is the "new" concept or the more abstract idea, and the source (B) often is the more familiar or concrete thing. When they are consciously created and used, analogies and metaphors generally have one of two goals. The first is to make A more understandable, and the second is to persuade the audience member to treat A as if it were B. The reasons for asking the audience member to treat A as if it were B might include any of the following: B is a similar but more familiar example; B provides an already-established category of examples; or B helps the reader see A in a new light, one more favorable for the speaker's purpose.[20]

2.2. The unconscious cognitive influence of barely visible metaphors

If a poet or a judge writes that "metaphor is the sun," is she using language in an interesting way or is she trying to affect the reader's thinking? Recent metaphor research supports the second option, the theoretical claim that metaphor is not "mere rhetoric." Because metaphor affects our thinking, it is not solely figurative or literary, but has cognitive status. Metaphor is "not only a way of seeing or saying" but also "a way of thinking and knowing, the method by which we structure and reason, and it is fundamental, not ornamental."[21] Most experts agree that metaphor shapes our thinking processes by "mapping

---

19. *Id.* at 13–15.

20. "We have suggested that metaphor is like analogy—that the basic processes of analogy are at work in metaphor." Dedre Gentner et al., *Metaphor Is Like Analogy, in* THE ANALOGICAL MIND: PERSPECTIVES FROM COGNITIVE SCIENCE, *supra* note 11, at 199, 243.

21. Linda L. Berger, *What Is the Sound of a Corporation Speaking? How the Cognitive Theory of Metaphor Can Help Lawyers Shape the Law*, 2 J. ALWD 169, 170 (2004).

onto the new experience the structures, inferences, and reasoning methods of the old."[22] Moreover, when the metaphor is conventional or long-established, mapping occurs automatically and unconsciously. Such unconscious influence can, of course, be very effective for persuasive purposes.

Theoretical and scholarly descriptions of metaphor often start with Aristotle's formal definition: "Metaphor consists in giving the thing a name that belongs to something else; the transference being either from genus to species, or from species to genus, or from species to species, or on grounds of analogy."[23] Over the centuries, some critics thought this description fell short because it restricted metaphor to words, rather than also including phrases or sentences, and because it depicted metaphor as a departure from ordinary language use.[24] If that was what the definition meant, the metaphor theorists of the twentieth century disagreed.

Early in the twentieth century, I.A. Richards—a rhetorician, poet, and literary critic—made the then-groundbreaking claim that metaphor was a principle of thought, rather than a "trick" of language. He suggested that thought itself, not only the language used for the expression of thought, was "metaphoric, and proceeds by comparison, and the metaphors of language derive therefrom."[25] Metaphor was not a departure from ordinary language, but instead permeated ordinary thought and language and raised issues about the nature of knowledge and reality.[26] Richards's view was that metaphor worked as "two thoughts of different things active together and supported by a single word, or phrase, whose meaning is a resultant of their interaction."[27] As implied by his claim that metaphor was a principle of thought, Richards expanded the reach of metaphor to include not only images and similarities, but also concepts and dissimilarities.[28]

---

22. *Id.* at 171.

23. Aristotle, *The Poetics, in* The Rhetoric and The Poetics of Aristotle, 223, 251 (7457b lines 8–11) (Ingram Bywater trans., Random House 1954).

24. *See* Mark Johnson, *Introduction: Metaphor in the Philosophical Tradition, in* Philosophical Perspectives on Metaphor 3, 3–4 (Mark Johnson ed., 1981); *but see* Michael Frost, *Greco-Roman Analysis of Metaphoric Reasoning*, 2 Leg. Writing 113, 118 (1996) (arguing that Aristotle thought that metaphor provides insights not achievable by other means).

25. Richards, *supra* note 14, at 92–94.

26. *Id.*

27. *Id.*

28. *Id.*

Richards's argument that metaphor should be seen as a *container* of cognitive content was further developed by the philosopher Max Black. Black argued that we understand a metaphor by engaging in a distinctive intellectual endeavor.[29] This endeavor involved the use of one complex system—made up of the properties associated with one part of the metaphor, the source—as a filter or a screen to select, emphasize, and organize relations among the properties associated with the target.[30] The meaning that the listener derived from metaphorical thinking could not be explained either as a comparison or through a literal paraphrase. Rather than merely reflecting similarity, the metaphor created it. In Black's conception, new meaning was generated in much the same way that rubbing two sticks together lights both.

Other rhetoricians, linguists, literary theorists, and cognitive scientists fleshed out this view of metaphor as going beyond literary tricks. Among the most influential was Michael Osborn, whose co-authored 1962 essay about metaphors in public speaking influenced a range of thinkers in understanding how metaphors persuade.[31] He followed up with a landmark essay, "Archetypal Metaphor in Rhetoric: The Light-Dark Family," providing a name for metaphors that retained their power over and across time, culture, and space.[32] Osborn suggested a continuum of archetypes "bounded at one end by vital phenomena of nature such as light-and-darkness, the sea, mountains and valleys, and the cycle of seasons" and at the other end by "thematic motifs... represent[ing] narrative impulses... such as the quest, the journey, sacrificial rituals, and revenge and conquest scenarios."[33] Also on the continuum from image to story "are potent sources of figuration, such as disease, family relationships and war."[34] Projecting a similar range of rhetorical applications, Osborn further

---

29. Max Black, Models and Metaphors: Studies in Language and Philosophy 41 (1962) ("We can say that the principal subject is 'seen through' the metaphorical expression—or, if we prefer, that the principal subject is 'projected upon' the field of the subsidiary subject.").

30. *Id.* at 38–44.

31. Michael Osborn & Douglas Ehninger, *The Metaphor in Public Address*, 29 Speech Monographs 223–34 (1962), *reprinted in* Michael Osborn, Michael Osborn on Metaphor and Style 3 (2018).

32. Michael Osborn, *Archetypal Metaphor in Rhetoric: The Light-Dark Family*, 53 Q. J. of Speech 115–26 (1967), *reprinted in* Osborn, *supra* note 31, at 59.

33. Osborn, *supra* note 31, at 80–81.

34. *Id.*

theorized ways in which stylistic devices beyond metaphor (metonymy, irony, anaphora, and so on) affected persuasive communication.[35]

In 1980, George Lakoff and Mark Johnson upended the conversation, focusing on the use of metaphor in everyday talk when they published *Metaphors We Live By*.[36] Lakoff, a professor of linguistics, and Johnson, a professor of philosophy, added cognitive science to the disciplines supporting the argument that metaphor shapes thinking. In the emerging theory labeled experientialism, metaphor referred to "a cognitive process by which we use a concrete, experienced source domain to structure and understand a more abstract domain."[37] As an example, Lakoff and Johnson pointed to the commonly understood cognitive metaphor that argument is war. The metaphor not only shapes our language uses, they emphasized, it also shapes our understanding and our actions:

> [W]e don't just *talk* about argument in terms of war. We win or lose arguments. See the person as an opponent. We attack his positions and we defend our own. We plan and use strategies.... [M]any of the things we do in arguing are partially structured by the concept of war.[38]

If experts agree that metaphor affects thought and conveys meaning, how do these outcomes happen? In other words, how does metaphor work?

---

35. Michael Osborn, *Toward Rhetorical Depiction, in* Osborn, *supra* note 31, at 135. Although less well-known outside their own fields of study, scholars from a range of disciplines provided insights that could be applied to persuasive lawyering. For example, philosophy professor Elisabeth Camp distinguished poetic from propositional metaphor. Camp, *supra* note 10. A propositional metaphor, although not literally true, suggests that one thing should be seen as and treated as if it were another (the First Amendment is a wall of separation). In contrast, a poetic metaphor (all the world's a stage) proposes a shift in viewpoint or perspective, a new take, a way of seeing that makes you consider a familiar concept in a new light.

36. Lakoff & Johnson, *supra* note 11.

37. Steven L. Winter, *Transcendental Nonsense, Metaphoric Reasoning, and the Cognitive Stakes for Law* , 137 U. Pa. L. Rev. 1105, 1115 n.25 (1989).

38. Lakoff & Johnson, *supra* note 11, at 4. Osborn wrote that his approach differed from the approach taken by Lakoff and Johnson because they were interested in metaphor "as it passes into ordinary language but continues to structure thought, attitude, and action." In contrast, "my research emphasizes conspicuous vivid instances of metaphor that are more self-conscious and more dependent upon artistic development by speakers." While Lakoff and Johnson were interested in metaphors that are "unconscious symptoms of culture," Osborn wrote that he was interested in metaphors that are "more calculated instruments of persuasive design." Osborn further characterized the Lakoff and Johnson approach as more sociological, and his as "rhetorical analysis." Osborn, *supra* note 31, at 90–91 n.39.

Starting with Aristotle, most experts who wrote about metaphor described the work of metaphor in much the way the word itself suggested. Derived from the Greek words meaning "to carry over," the word metaphor implied that the ideas and meanings associated with one thing were carried over to another. From the time of Aristotle until the advent of the cognitive theory of metaphor, many theorists argued that metaphorical meanings were based on a "carrying over" of ideas through substitution or comparison. In either substitution or comparison, metaphor was an indirect way of saying that A is like B in certain respects. The substitution and the comparison views were criticized on various grounds. Not only are many objects similar in some respects, but the comparison view also did not explain how we select relevant similarities. The theories did not account for differences nor for the anomaly that many metaphors are not based on literal similarities. As an example, Lakoff and Johnson's conceptual metaphor that "More is Up" is based not on similarity, but on our past experiences in the physical world. When we add more things to a pile, the top of the pile rises or goes "up."[39]

The third view—that the meaning of a metaphor was generated through a transaction or interaction between the contexts of the source and the target—grew out of Richards's argument that metaphorical understanding comes from stirring together two thoughts present at the same time.[40] Black's version of this theory was illustrated through the metaphor "Man is a Wolf." According to Black, the system of properties and relationships commonly believed to be true of the target (Man)—properties and relationships that he called "associated commonplaces"—interacted with the associated commonplaces of the source. Rather than comparing the two systems, Black suggested that we used one system of commonplaces—those associated with the source (Wolf)—as a kind of screen or filter to select, emphasize, suppress, and organize the system of commonplaces associated with the target (Man). For example, in this metaphor, we might see Man as brave, hairy, mean, and a loner. The other characteristics of Man are screened or filtered away to fall outside.[41]

The remainder of this chapter concentrates on two current theories of how metaphors work. First, for conventional metaphors, the chapter discusses conceptual metaphor theory as developed by Lakoff and Johnson,[42]

---

39. Lakoff & Johnson, *supra* note 11, at 15–16.

40. Richards, *supra* note 14, at 93.

41. Black, *supra* note 29, at 39–45.

42. An extensive statement of their cumulative theory and research can be found in George Lakoff & Mark Johnson, Philosophy in the Flesh: The Embodied

and second, for novel metaphors and analogies, the chapter explores analogy processing as described by Dedre Gentner and her colleagues.[43] Lakoff and Johnson advanced the theory that we absorb a system of primary metaphors automatically and involuntarily through long, constant, consistent, and unconscious experiences in the world. This explains such metaphors as the already-mentioned More is Up (the piling up of helpful things like grain, flowers, and jewels) and Life is a Journey (we age as we physically move from event to event through our lives). Our understanding of these metaphors comes not from studying the words themselves nor from any interaction between the contexts of the target and the source, but instead from our interaction with the physical and cultural environment. Through our experience, we form categories, frameworks, and scripts that give us a sense of coherence. Some come directly from a prior interaction with the environment, but we also understand new experiences by using a category, framework, or script from one domain to provide a structure for an experience in another. For example, we may transfer the experience of grasping a cup to the experience of understanding or *grasping* a new concept.[44]

According to Lakoff and Johnson, "by functioning normally in the world, we automatically and unconsciously acquire and use a vast number of [primary] metaphors."[45] Both basic or primary metaphors and the more complicated conventional metaphors that we use regularly become physically, environmentally, and culturally embedded over time. In the case of complex metaphorical systems like the one associated with the *marketplace of ideas*, both the mental concept and the organizational structure that surrounds it are unconsciously imported. We may even borrow the accompanying patterns of inference and methods of evaluation.

During the forty years since publication of *Metaphors We Live By*, Lakoff and Johnson's work has been critiqued,[46] but it remains widely applied and continues to be developed by the primary authors as well as by experts in a range of disciplines. Among others, cognitive scientist Raymond Gibbs has

---

Mind & its Challenge to Western Thought (1999).

43. *See* Dedre Gentner, *supra* note 20, at 227–36.

44. Lakoff & Johnson, *supra* note 11, at 59.

45. *Id.* at 58–59.

46. *See, e.g.*, Zoltán Kövecses, *Conceptual Metaphor Theory: Some Criticisms and Alternative Proposals*, 6 Ann. Rev. Cog. Ling. 168–184 (2008).

supported most tenets of Lakoff and Johnson's conceptual metaphor theory.[47] Gibbs concluded that "embodied simulation processes are central to the tacit, fast-acting, unconscious ways that we make sense of both concrete and abstract objects and events in the world, including legal ideas."[48] In other words, audience members understand what speakers and writers intend to communicate in context because they "automatically imagine themselves participating in the activities...even when [the actions described] refer to abstract activities."[49] Gibbs similarly linked the persuasive properties of storytelling with metaphor. When we are persuaded through argument, it is because we have engaged in embodied metaphorical thinking: "Persuading people via narratives to embrace different ideas requires that both writers and readers jointly participate in a metaphorical journey beginning at a starting point (the source), taking readers along some path (the path), overcoming relevant obstacles along the way, and ending at a particular location or destination (the goal)."[50] According to Gibbs, this journey metaphor is the basis for our intuitive understanding of stories.

From the rhetorical perspective, cognitive metaphor theory opens persuasive vistas because it changes traditional views of category creation and rule interpretation. In contrast to the formalist concept of categories as rigidly bounded, metaphors illustrate that category formation is imaginative and flexible. More important, categories are created, and rules are interpreted within larger frames, folk theories, or cultural models that organize knowledge and capture our normal expectations. For example, when it comes to the marketplace of ideas metaphor to be discussed later in the chapter, the words *buy*, *sell*, and *cost* are meaningful because of the model of a commercial transaction. Once the model pulls them together into a structural activity, the use of any of these words evokes an entire picture. Similarly, "the marketplace of ideas entails a variety of speakers, listeners, arguments, debates, openings, closings, claims, responses, buyers, sellers, markets, products, competition, regulation, free trade."[51] No matter how clear and simple the language, almost every legal

---

47. Raymond W. Gibbs, Jr., *Evaluating Conceptual Metaphor Theory*, 48 DISCOURSE PROCESSES 529–562 (2011).

48. Raymond W. Gibbs, Jr., *Embodied Metaphor in Persuasive Legal Narrative*, *in* NARRATIVE AND METAPHOR IN THE LAW 92 (Michael Hanne & Robert Weisberg eds., 2018).

49. *Id.*

50. *Id.* at 91.

51. Berger, *supra* note 21, at 169.

rule makes sense only "against the backdrop of a massive cultural tableau that provides the tacit background assumptions that render it intelligible."[52]

As noted earlier, just as metaphor helps writers explain, clarify, and support their arguments, metaphor is key to the rhetorical process of invention.[53] Thinking metaphorically can aid in problem solving and in increasing understanding. As Kenneth Burke pointed out, "If we are in doubt as to what an object is... we deliberately try to consider it in as many different terms as its nature permits: lifting, smelling, tasting, tapping, holding in different lights, subjecting to different pressures, dividing, matching, contrasting...."[54] In a similar way, when the Supreme Court first began to apply the First Amendment to the punishment of speech criticizing the government, the justices were feeling their way to determining what this object was, deliberately trying to consider First Amendment principles in as many different terms as possible.[55]

Because metaphor guides audience members to notice resemblances and patterns on their own, without specific guidance, metaphor may be especially persuasive. And because metaphor is inherently open to interpretation, metaphors can be used to advance uncertain or contradictory ideas. However, like all words, metaphors are prone to misunderstanding, and like most words, they carry emotional baggage and unintended ramifications. But both tendencies are exaggerated when it comes to metaphor. For one thing, metaphors are imprecise on purpose. When we use metaphors, we do not intend them to be literally true, and ambiguity or confusion may easily result. For example, the metaphor of evidence being weighed can be understood to refer to two different kinds of scales. If we want the listener to understand the metaphor by reference to weighing something on a bathroom scale, it would mean to find out whether the evidence is heavy or light, seemingly without reference to another item. But if we want the listener to understand the metaphor by reference to the scales of justice, it would mean to compare the weight of the

52. Steven L. Winter, A Clearing in the Forest: Law, Life, and Mind 101–03 (2001) (explaining how we know, without having to think about it, that humans are not animals for purposes of the rule prohibiting "live animals on the bus").

53. *See, e.g.*, Donald A. Schön, *Generative Metaphor: A Perspective on Problem-setting in Social Policy*, *in* Metaphor and Thought, *supra* note 11, at 137, 147.

54. Kenneth Burke, A Grammar of Motives and a Rhetoric of Motives 504 (1962).

55. *See* James Boyd White, *Legal Knowledge*, 115 Harv. L. Rev. 1396, 1414 (2002) ("A person writing about the First Amendment needs above all a way of imagining what it means that human beings have language, and can think and speak; what it means, or can mean, to be a speaking person, including in the law.").

evidence on one side or to balance it against the weight on the other. Choosing one interpretation of weighing the evidence over the other (did the plaintiff introduce some evidence or did the plaintiff introduce enough evidence to outweigh the evidence on the other side) could lead to very different outcomes.

As for the baggage carried by metaphor, think about the unintended consequences of the commonplace claim that argument is war. For many people, the metaphor raises an image of no-holds-barred battle and scorched-earth tactics. By invoking these images, we may create fear and anxiety. Simply using the metaphor prompts the listener to perceive and judge the process very differently than she would if she were presented with a perspective that argument is dialogue. Similarly, when we refer to criminal defendants in terms reflecting disease, lack of humanity, or filth, our listeners may approach individual defendants and the criminal justice system very differently than they would if we referred to criminal defendants more neutrally (for example, by their family status, age, gender, employment, or community position).

2.3. The more elusive persuasive effects of analogies and novel metaphors

If cognitive metaphor theory tells us that conventional and deeply embedded metaphors work automatically and unconsciously—because we have acquired them through long, constant, and unthinking experience in the world—where does that leave us as far as understanding how novel metaphors and analogies work? For example, in the cheerleader example used to open this chapter, the attorney representing the school board might have decided that the theme for the board's argument should come from a novel metaphor. Rather than relying on the marketplace of ideas (an unfavorable image for the school board's argument), the attorney might have constructed a comparison of unlike items that had not been used before for this purpose, claiming, for example, that the social media post would *pollute* or *poison* the conversation among students, faculty, coaches, and parents in the high school community.

The so-called novel metaphor is potentially helpful to the advocate when the traditional metaphor favors the other side as well as when the attorney wants the listener or reader to be surprised, almost taken aback, by the apparent incongruity of the proposed comparison. After the initial surprise, when the audience member thinks again, the audience member may be more (or less) inclined to accept the metaphor as a helpful frame for understanding the argument.

Supporting the advocate's choice of a novel metaphor in some circumstances, rhetorical scholar Michael Osborn theorized that some metaphors are more powerful because they are archetypal and others, paradoxically, because they surprise or shock the listener.[56] The more unusual or unexpected the relationship between the target and the source, "the greater the strain placed upon the associative threads necessary to hold the divergent elements together." With a novel metaphor, Osborn suggested that "a state of high tension exists, and when this tension is suddenly relieved by insight into the intended meaning, the metaphor, like a taut bowstring, drives the arrow of its meaning deep." On the other hand, the strings may snap, and the metaphor may fall apart.[57]

Recent analogy research concludes that the most important distinction in how metaphor and analogy are understood is not between analogy and metaphor but between conventional metaphor and novel metaphor.[58] This research suggests that novel characterizations and metaphors spark an analogy-like comparison, and the resulting process of comparison may in turn generate new understanding. This new understanding emerges not because new information has been provided to the reader, but instead because the reader is able to perceive and interpret the available information in a new way. The shift is not in *what we see* (content) but in *how we see* (perspective).

Novel metaphors and characterizations are not necessarily "novel" in the sense of being completely far-fetched, unique, or unusual.[59] Instead, they are novel because they have not previously been used within this specific context or as a basis for comparison to this particular target. For example, although property rights are often described as a bundle of sticks, it might be considered novel to describe privacy rights in that way. But if this novel metaphor were

---

56. Osborn & Ehninger, *supra* note 31, at 18–19.

57. *Id.*

58. Dedre Gentner, *Structure-Mapping: A Theoretical Framework for Analogy*, 7 Cognitive Sci. 155, 162 (1983); Gentner et al., *supra* note 20, at 227–36 (discussing results indicating that processing varies as a metaphor moves along a continuum from novel to conventional).

59. For example, one of the novel metaphors used by Gentner was "A Mind is a Kitchen." Gentner et al., *supra* note 20, at 231. In another study, the examples of novel metaphors were more unusual: His handshake was a mumble; the insults hopped on her tongue. Eileen R. Cardillo et al., *From Novel to Familiar: Tuning the Brain for Metaphors*, 59 Neuroimage 3212, 3214, 3219–20 (2012).

advanced, and if the reader had a stake in what was being argued, as will be discussed below, the reader would try to align surface features and underlying relationships found in the source (a bundle of sticks) with those found in the target (privacy rights). If the matching of surface features and underlying relationships seemed to be working (how might privacy rights be seen as divided over time and among interests and parties?), the reader would go on to transfer information by inference from the concept of a bundle of sticks to the concept of privacy rights, thus generating a new perspective on privacy rights.

Fittingly, research into cognitive processes emerged from a potential analogy: could human cognition be studied like a form of computation?[60] Seeking an alternative to rule-based reasoning, analogy researchers studied whether it would be more useful to retrieve "cases or analogs stored in long-term memory" in order to solve new problems.[61] Many of the recent studies have reached a consensus on the "structural alignment" model of analogy processing. In this model, as described by Dedre Gentner and her fellow researchers, analogy processing moves through stages of "structural alignment, inference projection, progressive abstraction, and rerepresentation."[62]

The researchers distinguished this model from processes that depend on either literal similarities or category-like abstractions, using the following examples. When you rely on a literal similarity—the X12 star system in the Andromeda galaxy is like our solar system—you are emphasizing that there are real, physical similarities both in the characteristics of the objects involved (the X12 star is yellow and mid-sized, as is our sun) and in the relationships among them (the planets revolve around the X12 star, as they do around our sun).[63] But when you make an analogy between unlike items—the hydrogen atom is like our solar system—you are relying mostly on similarities in the structure of relationships between elements in the target and the source: an electron revolves around the nucleus like the planets revolve around the sun. There may be some similar characteristics, but different characteristics become irrelevant. Conversely, when you formulate an abstraction—The hydrogen atom is a central force system—you are drawing on the similarities in relationships absent any similar characteristics.[64]

---

60. K.J. Holyoak et al., *Introduction: The Place of Analogy in Cognition*, *in* THE ANALOGICAL MIND: PERSPECTIVES FROM COGNITIVE SCIENCE, *supra* note 11, at 1, 7.

61. *Id.* at 7.

62. Gentner, *supra* note 58, at 159–61.

63. *Id.* at 159.

64. *Id.* at 159–61.

Gentner and her colleagues found that (1) the similarities in analogy lie mostly within the relationships present in both the target and source domains rather than in the features of the individual objects within those domains, and (2) some analogical similarities depend on higher-order relations, or relations between relations.[65] The "structural alignment" model of analogy processing incorporates alignment (between the target and the source) and projection (from the source to the target). According to the model, the first step in processing an analogy is that one or more relevant analogs (or schema) are accessed from long-term memory. The processor (or reader) then begins comparing the source and the target to identify matches and to align the corresponding parts of the target and the source. After that, the reader maps source attributes onto the target. The mapping allows analogical inferences derived from the source to transfer to the target. These inferences are evaluated and adapted to fit the target if necessary. In addition, new categories and schemas may be generated and new understandings of old schemas may be added to memory banks.[66]

But there are constraints on analogy making, primarily constraints of consistency and systematicity. Not only must there be a one-to-one correspondence between the aligned elements in the target and the source, but also there must be parallel connections. In addition to structural consistency, alignment is guided by the principle that a system connected by causal relationships is preferred over independent matches. Thus, the reader does not project inferences that are unconnected but instead only those that "complete the common system of relationships." According to Gentner, this occurs because of "our tacit preference for coherence and deductive power in interpreting analogy."[67]

A more specific multi-constraint theory of analogy has been applied to the lawyer's use of analogies in legal persuasion. Dan Hunter describes these as constraints at the surface or feature level, constraints at the structural or relationship level, and constraints of purpose.[68] At least some surface-level similarity appears to be necessary. But even though simple factmatching often

---

65. *Id.*

66. *Id.*

67. *Id.*

68. Hunter, *supra* note 13, at 159–67 (relying on Keith J. Holyoak & Paul Thagard, *A Computational Model of Analogical Problem Solving*, *in* Similarity and Analogical Reasoning 242 (Stella Vosniadou & Andrew Ortony eds.,1989); Keith J. Holyoak & Paul Thagard, Mental Leaps: Analogy in Creative Thought (1995)). *See also* Hunter, *supra* note 13, at 159–60 (discussing studies demonstrating that surface-level similarities predict outcomes and noting that surface-level similarities may be sufficient when a judge must decide many cases in a short period of time).

appears to be the basis of legal arguments based on analogy, surface-level similarity is only the first step. The structural constraint requires a finding of consistent structural parallels between the target and the source. If the surface level describes objects, the structural level describes relationships between or among objects. The final constraint is the purpose for using the analogy, which, as Hunter points out, may be particularly important in using analogies for legal persuasion. If a particular analogy helps one side's case more than another, the lawyer's purpose will influence others' perceptions of whether the analogy is appropriate or not.

In his book applying cognitive theory to the law, Steven Winter critiqued Gentner's taxonomy of literal similarity/analogy/abstraction and suggested that the difference between an analogy and a literal similarity depends on whether we are surprised by the analogy, that is, the degree of conventional connection between the target and the source.[69] If the connection between the target and the source is conventional, as in *A tabby is a cat*, the statement is viewed as a literal similarity. When the connection disrupts entrenched patterns, as in *A woodshed is like a house*, we label the sentence or phrase as an analogy.[70] Professor Winter characterized an analogy as "a conceptual mapping (whether of attributes or relations) that highlights connections that are otherwise not well established in our conceptual system."[71] Recognizing that the advocate must invent new analogies and metaphors when new circumstances don't fit existing categories, he predicted that "the analogy or metaphor with the best chance of adoption is the one that opens up the most useful possibilities." As an example, he cited the concept of "windows" for organizing data on a computer, an idea introduced at Xerox, more widely distributed by MacIntosh, and eventually commandeered by Microsoft to such an extent that it now seems like the only possible way to describe the concept.[72]

69. WINTER, *supra* note 52, at 236–37.
70. *Id.* at 236–37.
71. *Id.* at 237.
72. *Id.* at 248–49.

3. The roles of metaphor and analogy in constructing the law

In April 1968, while on his way to testify as a witness in an unrelated case, nineteen-year-old Paul Robert Cohen wore a jacket bearing the words "Fuck the Draft" into a Los Angeles courthouse.[73] A police officer arrested him and charged him with disturbing the peace by engaging in "offensive conduct." Cohen was convicted and sentenced to thirty days in jail. A California court of appeals affirmed his conviction; the Supreme Court of California declined review; and Cohen appealed to the U.S. Supreme Court, which reversed his conviction.

Using *Cohen* as its axis, the remainder of this chapter looks backward and forward at how metaphor and analogy interact with the development of the law. Judicial opinions interpreting the reach of the First Amendment protection for free speech are a sort of metaphorical palimpsest: as decisions come and go, their authors document the omissions and alterations to the original text to make room for later writing while retaining traces of the original.[74] Through metaphor and analogy, one precedent builds on another, sometimes smoothing off the rough corners of one, or even shattering the next.[75]

Even though First Amendment law can be charted as a complex doctrinal framework, real understanding of the law's development depends on understanding how metaphor and analogy (and storytelling) contributed. As one author explained, "metaphor does more than just draw or deflect a reader's attention. It triggers powerful, recurring frameworks of meaning and patterns of belief, and it sets in motion deeply rooted folk images, archetypes, and story lines."[76] Analogy works more directly, if more narrowly, in guiding the development of the law, each instance serving as the template for adding onto or carving away the next step in the design.

---

73. Cohen v. California, 403 U.S. 15, 15 (1971).

74. *Palimpsest Definition*, Oxford English Dictionary (2d ed. 1989), https://www.oed.com/oed2/00169695 (last visited March 1, 2022). *See also* Bret D. Asbury, *Law as Palimpsest: Conceptualizing Contingency in Judicial Opinions*, 61 Ala. L. Rev. 121, 163 (2009) (using the palimpsest metaphor for judicial decision making "engenders an understanding of the law as a fluid work-in-progress reflective of our evolving societal needs, preferences, and expectations").

75. *See* Benjamin Cardozo, The Nature of the Judicial Process 149 (8th ed. 1985) (describing the process of common law precedent as bricklaying).

76. Robert L. Tsai, *Fire, Metaphor, and Constitutional Myth-Making*, 93 Geo. L.J. 181, 189 (2004).

3.1. Lawyers' and judges' two-faced views of metaphor and analogy

When metaphors leap from the page, no one fails to notice them. These are the obvious examples of metaphor in legal opinions, the explicitly stylistic ones intended to garner the readers' appreciation or stir the readers' dismay. For example, there is Justice Scalia's reference to one Supreme Court opinion as a "ghoul in a late night horror movie that repeatedly sits up in its grave and shuffles abroad, after being repeatedly killed and buried."[77] But it's likely that the more subtle and implicit metaphors used to frame arguments have more far-reaching persuasive implications—for example, when an advocate relies on images of the *western frontier* to support the freedom of landowners to exploit minerals on their land or when the government attorney exploits the characterization of *immigrant caravans* to foster adverse holdings on asylum applications.

Similarly, when a lawyer uses the phrases, "Like *Smith*, this case addresses...," or "In contrast with *Miranda*, the situation here...," the reader is encountering the most obvious example of lawyers' use of analogy. Such analogical reasoning explicitly compares and contrasts case precedents along a series of vectors, including facts, language, history, policy, changing times, and so on. But the ability to analogize has persuasive applications far beyond arguments based on case precedents. Bringing up the kinds of comparative fact examples that we use every day to persuade each other is essential when there is no case precedent and powerful when there is.

Suspicious of the use of metaphor by others, lawyers and judges knowingly and unknowingly leaven their own writing with metaphor. Still, these legal authors make their suspicions known by repeating the Cardozo quotation that "[m]etaphors in law are to be narrowly watched, for starting as devices to liberate thought, they end often by enslaving it."[78] Or these authors follow up on an image with the Quintilian caution that "[w]hile a temperate and timely use of metaphor is a real adornment to style...its frequent use serves merely to obscure our language."[79] Only in the last few decades have some legal authors openly advocated the creative, deliberate, and insightful use of metaphor.

---

77. Lamb's Chapel v. Center Moriches Union Free School District, 508 U.S. 384, 398–99 (1993) (Scalia, J., concurring).

78. Berkey v. Third Avenue Ry. Co., 155 N.E. 58, 61 (N.Y. 1926).

79. QUINTILIAN, INSTITUTIO ORATORIA 8.6.14 (H.E. Butler ed.) (English translation available at http://www.perseus.tufts.edu/hopper/text?doc=Perseus%3Atext%3A2007.01.0066%3Abook%3D8%3Achapter%3D6%3Asection%3D14) (last visited March 1, 2022).

In the law as elsewhere, metaphor is often hidden. When it goes unnoticed, it is thought to have even more potential to affect audience values, beliefs, and attitudes. Operating mostly beneath the surface, conventional or long-embedded metaphors—the rates of violent crime are *up*, or the defendant was *lying in wait*—exercise their influence without objection. Novel or particularly vivid metaphors may play more noticeable roles in persuasion—for instance, the decision-making process was *contaminated* with bias—but they tend to evoke both positive and negative responses. Whether the novel or the conventional metaphor will be more effective depends on the setting in which they are used and the audience which receives them.

Metaphorically speaking, the law itself is viewed as an object, one that is shaped by the past and can mold the future; as a container holding rights and obligations; and as an entity, even a "being," that interacts with a writing-speaking-listening community. Both the written law, and the unwritten rules swirling around it, establish "roles and relations and voices, positions from which and audiences to which one may speak, and it gives us as speakers the materials and methods of a discourse."[80] The resulting community of speakers, writers, and listeners forms a culture of argument. Legal language and lawyers' advocacy roles support and encourage multiple arguments. Because of this culture of argument, lawyers and citizens often are engaged in making and remaking the meaning of legal language, and in the process, they are constructing and reconstructing the law itself. Even this way of thinking and writing about the law—as though it can be molded and shaped—illustrates how thoroughly the law is viewed in its metaphorical form.

Some legal scholars differentiate types or levels of metaphor.[81] Thinking about metaphor in this way may help the advocate decide when a particular metaphor is more fitting. For example, Professor Michael Smith identifies the first level of metaphor as doctrinal images, including such metaphors as the *marketplace of ideas* or the *wall of separation*. These concepts refer to aspects of doctrinal law but are expressed wholly in metaphor.[82] Smith's second level is the legal method metaphor, including metaphors referring to concepts of legal method and legal analysis, such as *elements* of a rule and *balancing* or *weighing*

80. James Boyd White, When Words Lose Their Meaning: Constitutions and Reconstitutions of Language, Character, and Community 266 (1984).

81. Michael R. Smith, *Levels of Metaphor in Persuasive Legal Writing*, 58 Mercer L. Rev. 919 (2007).

82. *Id.* at 921–28.

tests.[83] Smith's third level of metaphor affects not "what is said" by an advocate but "how it is said." These include overarching metaphoric themes, such as *the frontier*, and more extended metaphors relevant to specific points.[84] Smith labels his fourth level of metaphor "inherent metaphor"; these are the basic conceptual metaphors labeled primary metaphors by Lakoff and Johnson, including such concepts as "Happy is Up" and "Sad is Down," which are expressed in phrases like "I'm feeling up today."[85]

The criminal justice process provides especially vivid examples of metaphor's hold on the law. Criminal convictions are won and lost through metaphor. Even though "evidence" does not exist in nature, we believe that evidence *speaks for itself*. What constitutes evidence is understood as the result of a metaphorical process, a process in which potential items of evidence are compared with or implicitly analogized to prior models, stories, and experiences. Through this metaphorical process, lawyers, judges, defendants, plaintiffs, jurors, and witnesses determine whether specific pieces of testimony and exhibits will be "seen as" evidence of the guilt of this individual.

In addition to the process by which specific things become seen as evidence, the witnesses' testimony and the parties' exhibits are seen through metaphorical lenses. During discovery, lawyers go on *fishing expeditions* and attempt to use rules and procedures as a *shield* or as a *sword*. They advance arguments about whether certain found items can be considered evidence of guilt or instead are *forbidden fruit* because they come from *poisonous trees*. Lawyers ask jurors to *connect the dots* or the *links in the chain*, to *put the puzzle together*, or to *add bricks to build the wall*. Judges and juries *weigh the evid*ence to decide whether it leans toward the prosecution or the defense. Sometimes, they are asked to *put their thumbs on* one side or the other of *the scale*. Opposing lawyers portray criminal defendants as diseased or inhuman or both (*sick animals*), and they depict each other as manipulators (who *stack the deck*) and tricksters (who use *smoke and mirrors*). The good lawyer tries to *level the playing field*, while the other side is trying to *hit the lotto*.

If metaphor is a closely guarded suspect in the law, analogy is welcomed with open arms:

> Analogy is [seen as] central to legal reasoning, legal argument, and legal justification. Or so it is said. For many judges, scholars, and commen-

83. *Id.* at 928–32.
84. *Id.* at 932–42.
85. *Id.* at 942–43.

tators, analogical reasoning lies at the core of the common-law process. Indeed, many of those same judges, scholars, and commentators believe that analogical reasoning is at the heart not only of common-law decision-making, but also of the very idea of distinctively legal reasoning.[86]

Analogical reasoning gains emotional appeal from its resemblance to syllogistic reasoning. But the processes differ in several ways, especially in whether the outcome has been "proved" (as is the case in true syllogistic reasoning) or whether it has only been found persuasive enough for the time being to prevail (as is the case with most legal reasoning). Justice Benjamin Cardozo differentiated analogical reasoning from syllogistic logical deduction, depicting it as a process by which "the professional experts who make up the lawyer class" determine when two cases were "the same" and when they were not, leading to a similar result.[87] Analogies work best when speaker and audience agree on their context. For example, a nonlawyer likely would not understand why advocates and courts recognized "similarities between Nazis and the civil rights demonstrators of the 1960s." Still, "to the lawyer steeped in American First Amendment free speech doctrine, the similarity—groups subject to attempted viewpoint-based restrictions on their ability to march in public places—would again have seemed as obvious as the dissimilarity would seem to those outside of the First Amendment culture."[88]

In the prototypical analogical case argument, the decision maker compares the new case to the precedent case to decide whether the current case is analogous and should be decided the same or whether it is distinguishable and should be decided differently. It's not enough to have a small or insignificant similarity or difference, and lawyers test arguments by analogy by examining similarities of surface features, relationships, and purposes. One classic example is the case of the steamboat passenger whose billfold was stolen while he slept.[89] He argued that the owner of the steamboat should be treated like an innkeeper (and therefore responsible) rather than like the operator of a train with open-berth sleeping cars (not responsible). The New

---

86. Frederick Schauer & Barbara A. Spellman, *Analogy, Expertise, and Experience*, 84 U. Chi. L. Rev. 249, 249 (2017).

87. *Id.* at 253–54.

88. *See id.* at 264–65.

89. Adams v. New Jersey Steamboat Co., 45 N.E. 369 (N.Y. 1896).

York Court of Appeals agreed with the passenger, referring to the steamboat as a "floating inn."[90]

In opinions that appear to be based on arguments by analogy, some observers discern that the court is making a policy judgment about the most appropriate outcome rather than only a judgment about the similarities and differences between the cases.[91] As a result, some scholars criticize analogical reasoning as a stand-in for judges taking the law-making function into their own hands. But whether the analogy or the policy comes first, the common law develops as later cases are decided based at least in part on the comparison with prior precedents.

As noted earlier, analogical reasoning comparing past cases to current situations is only the periphery of a larger circle of analogy. When there are no precedent cases, lawyers must use the rhetorical method of invention to come up with other kinds of arguments. What did we do last time? Let's think of something similar. What is this situation like? What does it make you think about? At the top of the list of other kinds of arguments are factual analogies or explanatory examples. Advocates have, for example, argued that intellectual creations—books, poetry, musical recordings, video games—are like real property, that flag burning is an expression like speech, that a sentence to life without parole is like a death sentence. As in the prototypical analogous case argument, the advocate is arguing that there are similarities and that similar legal consequences should follow, but his argument does not carry the force of following precedent. Nonetheless, these analogies to fact examples are essential to predict, explain, or justify the favored outcome.

3.2. Tracing metaphor and analogy in the evolution of First Amendment law

When it comes to First Amendment protection for free speech, lawyers' and judges' use of metaphor and analogy influences the accumulation of precedent in at least three ways. First, metaphor and analogy contribute to First Amendment free speech doctrine by providing the images and examples that structure and explain the Court's and the public's understanding of how speech works

90. *Id.*

91. *See, e.g.*, Ronald Dworkin, *In Praise of Theory*, 29 ARIZ. ST. L.J. 353, 371 (1997) (arguing that "[a]n analogy is a way of stating a conclusion, not a way of reaching one, and theory must do the real work").

and how it affects society. Second, these images and examples contain implicit scripts, and the scripts provide settings and roles for various participants in the activities of free speech, especially for speakers, audience members, government bodies or regulators, and judges. Third, the images and analogies carry over emotions, values, attitudes, and beliefs that influence how the courts and the public react to various kinds of speech activities.[92]

More rarely, judges explicitly use metaphor and analogy in discussing how the law evolves. For example, to explain a legal point about the law's development and to highlight what he considered to be a significant problem using a precedent case, a Texas Court of Appeals judge in *Coyle v. Texas* connected the problem to the story of the woodcutter attempting to cut equal lengths of firewood. "Instead of measuring each successive log to the original he measured it to the log cut immediately before. At the end of the cord, he discovered that the last log bore no resemblance in length to the first."[93] In other words, the problem with the current state of the law was that the cases were no longer being measured by the original constitutional language, but instead they were being measured against the language in the immediately preceding opinion.[94]

3.2.1. The rapid spread of "speech as fire"

Compared with the legislative bodies that write statutes, the drafters of constitutions must cover more ground with fewer words. The First Amendment states only that "Congress shall make no law ... abridging the freedom of speech, or of the press" or affecting the related freedoms of religion and association. As law professor and literary scholar James Boyd White pointed out when writing about Justice Oliver Wendell Holmes's early decisions on the First Amendment: "Any thought about the possible bearing of the First Amendment had in a sense to be conjectural, for its language had been given no effective meaning."[95] Early in the life of constitutional interpretation, before a body of

92. Tsai, *supra* note 76, at 193.

93. Coyle v. Texas, 693 S.W.2d 743 (Tex. App. 1985). The case is discussed in Smith, *infra* note 94.

94. In this example, Professor Smith noted that a parable was used to "make an abstract legal point in concrete, immediate terms" and in a "compelling and credible manner," thus blending narrative and metaphor together by linking a familiar tale and a particular legal dispute. Michael R. Smith, *Metaphoric Parable: The Nexus of Metaphor and Narrative in Persuasive Legal Writing, in* NARRATIVE AND METAPHOR IN THE LAW, *supra* note 48, at 65.

95. White, *supra* note 55, at 1414.

case law precedent has accrued, the courts turn for interpretive cues not only to the historical record but also to historical and cultural metaphors, images, stories, and analogies. When judicial authority on the meaning of the constitutional provision emerges, it has been "framed, illuminated, and reinforced" by metaphor and analogy. And metaphor and analogy have not only developed the legal rules and doctrines, but also established acceptable roles and relationships for legal actors.[96]

The Supreme Court did not address the First Amendment clauses protecting free speech and the free press until early in the twentieth century. As social and cultural tensions rose in the years before World War I, free speech controversies began to find their way to the Court, and in 1907, the Court first interpreted the First Amendment Speech and Press Clause. The Court determined that when governments wished to regulate speech, the First Amendment applied, but only to prohibit prior restraints on publication.[97] Thus, the government could impose fines, but it could not stop publication. Soon, the enactment of the Espionage Act and the Sedition Act—both stemming from heightened fears about the dangers of certain kinds of speech in the circumstances surrounding World War I—brought increasing numbers of First Amendment challenges.

The Court's interpretive responses to these challenges drew on metaphors with historical and cultural resonance. Professor Winter characterized early American attitudes as reflecting a "coherent view of free speech with substantial historical roots."[98] John Milton, the English poet and intellectual who lived in the 1600s, was influential in both England and America. He argued that speech led to the truth, expressing the relationship between truth and falsehood as a battle and characterizing truth as a free-flowing stream of information. Echoing Lakoff and Johnson's primary metaphors that Argument is War and Knowledge is Water, Milton's metaphorical model foreshadowed the later argument that the truth will ultimately prevail in a contest of ideas.[99]

John Stuart Mill, the English philosopher of the 1800s, used a related battle metaphor, arguing that even though the truth did not always triumph,

---

96. Tsai, *supra* note 76, at 185–86.

97. Patterson v. Colorado, 205 U.S. 454, 462 (1907) (the main purpose of the Free Speech and Free Press Clause is to prevent previous restraints and not subsequent punishment). *See also* Near v. Minnesota, 283 U.S. 697, 707 (1931) (the liberty of the press and of speech is safeguarded by the Fourteenth Amendment against state action).

98. WINTER, *supra* note 52, at 266–67.

99. *Id.* at 267–68.

silencing expression would always deprive society. Suppose that an individual opinion was silenced, he suggested: if the opinion is right, society failed to learn the truth and if it is wrong, society missed out on the clearer perception produced by the collision of truth with error.[100] Although these early metaphors were accompanied by a powerful set of social values and conventions, Winter emphasized that they did not yet provide a comprehensive model for free speech. That model would develop over time.[101]

The first influential metaphor, the image of *speech as fire*, emerged from Justice Holmes's analogy between speech urging resistance to the draft and the dangers of shouting fire in a crowded theater. Although the analogy itself was criticized, his use of the image of fire to stand in for speech allowed the Court to treat speech as a "threat to our psychological well-being" while at the same time invoking the "heroic myth of the firefighter."[102] According to Professor Robert Tsai, this myth furthered the suggestion that when governments punished political expression, the lawmakers—like firefighters—were brave and selfless.

The metaphor was more fully developed in three opinions determining whether First Amendment protection existed for citizens expressing anti-war views or for publications affiliated with Socialist or Communist Labor Party organizations: *Schenck v. United States*,[103] *Frohwerk v. United States*,[104] and *Gitlow v. New York*.[105] In *Schenck*, Charles Schenck and Elizabeth Baer were convicted of violating the Espionage Act by distributing publications that urged draftees to oppose the draft. On appeal, Justice Holmes's opinion affirm-

---

100. John Stuart Mill, On Liberty 16 (Elizabeth Rapaport ed., Hackett Publ'g Co. 1978) (1859).

101. Winter, *supra* note 52, at 269.

102. Tsai, *supra* note 76, at 185–86.

103. Tsai identified these three decisions as igniting the *speech as fire* metaphor. *Id.* at 194. *Schenck v. United States*, 249 U.S. 47 (1919), was one of four cases, including *Debs v. United States*, 249 U.S. 211 (1919), *Frohwerk v. United States*, 249 U.S. 204 (1919), and *Abrams v. United States*, 250 U.S. 616 (1919), that tested the constitutionality of the Espionage Act of 1917. The fire metaphor in these decisions is also discussed in Bradley C. Bobertz, *The Brandeis Gambit: The Making of America's First Freedom, 1909–1931*, 40 Wm. & Mary L. Rev. 557, 591 (1997); Mark Kessler, *Legal Discourse and Political Intolerance: The Ideology of Clear and Present Danger*, 27 L. & Soc'y Rev. 559, 581 (1993); and Judith Schenck Koffler & Bennett L. Gershman, *The New Seditious Libel*, 69 Cornell L. Rev. 816, 838–39 (1984).

104. 249 U.S. 204 (1919).

105. 268 U.S. 652 (1925). *Gitlow* decided that the First Amendment imposed limits on the states by operation of the Fourteenth Amendment.

ing their sentences compared the defendants' actions with "falsely shouting fire in a theater and causing a panic," speech that would not be protected by the First Amendment. Illustrating how a vivid image captures attention and then becomes embedded, the analogy quickly became "a quotable conception of law"; "a prototype for unprotected expression"; and a "mantra of judicial influence" that elevated the Court's interpretation of free speech over those of other government bodies.[106]

A few days later, the Court upheld Jacob Frohwerk's conviction under the same law for publishing articles questioning the legality of America's conscription law. In this opinion, Justice Holmes wrote of the possibility "that the circulation of the paper was in quarters where a little breath would be enough to *kindle a flame* and that the fact was known and relied upon by those who sent the paper out."[107] By the time of the third speech-as-fire opinion six years later,[108] Justice Holmes had changed his views. While the majority opinion affirmed the conviction for publishing a Communist manifesto, with the opinion's author writing that "[a] single revolutionary spark may *kindle a fire* that, *smoldering* for a time, may *burst into a sweeping and destructive conflagration*,"[109] Justice Holmes was pointing out in his dissent that "[e]very idea is an incitement." Working his way toward principles that would become foundational, he suggested that if ideas he found repugnant eventually were to become dominant, that was the necessary result of the Constitution's protection for free speech: "If in the long run the beliefs expressed in proletarian dictatorship are destined to be accepted by the dominant forces of the community, the only meaning of free speech is that they should be given their chance and have their way."[110]

The *speech as fire* metaphor affected the Court's development of First Amendment doctrine as doctrine, and it determined the roles to be assigned to the constitutional actors, thus affecting the scope of judicial authority.[111] When the Court employed the metaphor of *speech as fire*, it cast the state "in the fabled role of firefighter, quick to stamp out the 'sparks' of revolt. The character

106. Tsai, *supra* note 76, at 195–97.

107. *Frohwerk*, 249 U.S. at 209.

108. *Gitlow*, 268 U.S. at 673.

109. *Id.* at 669. The Court's determination in *Gitlow* that the Free Speech Clause applied to the states ensured that more First Amendment controversies would reach the Court in the years ahead.

110. *Id.* at 673 (Holmes, J., dissenting).

111. Tsai, *supra* note 76, at 201.

of the firefighter, summoned from daily experience and our ancient desire for savior figures, is immensely comforting because it envelops the state in an aura of selflessness and bravery, and portrays the state's course of action as a socially beneficial, even regime-preserving endeavor."[112]

In each of these cases, the anti-war speaker was perceived as an arsonist, menacing the status quo. "[T]he story line signals that although the peril is great, social tension can be easily ameliorated through separation and isolation of the arsonist." As for the public, the metaphor "casts the People as vulnerable, fixed objects.... It treats the citizenry collectively as tinder, fuel for the sparks of revolution."[113]

The *speech as fire* metaphor and its matching script fit world events like a glove. And in cases involving criticism of the government, the Court would continue to label *speech as fire*. Thus, in *Whitney v. California* in 1927,[114] a majority of the Court upheld the conviction of a Communist Labor Party member for violating a state criminal syndicalism law.[115] As late as 1951, in *Dennis v. United States*, the Court upheld the convictions of Eugene Dennis and his collaborators for conspiracy to advocate overthrow of the government, emphasizing the "*inflammable nature* of world conditions."[116]

3.2.2. The upward trend of "speech as participation in the market"

Remarkably, the metaphor that would overtake *speech as fire* also emerged from Justice Holmes's 1919 opinions. Although he had affirmed the conviction of presidential candidate Eugene Debs for making speeches opposing World War I in *United States v. Debs*,[117] Justice Holmes dissented only a few months later in *Abrams v. United States*.[118] In *Abrams*, the majority of the Court upheld the conviction of five individuals who had circulated pamphlets critical of the

112. *Id.*

113. *Id.* at 202.

114. 274 U.S. 357 (1927).

115. In a concurring opinion, Justice Brandeis agreed that enough evidence existed to affirm Whitney's conviction, but he disagreed that the First Amendment might not protect future advocacy. Using *fire* in a different mode, he wrote: "Men feared witches and burnt women. It is the function of speech to free men from the bondage of irrational fears." 274 U.S. at 372, 376 (Brandeis, J., concurring).

116. 341 U.S. 494, 511 (1951).

117. 249 U.S. 204 (1919).

118. 250 U.S. 616, 630 (1919) (Holmes, J., dissenting).

government and its involvement in World War I. In his dissent, Justice Holmes provided the conceptual foundation for the marketplace metaphor.

Describing Justice Holmes's dissent in *Abrams*, Professor White pointed out that the readers of these early opinions on the First Amendment were "taking [their] first steps into a different world."[119] In this first articulation by any Supreme Court Justice of what free speech might mean in a constitutional democracy, Justice Holmes wrote:

> [W]hen men have realized that time has upset many fighting faiths, they may come to believe... that the ultimate good desired is better reached by free trade in ideas—that the best test of truth is the power of the thought to get itself accepted in the competition of the market, and that truth is the only ground upon which their wishes safely can be carried out. That at any rate is the theory of our Constitution.[120]

Complementing this conception of free speech, Justice Holmes provided his now well-known perspective on the Constitution itself, again using metaphorical terms: "It is an *experiment*, as all life is an experiment." The terms of the experiment require that "[e]very year if not every day we have to wager our salvation upon some prophecy based upon imperfect knowledge." Despite the inherent dangers of unrestricted speech, Justice Holmes cautioned that "we should be eternally vigilant against attempts to check the expression of opinions that we loathe and believe to be fraught with death, unless they so imminently threaten immediate interference with the lawful and pressing purposes of the law that an immediate check is required to save the country." Beyond his eloquent expression of views that would soon dominate the Court, Justice Holmes's main achievement in *Abrams* may be that he was able "to express any view at all. No other Justice had done so" at the time.[121]

As new circumstances arose, the Court expanded the ramifications of the metaphor first expressed as "free trade in ideas." In *Whitney v. California*, 274 U.S. 357 (1927), where, as mentioned earlier, the Court upheld the conviction

---

119. White, *supra* note 55, at 121.

120. 250 U.S. at 630. Although Justice Holmes wrote about the free trade in ideas in 1919, the phrase *marketplace of ideas* was not used in a Supreme Court opinion until 1965. Lamont v. Postmaster General, 381 U.S. 301, 308 (1965). One commentator argued that this change was substantive because it grounded the concept within the specific context of the market. David Cole, *Agon at Agora: Creative Misreadings in the First Amendment Tradition*, 95 YALE L.J. 857, 879 (1986).

121. White, *supra* note 55, at 121.

of a member of the Communist Labor Party for violating California's criminal-syndicalism law, Justice Louis Brandeis expanded on the reasoning that might flow from the concept of the marketplace. Speech should be protected, he wrote, because the remedy for false speech in most circumstances was more speech: "If there be time to expose through discussion the falsehood and fallacies, to avert the evil by the processes of education, the remedy to be applied is more speech, not enforced silence."[122]

Global war as well as national cultural and social forces created ebbs and flows in free speech protection. These were reflected in the shifting metaphors and analogies that resonated with speakers and audiences. In 1940, as World War II escalated in Europe, Congress passed the Smith Act, Title I of the Alien Registration Act of 1940, making it a crime to advocate the violent overthrow of the government.[123] But in the same year, in a case involving labor union action, the Court broadened free speech protection to encompass protection against both prior restraints and subsequent punishments. In *Thornhill v. Alabama*, the Court struck down an Alabama law prohibiting loitering and picketing "without a just cause or legal excuse" near businesses.[124] Echoing the public assembly image now associated with the marketplace metaphor, the Court declared that the "freedom of speech and of the press guaranteed by the Constitution embraces at the least the liberty to discuss publicly and truthfully all matters of public concern without previous restraint or fear of subsequent punishment."[125]

An especially stark illustration of the ebb and flow of free speech protection, punctuated by an eloquent metaphor, came in the Court's two flag salute opinions separated by only three years during the World War II years. In 1940, the Court upheld a Pennsylvania flag-salute law in *Minersville School District v. Gobitis* by a vote of 8–1.[126] A Jehovah's Witness family with two children who had been expelled from the public schools for refusal to salute the flag challenged their expulsion on First Amendment free speech (not freedom of religion) grounds. In the opinion upholding the law, Justice Felix Frankfurter emphasized the importance of national unity at a time of war. Three years later,

122. *Whitney*, 274 U.S. at 377 (Brandeis, J., concurring)..

123. Smith Act of 1940 (subsequently repealed and substantially reenacted as 18 U.S.C. § 2385).

124. 310 U.S. 88 (1940).

125. *Id.* at 101–02.

126. 310 U.S. 586 (1940).

in *West Virginia State Board of Education v. Barnette*,[127] Justice Robert Jackson wrote for the majority in finding unconstitutional a resolution of the West Virginia Board of Education ordering that the flag salute become "a regular part of the program of activities in the public schools," and requiring all teachers and pupils to participate, with "refusal to salute the Flag [to] be regarded as an Act of insubordination."

Justice Jackson's opinion combined a compelling story with a startlingly new First Amendment principle prohibiting compelled speech. He first explained that the Jehovah's Witnesses' objection to the flag salute stemmed from a literal interpretation of familiar Bible verses, thus making the objection seem a simple and logical result of applying to the flag as an image the Biblical language prohibiting the worship of "any graven image." He pointed out the real-life consequences of the rule: "[c]hildren of this faith have been expelled from school and are threatened with exclusion for no other cause"; officials had threatened "to send them to reformatories maintained for criminally inclined juveniles"; and their parents "have been prosecuted and... threatened with prosecutions for causing delinquency."[128] The Constitution, he wrote, protects the freedom to differ, and the freedom to differ "is not limited to things that do not matter much. That would be a mere shadow of freedom. The test of its substance is the right to differ as to things that touch the heart of the existing order." And finally, he concluded with an image that created a new free speech frame:

> If there is any *fixed star* in our constitutional *constellation*, it is that no official, high or petty, can prescribe what shall be orthodox in politics, nationalism, religion, or other matters of opinion or force citizens to confess by word or act their faith therein. If there are any circumstances which permit an exception, they do not now occur to us.[129]

Despite Justice Jackson's words, until the *Barnette* opinion, the Supreme Court had never before "fixed" a Constitutional interpretation that protected citizens against government officials' prescriptions of orthodoxy.[130]

---

127. 319 U.S. 624 (1943).

128. *Id.* at 630.

129. *Id.* at 642.

130. The *Barnette* decision was handed down in June of 1943, a time when American troops were engaged in combat in North Africa and the South Pacific. Between *Gobitis* and *Barnette*, there had been "hundreds of violent attacks against Witnesses and their property." Vincent Blasi & Seana V. Shiffrin, *The Story of* West Virginia State Board of Education v.

Relying on the ramifications of the market metaphor, the Court began to decide that certain kinds of speech carried little or no *value in the market*, carving out exceptions to First Amendment protection. For example, in 1942, the Court determined that so-called "fighting words" were not protected by the First Amendment because they are "no essential part of any exposition of ideas, and are of such slight *social value as a step to truth* that any benefit that may be derived from them is clearly outweighed by the social interest in order and morality."[131]

The fire metaphor appeared extinguished by the late 1960s, according to Professor Tsai's analysis. In *Brandenburg v. Ohio*,[132] a Ku Klux Klan member was prosecuted for giving a speech laden with racial invective at a Klan rally that featured a cross burning. The Court overturned Brandenburg's conviction under Ohio's criminal syndicalism law (overturning the decision in *Whitney* at the same time) and held that advocacy of force enjoyed First Amendment protection unless it is "directed to inciting or producing imminent lawless action and is likely to produce such action." Instead of analogizing Brandenburg's speech to the inflammatory rhetoric of the past, "the Court treated the Klan rally like the deliberative actions of a constituted body."[133]

Although the marketplace of ideas appeared on the First Amendment stage as a novel metaphor, it contained two basic conceptual metaphors: the Mind is a Container and Ideas are Objects. Such basic metaphors can become specific when the writer identifies particular containers or objects, in this context, for example, *The mind is a machine capable of production* and *ideas are products*. When readers combine these metaphors with the experiences they have had in an economic market, the result is to generate an entire set of relationships and inferences: "ideas are commodities; persuasion is selling; speakers are vendors; members of the audience are potential purchasers; acceptance is buying;

Barnette: *The Pledge of Allegiance and Freedom of Thought*, *in* MICHAEL C. DORF, CONSTITUTIONAL LAW STORIES 433 (2004).

131. Chaplinsky v. New Hampshire, 315 U.S. 568 (1942). Within the decade, relying on the underlying values it had espoused based on the market metaphor, the Court decided to limit the reach of the fighting words exception. After all, the Court wrote, the "function of free speech … is to invite dispute. It may indeed best serve its high purpose when it induces a condition of unrest, creates dissatisfaction with conditions as they are, or even stirs people to anger." Terminiello v. Chicago, 337 U.S. 1 (1949). Yet another category of speech of little value was added in 1957, when the Court determined that obscenity is not protected by the First Amendment. Roth v. United States, 354 U.S. 476 (1957).

132. 395 U.S. 444, 452 (1969).

133. Tsai, *supra* note 76, at 216.

intellectual value is monetary value; and the struggle for recognition in the domain of public opinion is like competition in the market."[134] In addition to carrying over from the economic domain the idea that the value of speech can be measured by the demand for it, the metaphor carries over from the concept of free trade the cultural values of freedom and autonomy.[135]

Choosing among metaphors has consequences. The fire and marketplace metaphors carried over very different ideological and cultural meanings. Professor Tsai pointed out the close association between *speech as fire* and the fear of political subversion by foreign ideas. In contrast, the *marketplace of ideas*—the much more "pro-speech metaphor of the deliberative assembly"—encouraged the Court to expand its vision of the public gathering or assembly. This expansion went beyond analogy: "[n]ever mind how incongruous the comparisons, union gatherings, sidewalk sermons, racist rallies, and eventually anti-segregation demonstrations were juxtaposed against and ultimately benefited from their metaphoric association with the archetype of the deliberative body."[136]

As the Court's dominant metaphor for speech evolved from fire to be replaced by the marketplace of ideas, the Court began to view government regulation of speech—not the speech itself—as the inflammation that was a threat to the constitutional order.[137] Pro-speech metaphors reached an apex with *Citizens United v. Federal Election Commission*, where the Court extended protection for metaphorical *free speech*—literally campaign spending—by corporations, including nonprofit corporations, labor unions, and other associations.[138] Before 2010, the underlying images of First Amendment protection tended to conjure up an individual speaker, protester, pamphleteer, or printing press. But in *Citizens United*, Chief Justice Roberts rejected such a limit, writing that the "Government urges us in this case to uphold a direct prohibition on political speech," allowing censorship "not only of television and radio broadcasts, but of pamphlets, posters, the Internet, and virtually any other medium that corporations and unions might find useful in expressing their views on matters of public concern."[139] If First Amendment rights were confined to individuals,

134. Winter, *supra* note 52, at 272.
135. *Id.*
136. Tsai, *supra* note 76, at 213.
137. *Id.* at 186.
138. 558 U.S. 310, 365–66 (2010).
139. *Id.* at 372–73 (Roberts, J., concurring).

he wrote, the Court would subvert "the vibrant public discourse that is at the foundation of our democracy."[140]

By the end of the twentieth century, the marketplace metaphor had become so embedded that it was almost impossible to discuss First Amendment values without referring to the concepts implicit within the metaphor. Marketplace beliefs supported unregulated competition among speakers, unrestricted information exchange, and acceptance in the market as proof of an idea's worth. Overwhelmingly positive images of the public assembly and the democratic arena erased the old connections between inflammatory words and impending civic unrest.[141]

4. Lawyers' and judges' use of metaphor and analogy to influence the law's development

Shortly before its decision in *Cohen*, the Court had distinguished between "speech" that was protected by the First Amendment against regulation by the government and "conduct"—such as burning a draft card—that went unprotected and thus could be punished.[142] Even though Cohen had been found guilty of violating a California statute prohibiting offensive "conduct," the brief written on Cohen's behalf did not explicitly distinguish Cohen's actions from the prior opinion nor did the brief analogize jacket-wearing to speech. Instead, the brief simply stated that Cohen "clearly was engaging in speech" when he was "in the courthouse corridor outside Division 20 of the Los Angeles Municipal Court [wearing] a jacket upon which were inscribed the words 'Fuck the Draft' (A. 18)." Justice John Marshall Harlan, writing for a majority of the Supreme Court, agreed that Cohen was engaging in protected speech.[143] But how did the brief writer, and then a majority of the Court, get to that conclusion? Fortunately for Cohen's lawyers, the inferences that emanated from the new images based on the market metaphor shifted the primary concerns of

140. *Id.*

141. Tsai, *supra* note 76, at 207 (noting the "the post-war rise of the pro-speech metaphor of the deliberative assembly, which was accompanied by its own set of scripts, roles, and stage directions").

142. United States v. O'Brien, 391 U.S. 367, 388 (1968).

143. Portions of this analysis of Justice Harlan's opinion were first written and published in Linda L. Berger & Jack L. Sammons, *The Law's Mystery*, 2 Brit. J. Am. Legal Stud. 1 (2013).

the majority of the Court away from the potential danger caused by Cohen's conduct or speech (which would have been the emphasis under the speech-as-fire metaphor) to their assessment of the speech's potential contribution to dialogue in the public square.

4.1. The briefs in *Cohen v. California*: no matter the form of expression, self-government requires that the *democratic dialogue* be free of government censorship.

The author of the brief for Cohen was Melville Nimmer, known primarily as an expert in copyright law.[144] In addition, the ACLU submitted an amicus brief written by Tony Amsterdam, a very well-known civil rights lawyer and professor, and others.[145] (Decades later, an appeal like Cohen's, raising a novel First Amendment question, likely would have attracted dozens of amicus briefs.) The Cohen brief's "statement of the case," which contains the legally relevant facts, started with this significant fact:

> While in the courthouse corridor outside Division 20 of the Los Angeles Municipal Court, Appellant wore a jacket upon which were inscribed the words "Fuck the Draft" (A. 18).

The brief went on to point out:

> Also inscribed on the jacket were the words "Stop War" and two "peace symbols" (A. 19). Women and children were present in said corridor (A. 18). Appellant neither engaged in, threatened, nor incited any acts of violence (A. 19), nor were any other persons in the said corridor engaged in, threatening, or about to engage in acts of violence (A. 19). Appellant at no time caused the emission of any loud or unusual noises (A. 19). Appellant testified that by wearing the jacket as thus inscribed the public was made aware of the depth of feeling against the draft shared by himself and his friends (A. 19–20), and that he had no wish to vex, annoy, or injure others (A. 20).

---

144. Brief for Appellant Paul Cohen, 1970 WL 122788, Cohen v. California (U.S.) (Appellate Brief), August 21, 1970.

145. Brief Amicus Curiae on Behalf of the American Civil Liberties Union of Northern California, 1970 WL 123485, Cohen v. California (U.S.) (Appellate Brief), October 12, 1970.

Following brief-writing conventions, the author went on in the "summary of the argument" to explicitly state that "Appellant was clearly engaging in speech, and such speech is entitled to First and Fourteenth Amendment protection because it neither contained nor was it accompanied by any of the elements which this Court has heretofore recognized as justifying abridgment of freedom of speech." The summary of argument just as explicitly struck out the reasons not present in this case which might in some cases justify regulation of speech: if it contained a threat of violence; if it constituted "fighting words"; if the words were "obscene."

The summary then moved to its legal reasoning—all of it based on images and principles derived from the metaphorical concept of the marketplace of ideas:

1. Fundamental First Amendment theory requires protection for speech such as that employed by Appellant.
2. A free *marketplace of ideas*, or *democratic dialogue*, is essential for a self-governing people to be able to make informed decisions.
3. The *democratic dialogue* would not function properly if the state could censor the form (i.e., particular words chosen to *express an idea*) of speech even if there were no censorship of the ideas conveyed.
4. In this case, if Appellant had expressed himself in a more polite manner, the self-governing people would not have been apprised of the depth of feeling against the draft shared by Appellant and his friends.
5. More fundamentally, if the state could censor the emotive content of speech, even though it did not censor the intellectual content, the state could thereby to a large extent determine to which members of the public a given speech will appeal, and could thus largely influence whether a particular idea will *prevail in the marketplace*.
6. For this reason, it is clear that speech to be protected by the First and Fourteenth Amendments need not be "polite."

The opening metaphor that wearing a jacket should be "seen as" speech and the conceptual metaphorical system produced by the principle that speech was essential to the "marketplace of ideas" were repeated with emphasis in the brief's main section entitled "Argument." Emphasizing the depth of feeling expressed by Cohen on his jacket, the brief leaned on the argument that censoring the emotive content of speech would affect whether a particular idea would *win the market competition.*

The ACLU brief focused on long-standing problems resulting from discretionary police enforcement of vague breach-of-the-peace laws,[146] arguing that the California statute was plainly overbroad and unconstitutional as applied by the trial court and that there was no evidence that Cohen's expression tended to create violence by others. Supporting their primary argument, the authors of the ACLU brief advanced the marketplace/public assembly rationale that free speech, even speech that causes unrest, is important speech.[147]

4.2. The opinion in *Cohen v. California*: whether it expresses ideas or emotions, speech in the *democratic arena* is protected.

By the time *Cohen* was decided, the author of the majority opinion, Justice John Marshall Harlan, had earned a reputation for judicial restraint. In this context, judicial restraint meant that rather than voting to have the Court intervene, he generally voted to uphold actions by other governmental entities as long as he could be persuaded that the governmental officials and agencies were acting within their authority or jurisdiction.[148] As an example, in *O'Brien*, the draft-card-burning case, Justice Harlan listed the important administrative reasons served by the prohibition against damaging selective service registration cards, and he voted to uphold O'Brien's conviction partly on the basis that without jeopardizing the administration of the selective service, O'Brien could have made his point in many other ways.[149]

146. ACLU Brief, *supra* note 145, at *3 ("Like the Court, the American Civil Liberties Union has had long experience with these breach-of-the-peace laws.... Hundreds of times every day, in every State, their applications are the occasions of arbitrariness and injustice, harassment, ideological repression.... They give color of law to ultimate lawlessness, to a state in which 'lawmaking is... entrusted to the moment-to-moment judgment of the policeman on his beat,' and 'a person may stand on a public sidewalk... only at the whim of any police officer....' ").

147. In fact, the brief argued, speech "may... best serve its high purpose when it induces a condition of unrest, creates dissatisfaction with conditions as they are, or even stirs people to anger." *Id.* at *26 (quoting Terminiello v. Chicago, 337 U.S. 1 (1949)).

148. William W. Van Alstyne, *The Enduring Example of John Marshall Harlan: "Virtue as Practice" in the Supreme Court*, 36 N.Y.L.S. L. Rev. 109, 119 (1991); Henry J. Bourguignon, *The Second Mr. Justice Harlan: His Principles of Judicial Decision Making*, 1979 Sup. Ct. Rev. 251, 320.

149. United States v. O'Brien, 391 U.S. 367, 388–89 (1968) (Harlan, J., concurring).

Despite this reputation and unlike Chief Justice Warren Burger, who was said to have tried to persuade Cohen's attorney not to say the word at oral argument, Justice Harlan did not seem disturbed by the use of the word "fuck" on Cohen's jacket. The Harlan opinion apparently was the first by the Supreme Court to contain the word.[150] Cohen's attorney reportedly thought that if he avoided saying the word, his reluctance would reinforce the idea that using the word was unacceptable, and so he kept his statement brief but complete. "What this young man did was to walk through a courthouse corridor... wearing a jacket on which were inscribed the words 'Fuck the Draft.'"[151]

Unlike the dissenters, Justice Harlan apparently had become persuaded that Cohen's wearing of the jacket was important. The case was before the Court in 1970 and 1971, a time of anti-war protests, and it seems likely that some Court clerks sympathized with Cohen or with the perceived message on his jacket. When Justice Harlan met with his clerks after the oral arguments in the case, one of them reportedly pointed out that based on Justice Harlan's earlier opinions, this "speech" was protected because none of the exceptions to First Amendment protection fit Cohen's situation.[152]

Several facts not found in the opinions provide additional context and indicate that neither the speaker's intent nor the audience's reaction was quite as clear-cut as might appear at first glance. Although the nineteen-year-old Cohen testified that he wore the jacket as a way to let the public know his feelings about the Vietnam war and the draft, it was not Cohen but someone else who wrote the words on his jacket the evening before.[153] When Cohen entered the courtroom where he was supposed to testify in an unrelated matter, the policeman who first saw the jacket sent the judge a note suggesting that Cohen should be held in contempt of court, but the judge said no. It was only after Cohen left the courtroom that the police officer arrested him for disturbing the peace.[154]

---

150. See Bob Woodward & Scott Armstrong, The Brethren: Inside the Supreme Court 152–53 (2005), for the anecdote about Chief Justice Burger, and Daniel A. Farber, *Civilizing Public Discourse: An Essay on Professor Bickel, Justice Harlan, and the Enduring Significance of Cohen v. California*, 1980 Duke L.J. 283, 290 n.47, for the claim that the opinion apparently was the first one to contain the expletive.

151. Woodward & Armstrong, *supra* note 150, at 153.

152. *Id.* at 154–55.

153. Farber, *supra* note 150, at 286.

154. *Id.*

Justice Harlan's opinion unfolds a story embedded in metaphor and analogy. Recall that cognitive scientist Raymond Gibbs suggested that a persuasive narrative invites writers and readers to participate together in a metaphorical journey through the story that follows.[155] In a similar way, Justice Harlan appeared to be inviting the audience to join him in the unveiling of the legal analysis and in foreshadowing the outcome. For example, as he opened the opinion, he framed the problem in a phrase designed to generate anticipation and build credibility:

> This case may seem at first blush too inconsequential to find its way into our books, but the issue it presents is of no small constitutional significance.[156]

In these phrases, he seemed to join the audience in an initial reaction that these facts were too trivial to be considered by the Supreme Court, but then to immediately reassure the reader that it would be worthwhile to stay on the path for the entire journey in order to find out what happens. Still building credibility and staying in the background as he recounted the facts, Justice Harlan quoted in large part from the opinion of the California Court of Appeal, declining the opportunity to tell the story in his own words. After this routine and matter-of-fact account of the facts and the appellate review process, he concluded by stating: "We now reverse."[157]

The narrative journey picked up momentum when Justice Harlan switched to a more assertive tone to reject any issue of jurisdiction. Because Cohen had consistently claimed that the statute as applied to him infringed his rights to freedom of expression, a constitutional question properly before the Supreme Court, "[t]he question of our jurisdiction need not detain us long."[158] To "lay hands on the precise issue," Justice Harlan's next movement would clear out most of the obstructions on the path to confronting the real question. To do so, he wrote, it is useful to talk first about matters "which this record does not present."[159] In these sentences, Lakoff and Johnson's conceptual metaphors get a workout, if an unconscious one. Together, writer and reader "lay hands" on the real issue by clearing away all the irrelevant underbrush, the matters not presented.

---

155. *See* Gibbs, *supra* note 48, at 91.
156. Cohen v. California, 403 U.S. 15, 15 (1971).
157. *Id.* at 16–17.
158. *Id.* at 17–18.
159. *Id.* at 18.

In the next movement of the opinion, Justice Harlan proceeded by subtraction. The California Court of Appeal had held that Cohen's wearing of the jacket was offensive conduct, which it defined as "behavior which has a tendency to provoke others to acts of violence or to in turn disturb the peace." The California appellate court further held that the state had proved offensive conduct because it was "certainly reasonably foreseeable that [Cohen's] conduct might cause others to rise up to commit a violent act against the person of the defendant or attempt to forceably remove his jacket."[160]

But Justice Harlan stated conclusively that Cohen's violation was not "conduct." Instead, "[t]he conviction quite clearly rests upon the asserted offensiveness of the words Cohen used to convey his message to the public." His only conduct was "the fact of communication." Because wearing the jacket conveyed a message, Justice Harlan wrote, the conviction "rests squarely upon his exercise of the freedom of speech" and "can be justified, if at all, only as a valid regulation of the manner in which he exercised that freedom."[161] Once that step of the journey is established—that is, once writer and reader have together agreed that the jacket is speech—then it is a short step to conclude that the "State certainly lacks power to punish Cohen for the underlying content of the message the inscription conveyed."[162]

Justice Harlan next invited the reader to join him in overcoming a series of obstacles—very temporary obstacles that took the concrete form of nearly all the categorical exceptions to free speech protection adopted by the Court. First, the California statute did not fall within the exception for time, place, and manner restrictions.[163] First Amendment law allows restrictions on the time, place, and manner of speech when the restrictions are reasonably designed to preserve something special about the locale where they are imposed, and when they are not directed at the content of the speech. But this statute applied everywhere in the state, and it contained no language indicating its purpose was to maintain the decorum of the courthouse. Tellingly, the judge in the courtroom Cohen entered wasn't upset enough to hold him in contempt.[164]

Second, Cohen's message did not qualify as incitement, failing to meet the very high standard necessary to be excepted from First Amendment protection

---

160. People v. Cohen, 1 Cal. App. 3d 94, 99–100 (1969).
161. Cohen v. California, 403 U.S. 15, 19 (1971).
162. *Id.* at 18.
163. *See, e.g.*, Police Department of Chicago v. Mosley, 408 U.S. 92 (1972).
164. 403 U.S. at 19 and n.3.

set by *Brandenburg v. Ohio*.[165] Even if Cohen's jacket reflected a position on "the inutility or immorality of the draft," the statement did not fall within the proscription of incitement because there was no showing of an intent to incite disobedience to or disruption of the draft.[166] And even though the phrase might be vulgar and have a sexual derivation, the message did not fit within the Court's definition of obscenity.[167] And it was not fighting words, falling outside the narrow exception for words thought likely to provoke an immediate reaction from a specific person.[168] And it was not an intentional provocation of a given group likely to have a hostile reaction because "there is... no showing that anyone who saw Cohen was in fact violently aroused or that appellant intended such a result."[169] And it was not enough that the message was thrust upon unwilling or unsuspecting viewers: they could look the other way, no one seemed to object, and the statute doesn't really seem concerned about the captive audience.[170]

Metaphorically and narratively, Justice Harlan had cut away most of the underbrush, isolating the real issue:

> As a result, the issue stands out in bold relief. It is whether California can excise, as "offensive conduct," one particular scurrilous epithet from the public discourse, either upon the theory of the court below that its use is inherently likely to cause violent reaction or upon a more general assertion that the States, acting as guardians of public morality, may properly remove this offensive word from the public vocabulary.[171]

Justice Harlan had already dismissed the "theory of the court below" as untenable because there was "no evidence that substantial numbers of citizens are standing ready to strike out physically at whoever may assault their sensibilities with execrations like that uttered by Cohen."[172] That left only one question: whether California can act as a guardian of public morality and arrest Cohen because the officer was offended by Cohen's jacket. Here, Justice Harlan expressed some hesitancy before moving on to the holding: "it is

165. 395 U.S. 444, 452 (1969).
166. 403 U.S. at 18.
167. *Id.* at 20.
168. *Id.*
169. *Id.*
170. *Id.* at 21–22.
171. *Id.* at 22–23.
172. *Id.* at 23.

not so obvious that the First and Fourteenth Amendments must be taken to disable the States from punishing public utterance of this unseemly expletive in order to maintain what they regard as a suitable level of discourse within the body politic."[173]

Before we go on, consider how the opinion has so far revealed the workings of metaphor, analogy, and storytelling. Justice Harlan structured and wrote the opinion as though he was recounting a narrative path through the working out of a problem rather than reciting a foregone conclusion. Although this case may first seem small, together we will find it is not. As we move along, some questions need not detain us. Others need to be addressed, but only to be removed. We move together along the path, clearing away what is not at issue. Through this process, we "flush" the issue out of the bushes.

After he carefully carved out the path to a single issue, he narrowed the opening. There were only two ways the state could completely outlaw the word "fuck": the theory that its use is inherently likely to provoke violence or the theory that the states, "acting as guardians of public morality, may properly remove this offensive word from the public vocabulary." The violence aspect was easily rejected, leaving only the argument that the state wanted to maintain "a suitable level of discourse within the body politic." And this argument "represented state censorship in its purest form."[174] And why is state censorship out of bounds? The marketplace metaphor, buttressed by the images and inferences added over the years since its introduction, made very little explanation necessary.

Justice Harlan approached the holding hesitantly, less as a pronouncement and more as if he was discovering something along with the audience:

> It is, in sum, our judgment that, absent a more particularized and compelling reason for its actions, the State may not, consistently with the First and Fourteenth Amendments, make the simple public display here involved of this single four-letter expletive a criminal offense. Because this is the only arguably sustainable rationale for the conviction here at issue, the judgment below must be reversed.[175]

In the following movement of the opinion, Justice Harlan sketched the constitutional backdrop for the decision:

173. *Id.* at 23.
174. *Id. See* Farber, *supra* note 150.
175. 403 U.S. at 26.

> [First,] we cannot overemphasize that... most situations where the State has a justifiable interest in regulating speech will fall within one or more of the various established exceptions [that we have already found do not apply here].
>
> [Second, the] constitutional right of free expression is powerful medicine in a society as diverse and populous as ours. It is designed and intended to remove governmental restraints from *the arena of public discussion*, putting the decision as to what views shall be voiced largely into the hands of each of us, in the hope that use of such freedom will ultimately produce a more capable citizenry and more perfect polity and in the belief that no other approach would comport with the premise of individual dignity and choice upon which our political system rests.[176]

The complex conceptual system associated with the market metaphor makes this reasoning possible. The underlying rationale for each step need not be tested in a formal syllogism; instead, each step is unconsciously and automatically agreed upon because of our prior understandings. In fact, the rationale for protecting Cohen's expression is almost indescribable in the ordinary sense of legal argument. Why should governmental restraints be removed from the arena of public discussion? In phrases that almost slide on top of one another, Justice Harlan justified the result: the decision about what can be said has been placed into the hands of each of us, in the hope that freedom will make citizens and governments better, and in the belief that individual dignity and choice are foundational.

Although the immediate result of such freedom of expression may seem like chaos, Justice Harlan found value in this image of the air being filled with people speaking:

> To many, the immediate consequence of this freedom may often appear to be only verbal tumult, discord, and even offensive utterance.... That the air may at times seem filled with verbal cacophony is, in this sense not a sign of weakness but of strength. We cannot lose sight of the fact that, in what otherwise might seem a trifling and annoying instance of individual distasteful abuse of a privilege, these fundamental societal values are truly implicated.[177]

---

176. *Id.* at 24–25.
177. *Id.*

In the democratic arena where citizens assemble and debate, verbal cacophony can be viewed as a strength. Again, the reasoning was not so much explained, as taken for granted: "we cannot lose sight of the fact that . . . fundamental societal values are truly implicated." In this setting, Justice Harlan highlighted the emotional content of the speech. He pointed out that "much linguistic expression serves a dual communication function: it conveys not only ideas capable of relatively precise, detached explication, but otherwise inexpressible emotions as well. In fact, words are often chosen as much for their emotive as their cognitive force."[178] Thus, the Constitution protects both the cognitive content and the emotive function of the message being communicated.[179]

Late in the opinion, Justice Harlan finally unveiled the backing of First Amendment history and precedent on which he rested the final section of his opinion. The core principle, as noted earlier, is that the First Amendment relies on every individual to decide what views he or she will express, hoping that freedom will make every individual a better citizen and believing that no other choices "comport with our faith in individual dignity and choice."[180] As support for this principle, Justice Harlan provided only a glancing "see" citation to Justice Brandeis's concurrence in *Whitney v. California*,[181] discussed earlier in this chapter. In *Whitney*, Justice Brandeis wrote:

> Those who won our independence believed that the final end of the State was to make men free to develop their faculties, and that, in its government, the deliberative forces should prevail over the arbitrary. They valued liberty both as an end, and as a means. They believed liberty to be the secret of happiness, and courage to be the secret of liberty. They believed that freedom to think as you will and to speak as you think are means indispensable to the discovery and spread of political truth; that, *without free speech and assembly, discussion would be futile*; that, with them, *discussion affords ordinarily adequate protection against the dissemination of noxious doctrine*; that the greatest menace to freedom is an

178. *Id.* at 25. Some commentators focused on Justice Harlan's apparent reliance on the difficulty of distinguishing the quality of speech: "[O]ne man's vulgarity is another's lyric." *Id.*

179. *Id.* at 25–26.

180. *Id.* at 24.

181. 274 U.S. 357, 372 (Brandeis, J., concurring).

> inert people; that public discussion is a political duty, and that this should be a fundamental principle of the American government.[182]

From Professor White's perspective, this passage shows Justice Brandeis (like Justice Holmes in *Abrams*) engaged in the rhetorical process of invention that is necessary to the work of judicial lawmaking. When it comes to interpretation of constitutional provisions, judges and lawyers must imagine and invent "[f]or the words of the text alone do not mean much nor do they carry much force even if understood."[183] In *Whitney*, Justice Brandeis "create[s] a whole language, a way of talking and thinking." Justice Brandeis's voice in *Whitney* is singular because "in a sense it defines a standard of civilization, an ethical and political standard, [one] that is so secure that it can be unafraid of argument, dissent, or even passionate and determined hostility."[184]

After *Cohen*, the Court's free speech doctrine encompassed not only the *market*, but ever-more-expansive images of public assemblies, democratic arenas, public discourse, and protected speakers.[185] The inferences emanating from the market metaphor and its offshoots, as stated by Justices Holmes in *Abrams* and Brandeis in *Whitney*, had taken root and spread:

> The *ultimate good* desired is best reached by the *free trade in ideas*....[186]

> [T]he best *test of truth* is the *power of the thought* to get itself accepted in the *competition of the market*....[187]

> [F]reedom to think as you will and to speak as you think are means *indispensable to the discovery and spread of political truth*....[188]

> [W]ithout *free speech and assembly*, discussion would be futile.... [189]

---

182. *Id.* at 375 (Brandeis, J., concurring).

183. White, *supra* note 55, at 1426.

184. *Id.*

185. Although it found constitutional a state law banning cross-burning, Virginia v. Black, 538 U.S. 343 (2003), and allowed a school principal to punish a student for displaying a sign favoring drug use, Morse v. Frederick, 551 U.S. 393 (2007), the Court protected against enforcement of state law the burning of the American flag, Texas v. Johnson, 491 U.S. 397 (1989), and a church's protest against same-sex relationships at the funeral of a slain marine, Snyder v. Phelps, 562 U.S. 443 (2011).

186. *Abrams*, 250 U.S. at 630 (Holmes, J., dissenting).

187. *Id.*

188. *Whitney*, 274 U.S. 372, 375 (Brandeis, J., concurring).

189. *Id.*

> [W]ith them, *discussion* affords ordinarily adequate *protection against the dissemination of noxious doctrine....*[190]

Together, these now-embedded principles favored the Court's stepping in to protect from government regulation *metaphorical speech* by a range of speakers on an unending array of platforms. In every instance, the Court was likely to decide that protecting free speech is the best method to reach the truth and the best protection against the dissemination of falsity. Not only did the metaphors of the market, public assembly, and democratic arena provide rhetorical settings for the Court's First Amendment free speech decisions, they supplied scripts that cast the Court in the role of resisting interference by other government actors.

In the lawsuit discussed briefly at the beginning of this chapter, the Court applied the market metaphor to the social media posting of the high school cheerleader, calling America's public schools the "nurseries of democracy." In *Mahanoy Area Sch. Dist. v. B.L.*,[191] the Court held that the high school violated the First Amendment when it punished B.L. with a year's suspension from cheerleading for posting an image on Snapchat showing her and a friend with raised middle fingers and a vulgar caption. Despite the surface-level similarity in the phrases used, Fuck the Draft, Fuck Cheer, Cohen's phrase can more easily be interpreted as referring to a matter of public concern, an expression of his feeling about a matter of public debate and discussion. Still, the Court found B.L.'s phrase to be analogous.[192] Justice Breyer wrote: "Putting aside the vulgar language, the listener would hear criticism, of the team, the team's coaches, and the school—in a word or two, criticism of the rules of a community of which B.L. forms a part."[193]

Relying on the marketplace of ideas metaphor, Justice Breyer also found sufficient structural parallels between Cohen and B.L. He wrote that "the school itself has an interest in protecting a student's unpopular expression, especially when the expression takes place off campus [because our] representative democracy only works if we protect the 'marketplace of ideas.'"[194] In the end, quoting *Cohen*, Justice Breyer acknowledged that while it "might be tempting to dismiss B.L.'s words as unworthy" of First Amendment protection, funda-

---

190. *Id.*
191. 141 S. Ct. 2038, 2046 (2021).
192. *See* Gentner, *supra* note 58; Hunter, *supra* note 13.
193. 141 S. Ct. at 2046.
194. *Id.*

mental societal values were still implicated in what "might seem a trifling and annoying instance of individual distasteful abuse of a privilege."[195] As a result, for Justice Breyer and the majority, the high school student's lawsuit called for a straightforward application of *Cohen*, the fifty-year-old precedent.

5. Conclusion

Because metaphor and analogy draw on our capacity to see one thing as another, they fuel the rhetorical process of invention. As discussed earlier, when we want to solve a complicated problem or explain a complex issue, "[w]e deliberately try to consider it in as many different terms as its nature permits: lifting, smelling, tasting, tapping, holding in different lights, subjecting to different pressures, dividing, matching, contrasting."[196]

Knowing that metaphor and analogy aid in invention, how might an advocate think about constructing alternatives to the Court's *marketplace of ideas* jurisprudence? We cannot object merely on the basis that the *marketplace of ideas* is a metaphor. When "the words of the text alone do not mean much,"[197] legal interpreters look elsewhere, and metaphor, analogy, or story are among the sources most likely to provide meaningful framing, explanation, or example. The objection more likely would be that the metaphor no longer fits or that its underlying assumptions have proven unjustified: more speech has failed to provide adequate protection against the dissemination of false and harmful speech. If the now-conventional concepts and categories that flow from the *marketplace of ideas* have failed to keep up with "changing social circumstances" or "strongly felt social needs,"[198] the advocate turns to invention.

In turning to invention, the advocate first considers alternatives without regard to constraints, setting to one side the desires of a client for a particular outcome as well as the apparent precedential landscape. Considering First Amendment protection for speech in "as many different terms as its nature permits," the advocate explores what "free speech" *could* mean in the current social, cultural, and historical setting. Rather than beginning with metaphorical substitutes for *speech as fire* or the *marketplace of ideas*, the advocate might begin with Justice Harlan's protection for both ideas and feelings and argue that *any* expression of ideas or emotions should be protected. Concerned that

195. *Id.* at 2047 (quoting *Cohen*, 403 U.S. at 25).
196. Burke, *supra* note 54.
197. White, *supra* note 55, at 1426.
198. Winter, *supra* note 52, at 248–50.

this concept has no limits, the advocate might instead propose that the First Amendment protects only truthful expressions or valuable ones, that is, speech with particular natures and qualities.[199] But how would constitutional decision makers decide the nature and quality of speech that deserves protection? These are the questions that likely prompted the Supreme Court to protect all speech except speech that fell within narrowly defined categories, thinking it easier to define the unprotected than the protected. But the current approach assumes that almost all speech serves the purposes of the First Amendment. And the core criticism of the Court's free speech holdings is that some speech is protected that does not serve those purposes but instead harms democracy or self-government, threatens equal justice, or undermines the rule of law.[200]

Echoing this process of invention in the writing of his opinion, recall that in *Cohen*, Justice Harlan entertained nearly every potential alternative under First Amendment law before settling on the issue before him. In this way, he created "a space for real thought" and addressed the "argumentative opposition between lawyers" that can lead to new discoveries.[201] Justice Harlan called up barely-there precedent (Justice Brandeis's dicta) to construct an image of what the First Amendment was intended to do. Using this perspective, he "dissolved the distinction between ideas and feelings." This movement freed later advocates to argue that the First Amendment extended to all kinds of artistic expression, rather than only to political speech that contributes to the marketplace of ideas.[202]

---

199. The radical suggestion that inherently valuable speech—and only such speech—should be protected by the First Amendment was made by James Boyd White. White proposed that speech should be considered inherently valuable when the speaker intends to make "a claim of meaning" because "at its heart democracy works... by speech that is seriously meant." James Boyd White, Living Speech: Resisting the Empire of Force 211 (2006).

200. Professor Schauer suggested bypassing the First Amendment because many false communications are not even governed by the First Amendment. Instead, they are controlled by private corporations and entities. If that is the case, the answer to concerns about falsity might lie elsewhere, not with the First Amendment and perhaps not with the Constitution at all. Frederick Schauer, *Facts and the First Amendment*, 57 UCLA L. Rev. 897, 919 (2010).

201. White, *supra* note 199, at 190–91.

202. *Id.* at 194. Picking up on Chapter 1's distinction between rhetorical and legal thought, Justice Harlan's opinion in *Cohen* might be viewed as illustrating the rhetorical perspective while Justice Breyer's opinion in *B.L.* falls into the "legal" category. Justice Breyer's path was the more familiar one, following a Supreme Court opinion whose holding had not been questioned and whose facts might be considered similar, thus "controlling" the outcome.

In support of his suggestion that only inherently valuable speech (that is, speech that is "seriously meant") should be protected by the First Amendment, Professor White pointed to the opinions by Justice Harlan in *Cohen*, Justice Brandeis in *Whitney*, and Justice Jackson in *Barnette*. What rhetorical choices in these opinions indicated that they were "seriously meant" and therefore inherently valuable? White argued that they demonstrated the authors' "openness to other ways of thinking; responsiveness to questions; honesty in facing difficulties; sensitivity to historical and social content; understanding of the situations and motives of others; [and] awareness of the real costs and dangers of a particular decision."[203] At first glance, these standards contradict the rhetorical commitments that bind lawyers representing clients and lower-court judges obligated to follow precedent. Rather than showing "openness to other ways of thinking," the briefs and opinions of these writers will observe conventions, rules, and practices that emphasize hierarchy and authority, and they will advocate a yes-or-no judgment to end the current dispute.[204]

Still, even as they are bound by the rhetorical commitments of the law, experienced lawyers and judges recognize that they are engaged in a thoroughly rhetorical practice. In an image that might serve as a metaphor for both free speech and legal argument, the arena imagined by Justices Holmes, Brandeis, and Harlan "is populated with people who are striving to understand and speak, disagreeing to the point of war, claiming power, asserting truth."[205] The practice of legal argument is open-ended, messy, and recursive. The language of the law is full of plural possibilities, ambiguities, and alternatives, and so the meaning of the law is necessarily contingent, contextual, and uncertain. Legal rules and practices establish boundaries that govern the current context for the time being, but countless rhetorical choices are being made within those boundaries. By better understanding how metaphor and analogy intersect with the past, present, and future development of the law, lawyers and judges may be able to make those choices more meaningfully.

---

203. *Id.* at 211–12.

204. Gerald B. Wetlaufer, *Rhetoric and Its Denial in Legal Discourse*, 76 VA. L. REV. 1445, 1551–52 (1990).

205. White, *supra* note 55, at 1422.

Summing It Up

- Metaphor and analogy provide meaningful frames for legal problems and questions. From a rhetorical perspective, these frames are persuasive when they guide readers and listeners into a particular way of thinking.
- For example, an advocate may rely on the metaphor of the *western frontier* to support the freedom of landowners to develop mineral rights, or an attorney may exploit the example of *immigrant caravans* to foster restrictive immigration practices.
- Because metaphor and analogy prompt us to see one thing as another, they support writers and speakers as they invent and present arguments. The capacity to see one thing as another is the root of imagination. And the process of metaphor and analogy—our propensity to make connections and to find similarities across difference—underlies all our thinking and decision making.
- Metaphor and analogy necessarily highlight some elements of a concept or situation and leave others in the shadow. Readers and writers, speakers and listeners should take care to remember that metaphor and analogy are necessarily incomplete and may be culturally and ideologically biased.
- Conventional metaphors have become embedded over time and are understood automatically and almost unconsciously. This is why we are able to envision the long, drawn-out months of a political campaign as a *race* in which some *pull ahead* and some *fall behind*.
- Like analogies, novel metaphors spark a more active comparison process that may generate new understanding. The shift in our views that occurs when the writer asks how the *stench* of judicial politicization can be overcome is not in *what we see* (content) but in *how we see* it (perspective).
- Legal interpretation depends on metaphor and analogy. In the First Amendment arena, the metaphors of *speech as fire* and the *marketplace of ideas* triggered "powerful, recurring frameworks of meaning and patterns of belief, and [they set] in motion deeply rooted folk images, archetypes, and story lines."[206]

---

206. Tsai, *supra* note 76, at 189.

- Analogies—even ones that seem to stretch credulity—ease the further evolution of the law, each instance serving as the template for adding onto or carving away the next step in the design.

Suggestions for Further Reading

LINDA L. BERGER & KATHRYN M. STANCHI, LEGAL PERSUASION: A RHETORICAL APPROACH TO THE SCIENCE (2018).

Linda L. Berger, *Metaphor and Analogy: The Sun and Moon of Legal Persuasion*, 22 J. L. & POL'Y 147 (2013).

______, *What is the Sound of a Corporation Speaking? How the Cognitive Theory of Metaphor Can Help Lawyers Shape the Law*, 2 J. ALWD 169 (2004).

MAX BLACK, MODELS AND METAPHORS: STUDIES IN LANGUAGE AND PHILOSOPHY (1962).

Michael Frost, *Greco-Roman Analysis of Metaphoric Reasoning*, 2 LEG. WRITING 113 (1996).

Dedre Gentner et al., *Metaphor is Like Analogy*, *in* THE ANALOGICAL MIND: PERSPECTIVES FROM COGNITIVE SCIENCE 199 (Dedre Gentner et al. eds., 2001).

______, *Structure-Mapping: A Theoretical Framework for Analogy*, 7 COGNITIVE SCI. 155 (1983).

Raymond W. Gibbs, Jr., *Embodied Metaphor in Persuasive Legal Narrative*, *in* NARRATIVE AND METAPHOR IN THE LAW 92 (Michael Hanne & Robert Weisberg eds., 2018).

______, *Evaluating Conceptual Metaphor Theory*, 48 DISCOURSE PROCESSES 529 (2011).

Douglas R. Hofstadter, *Epilogue: Analogy as the Core of Cognition*, *in* THE ANALOGICAL MIND: PERSPECTIVES FROM COGNITIVE SCIENCE 499 (Dedre Gentner et al. eds., 2001).

K.J. Holyoak et al., *Introduction: The Place of Analogy in Cognition*, *in* THE ANALOGICAL MIND: PERSPECTIVES FROM COGNITIVE SCIENCE 1 (Dedre Gentner et al. eds., 2001).

Dan Hunter, *Teaching and Using Analogy in Law*, 2 J. ALWD 151 (2004).

Mark Johnson, *Introduction: Metaphor in the Philosophical Tradition*, *in* PHILOSOPHICAL PERSPECTIVES ON METAPHOR 3 (Mark Johnson ed., 1981).

GEORGE LAKOFF & MARK JOHNSON, PHILOSOPHY IN THE FLESH: THE EMBODIED MIND & ITS CHALLENGE TO WESTERN THOUGHT (1999).

______, METAPHORS WE LIVE BY (1980).

George Lakoff, *The Contemporary Theory of Metaphor*, *in* METAPHOR AND THOUGHT 202 (Andrew Ortony ed., 2d ed. 1993).

MICHAEL OSBORN, MICHAEL OSBORN ON METAPHOR AND STYLE (2018).

I. A. RICHARDS, THE PHILOSOPHY OF RHETORIC (1936).

Frederick Schauer & Barbara A. Spellman, *Analogy, Expertise, and Experience*, 84 U. CHI. L. REV. 249 (2017).

Michael R. Smith, *Levels of Metaphor in Persuasive Legal Writing*, 58 MERCER L. REV. 919 (2007).

Paul H. Thibodeau & Lera Boroditsky, *Natural Language Metaphors Covertly Influence Reasoning*, PLOS ONE 8(1) (2013).

______, *Metaphors We Think with: The Role of Metaphor in Reasoning*, PLOS ONE 6(2) (2011).

Robert L. Tsai, *Fire, Metaphor, and Constitutional Myth-Making*, 93 GEO. L.J. 181 (2004).

JAMES BOYD WHITE, LIVING SPEECH: RESISTING THE EMPIRE OF FORCE (2006).

______, *Legal Knowledge*, 115 HARV. L. REV. 1396 (2002).

______, WHEN WORDS LOSE THEIR MEANING: CONSTITUTIONS AND RECONSTITUTIONS OF LANGUAGE, CHARACTER, AND COMMUNITY (1984).

James R. Wilcox & H.L. Ewbank, *Analogy for Rhetors*, 12 PHIL. & RHETORIC 1 (1979).

STEVEN L. WINTER, A CLEARING IN THE FOREST: LAW, LIFE, AND MIND (2001).

Chapter Six

The Pervasiveness of Rhetoric in Lawyering

MARK A. HANNAH

MICHAEL J. CEDRONE

1. Introduction: the rhetorically sensitive lawyer

We may typically think of law and persuasion in big-picture terms, centered on the climactic and dramatic setting of the trial scene with the attorney addressing the jury. However, the mass of legal persuasion presents itself in more intimate and ubiquitous settings characteristic of interpersonal communication. Meeting with clients, negotiating contracts, and interacting with colleagues all consume a great deal of a lawyer's time. The burgeoning field of alternative dispute resolution also encompasses communication focusing on individual interactions among lawyers, clients, and other interested third parties.

The theory of rhetorical sensitivity presents a solid foundation for understanding interpersonal communication in your role as an attorney. Hart and Burks in their seminal article on rhetorical sensitivity introduce the concept: "The rhetorically sensitive person, then, (1) tries to accept role-taking as part of the human condition, (2) attempts to avoid stylized verbal behavior, (3) is characteristically willing to undergo the strain of adaptation, (4) seeks to distinguish between all information and information acceptable for communication, and (5) tries to understand that an idea can be rendered in multi-form ways."[1] Developing these critical abilities is helpful for young lawyers to anticipate the kinds of interactional demands they will experience in their work.

Across each of these features is a fundamental concern with audience. Regardless of the role(s) they may assume—as trusted advisor, as adversary, as friend—rhetorically sensitive lawyers strive to develop discourse (written, oral, visual) that is responsive to audience needs and establishes the grounds upon which successful interaction will occur.[2] They will select language that is appropriate and avoid the ornamental, stylistic flourishes associated with "mere rhetoric."[3] They will identify and distill information from rhetorical situation(s) that directly addresses relevant legal issues.[4] They will adapt language choices in the face of competing claims and emerging audience needs.[5] They will be empathetic to audience values and diversity and try to accommodate them within the constraints of formal legal argumentation. They will guide audience members through trappings of the law, such as procedural filing guidelines or even the majesty of the courtroom, that are not only unfamiliar, but daunting.

In some ways, the goal of this entire book has been to train you in the ways of a rhetorically sensitive lawyer. We began in Chapters 1 and 2 with an overview of rhetorical concepts and with rhetoric's ancient roots, and we have proceeded through studies of argumentation, narrative, and metaphor with an eye to mining the riches of rhetorical scholarship for the insights they can provide to lawyers. Many of these discussions have considered large

---

1. Roderick P. Hart & Don M. Burks, *Rhetorical Sensitivity and Human Interaction*, 39 Speech Monographs 75, 76 (1972).

2. *Id.* at 88 ("Because ideas themselves do not themselves prescribe forms of verbalization, the rhetorically sensitive person tries to understand that an idea can be rendered in multi-form ways.").

3. *Id.* at 79.

4. *Id.* at 88 (describing the two procedures thus required: "(1) determination of which ideas are to be made known, and (2) consideration of how such information is to be presented.").

5. *Id.* at 82.

scale concerns: how a lawyer initially conceptualizes a client's story as a legal matter, how a lawyer selects the most persuasive arguments or legal positions to accomplish the client's goals, and how law's meanings evolve over time. This chapter seeks to address in a more intentional way the multiplicity of communications that lawyers undertake in their representation of clients. By examining the rhetorical situation, rhetorical circulation, rhetorical framing, and revisiting the concept of audience in the context of an imagined but typical representation, the following sections seek to build strategies and develop insights for how rhetorical sensitivity is not only a productive tool for large-scale legal matters, but for creating workaday legal communications that ultimately lead to the resolution of legal problems.

2. The basic outline of a medical malpractice representation and the case of *Arbury v. Sorio*

For purposes of this chapter in helping you further contextualize what you are learning about rhetoric in this book, we will examine a medical malpractice claim.[6] These cases are legally straightforward: medical malpractice is a tort. Your jurisdiction has ample case law clarifying the legal requirements. Occasionally, new issues arise, but in a basic case, the plaintiff must prove that the doctor failed to treat the patient as a reasonable, competent doctor in her area of specialty would. The plaintiff must further prove that the doctor's breach caused damages. While the law of these cases is not hard, the facts are often quite complicated. Expert testimony is generally required to establish the standard of care and to assist the jury and the court in interpreting the medical records at issue in each case. Attorneys who practice in this area become skilled in reading medical records, understanding a wide variety of medical conditions, and working with expert witnesses in the field of medicine.

Every person injured through the negligence of a healthcare provider (or survivors of those who die) does not become a plaintiff in a malpractice suit. Lawsuits typically result from both legal grounds for a suit and a party who is disposed to file a claim. In recent years, providers and hospitals have worked toward maintaining positive relationships with patients and families so that they are less likely to seek to assign blame or extract vengeance when errors occur. Further, some patients view doctors with suspicion based upon prior experience or other environmental or cultural factors. Other patients tend to assign

6. The facts outlined here are fictitious to allow emphasis on selected rhetorical ideas.

unwarranted godlike status to doctors. These background factors, combined with the strength or weakness of the doctor-patient relationship, all contribute to a party's decision whether to file suit when a medical error occurs.

Further, filing a lawsuit requires finding an attorney willing to do so. Most medical malpractice attorneys are compensated on a contingent-fee system. They receive a percentage (typically a third) of any recovery, whether obtained through settlement or jury verdict. As a result, plaintiff attorneys are unlikely to file weak claims. Stronger claims tend to filter to skillful attorneys, while some less experienced or less skilled attorneys pursue weaker claims.

On the defense side, nearly all doctor-clients are insured. In fact, defense attorneys typically have long-standing relationships with insurers. Although the doctor is the client, the insurance company has hired the attorney and pays the attorney fees, typically billed by the hour. Under the terms of its policy with the doctor and under the law, the insurance company has a duty to defend the doctor against claims, a duty to indemnify the doctor against liability, and a duty to settle claims once liability becomes reasonably clear. In some cases, it can settle a matter even without the doctor's consent. In support of these rights, defense attorneys are allowed to share most information about the matter with the insurer.

Complicating the situation to some degree is the fact that the insurance company is a repeat player with defense attorneys. Doctor-clients, on the other hand, largely are not repeat players; doctors typically do not have repeat claims against them unless they practice in the highest-risk medical specialties. Thus, while defense attorneys owe duties of the attorney-client relationship to their doctor-clients, their relationships with insurers keeps them in business. They must achieve cost-effective resolutions of cases in order for insurers to continue referring clients.

The defendant-doctor in this matter, Dr. Samuel Sorio, is an anesthesiologist at a suburban hospital near a major metropolitan area. As part of his duties at the hospital, he supervised an intensive care unit (ICU). On days he was working, he completed rounds on ICU patients twice, first thing in the morning, then later in the afternoon, both times receiving reports from patients' critical care nurses and other medical personnel. Since the onset of the COVID pandemic in 2019, resources in nearly all areas of the hospital including the ICU have been stretched thin. There has been a small uptick in claims involving the ICU. Before 2019, the ICU experienced a major claim every three to four years. There have been three such claims, of which Dr. Sorio's is one, in the three years 2019–2021. One of the other claims involved negligent observation of a patient in a manner similar to Dr. Sorio's claim; the other did not. No prior claims have been made against Dr. Sorio.

The plaintiff Amanda Arbury is a 67-year-old woman treated in the ICU at times when Dr. Sorio was working. The medical evidence, while complicated, would support the following series of events in her case:

Ms. Arbury was admitted to the ICU to manage cardiac conditions and various complications. Her medical history includes diabetes with neurological, vision, and cardiac complications. When the skin is breached on a person with diabetes, the wound is typically slow to heal. An open wound leaves the individual at greater risk of infection and complications. When Ms. Arbury entered the intensive care unit, a wound, or ulcer, was noted on the calf of her left leg. The ulcer was regularly cleaned and dressed by medical staff in the unit, and it did not change during her first two days in the unit. Dr. Sorio and the team included information in Ms. Arbury's chart about the existence of the ulcer and their treatment of it.

On the morning of day three, the area of redness around the ulcer appeared to be much larger. In accordance with the standard of care, Dr. Sorio ordered lab tests, including a culture of the tissue and discharge at the site of the ulcer. He also ordered broad spectrum antibiotics to be delivered intravenously, with a plan to switch to more targeted antibiotics pending the results of the lab tests. During the next twenty-four hours, the ulcer did not respond to these treatments. The situation progressed rapidly, and the appearance of the ulcer worsened significantly. In medical terms, the chart and experts for both parties agree that the infection became fulminant; that is, it suddenly escalated quickly, to the point of threatening Ms. Arbury's life. Ultimately, Ms. Arbury's left leg was amputated below the knee. A week following surgery, and after significant suffering, Ms. Arbury was discharged from the ICU and eventually the hospital. The leg injury caused a significant impairment to Ms. Arbury's mobility.

Ms. Arbury has an expert witness who is prepared to testify that Dr. Sorio deviated from the standard of care by not requiring the boundaries of the red area surrounding the ulcer to be marked and observed from her first moment in the ICU. The expert will testify that if these steps had been taken, there is a chance the fulminant infection could have been discovered and stopped sooner, thus saving Ms. Arbury's leg. Dr. Sorio's expert, on the other hand, is prepared to testify that the infection became fulminant so quickly that more intensive observation in the days prior would not have made a difference. Further, Dr. Sorio's expert will testify that Ms. Arbury's diabetes, cardiac issues, and other complications would have kept her in the ICU for at least as long on their own even if the ulceration did not develop into a fulminant infection. Further, the expert will testify that her quality of life would be no better even if the leg amputation were unnecessary due to mobility limitations arising from her underlying conditions.

Discovery in the matter is nearing completion. Documentary evidence has been exchanged, and the parties, their experts, and other witnesses have been deposed. The remainder of this chapter will examine how rhetorically sensitive lawyers might proceed through this case. By examining various approaches to rhetorical situations, rhetorical circulation, rhetorical framing, and audience, this chapter will explore ways that rhetorical awareness can assist an attorney to resolve this dispute. Key moments in the case include initial decisions made by attorneys involving how to present claims and defenses, and later efforts to resolve the dispute through litigated or negotiated resolution. To be sure, there is much discourse and rhetoric throughout a lawsuit, from the underlying events that lead to the claim through final resolution. However, at the key moments of framing and resolving legal conflict, the effects of rhetoric can be seen most clearly.

3. The rhetorical situation

Conceptualizing how rhetoric occurs in situations can help lawyers anticipate the impacts of the language choices they make. Rhetorical theorists have written about rhetorical situations over the years, each emphasizing new features that illustrate how discourse stems from or is shaped by contextual factors.

3.1. Situating rhetoric as bounded: Lloyd Bitzer's theory

The concept of rhetorical situation was introduced by Lloyd Bitzer in 1968 to answer his question regarding the nature of the contexts in which speakers or writers create rhetorical discourse in response to an exigence, which is generally understood as an event or occurrence that demands a response or remedy.[7] Bitzer defines a rhetorical situation "as a complex of persons, events,

7. Lloyd F. Bitzer, *The Rhetorical Situation*, 1 Phil. & Rhetoric 1, 1 (1968). For a more in-depth discussion of rhetorical situation in the context of law, see Mark A. Hannah & Susie Salmon, *Against the Grain: The Secret Role of Dissents in Integrating Rhetoric Across the Curriculum*, 20 Nev. L.J. 935, 935 (2020).

objects, and relations presenting an actual or potential exigence[,] which can be completely or partially removed if discourse, introduced into the situation, can so constrain human decision or action as to bring about the significant modification of the exigence."[8] Bitzer descriptively casts rhetorical situations as bounded units or contexts that exist out there in the world waiting to be perceived and found by rhetors and then addressed through their discourse.[9]

Bitzer's account of rhetorical situation goes a long way towards explaining the conduct of litigation in Arbury v. Sorio. One may view Arbury's attorney's decision to file a claim in Bitzerian terms. Presented with the exigence of a client's injury, Arbury's attorney turns to the legal system's defined opportunities to seek recompense and resolution by filing a lawsuit. Within the lawsuit, multiple further exigences arise. At the start of the case, the attorney must define the claim, selecting from the causes of action defined at law. In Arbury's case, the appropriate claim is for medical malpractice. Later in the process, the attorney must marshal facts and evidence to make or respond to motions and ultimately to try the case. These acts may be viewed in Bitzerian terms as actions designed to resolve given exigences.

In defending the claim, Dr. Sorio's attorney will likely take advantage of opportunities provided by the rules of civil procedure during the litigation. She will likely file a motion for summary judgment at the close of discovery. Summary judgment is a procedural vehicle allowed under the rules which allows a defendant to argue to the court that there is no genuine dispute of material fact, and that he is entitled to judgment as a matter of law. It allows Dr. Sorio's attorney to bring together evidence and legal arguments in an effort to convince the court that a jury trial is not needed. Again, on a Bitzerian view, the law provides moments to defend the claim; the attorney's job is to create discourse that meets the moment.[10]

---

8. Bitzer, *supra* note 7, at 6.

9. *Id.* at 5, 9.

10. Just as the plaintiff's attorney must make decisions in order to meet the moment defined by the law, so too must the defense attorney. The arguments of the parties require attorneys to make strategic choices: should the plaintiff's attorney argue that ultimate responsibility lies with the negligence of Dr. Sorio, or should the plaintiff fit Dr. Sorio's negligence into a larger narrative about declining quality of care at the hospital? Does the defense attorney have a strong enough argument on summary judgment that the plaintiff would have done poorly even if the wound was more aggressively monitored when she first entered the ICU? The shortcomings of Bitzer's views begin to become apparent: even "meeting the moment" involves lawyer-rhetors in making choices and working towards what Richard Vatz would call creating the rhetorical situation. *See infra* section 3.2.

Not only does Bitzer's understanding of rhetorical situations explain what happens at various stages of the litigation process, but it also tends to dominate how the law is framed and taught in law school. The traditional case study approach to legal education is built on bounded rhetorical situations, i.e., the prepackaged appellate opinions that students encounter in their casebooks.[11] Those opinions are constrained to a particular fact pattern and application of law that led to a specific legal outcome. Further, they arise in a procedural posture—appeal—which is itself highly formalized and which bounds acceptable discourse. By the appellate stage of a case, factual disputes have been resolved either by a jury or by presumption, and communications among and between the parties and the court are fewer and more formal.

In law classes, students try to discern legal principles and doctrine through principles of legal reasoning as they think through how the exigence, the audience, and the constraints within the case work together and lead to the eventual holding. Importantly, students do consider other rhetorical situations or cases through discussions and acknowledgement of precedent and other historical cases that influence the holding in a case; however, they often are not prompted to fully consider a range of other factors—historical, political, social, economic, religious, interpersonal, etc.—that influenced the production of discourse in the case initially selected for review. Rather, they typically are asked to distinguish cases on fine, nuanced grounds, thus reifying Bitzer's isolated conception of rhetorical situations as being found. Put differently, in this constrained classroom environment, student views of and voices about law can become unduly constrained.

3.2. Situating rhetoric as choice: Richard Vatz's critique of Bitzer

Shortly after its publication, Bitzer's bounded conception was challenged as too limited and constraining.[12] For example, Richard Vatz, Professor of Rhetoric at Towson University, argued that rhetorical situations do not simply exist

---

11. As an example, in her discussion of the schism between doctrinal and skills courses, Kristen Tiscione cites Bitzer as her initial scholarly source for rhetorical situation awareness. Kristen Konrad Robbins-Tiscione, Rhetoric for Legal Writers: The Theory and Practice of Analysis and Persuasion 83 (2009).

12. Nevertheless, in rhetoric and communication scholarship, Bitzer's rhetorical situation analysis is generally the standard citation for defining this concept and grounding subsequent theorizing. See *infra* notes 15–18 for some examples of subsequent theorization.

out there waiting to be perceived. Rather, they are created by rhetors through the choices they make when describing a context of events.[13] Retheorizing rhetorical situations in this way, Vatz shifted agency to the rhetor. Namely, Vatz endowed rhetors with a capacity to shape conditions for discourse and create rhetorical situations, thereby freeing rhetors from the constraints of a pre-determined, bounded situation.

Vatz's theory sees rhetorical situations as fluid and changeable. A plaintiff's attorney pursuing a more Vatz-like vision of her role selects deliberately among possible ways to name the claim. Conceiving of the claim as a broader story about declining hospital care could lead the attorney to pursue multiple claims against multiple defendants, including possibly the hospital itself. Thus, the attorney takes a more active role in defining the situation. She is not entirely unconstrained; law still limits the claims and arguments she can and cannot make. However, through assiduous investigation and careful study and preparation of her case, she can determine, to some extent, the shape of the claim.

For attorneys, this leads to an interesting tension that is partly addressed in the Rules of Professional Conduct. Model Rule 1.2(a) recognizes that the client determines the objectives of the representation, while the lawyer determines the means for pursuing those objectives in consultation with the client.[14] However, a Vatz-oriented lawyer may hear a client's story and present wider possibilities for relief than the client initially envisioned. Consider, for example, attorneys who collate individual client wrongs into class action lawsuits. In those cases, the situation for which recovery is sought even extends beyond the initial client. While the rules require an attorney to defer to the client's ultimate determination of the objectives of the representation, the attorney can take a very active role in advising and collaborating with the client on those objectives. In a case where the client has limited knowledge of law, the attorney's guidance on possible objectives may blur the line between attorney and client which the Rules establish.

To resolve a case through settlement, attorneys for either side must proceed in Vatz-like fashion to create situations in which the clients will be willing to resolve the case. For instance, once Dr. Sorio's attorney files a summary judg-

13. Richard E. Vatz, *The Myth of the Rhetorical Situation*, 6 Phil. & Rhetoric 154, 154, 156 (1973). There is some precedent in legal scholarship for acknowledging the capacity of expert writers to construct rhetorical situations. *See* Linda L. Berger, *Studying and Teaching Law as Rhetoric: A Place to Stand*, 16 Legal Writing 3, 61–62 (2010).

14. Model Rules of Prof'l Conduct r. 1.2(a) (Am. Bar. Ass'n 2021).

ment motion, she might have some uncertainty as to how the judge will likely rule. She will gain a bit more information when she sees the opposition filed by Ms. Arbury's attorney. At that point in time, Dr. Sorio's attorney will decide whether the situation for settlement negotiations exists. If Dr. Sorio's summary judgment motion is strong on the merits, it will incentivize Ms. Arbury to negotiate. After all, a successful summary judgment motion would deprive Ms. Arbury of any recovery. If the matter is successfully settled, a negotiated resolution removes decision making power from the court and places it in the hands of the parties. Each party can determine their various positions through a complex of factors including their perception of their likelihood of success on summary judgment; their likelihood of success at trial; the sympathy they can muster for their client; their own financial condition; their tolerance for risk; and numerous others. Vatz's work helps us understand negotiation: a settlement occurs when parties create rhetorical situations that allow for a negotiated resolution.

Moreover, settlements provide even further opportunities for creativity; settlements can include terms that are unavailing in resolutions provided by the courts. For example, many settlement agreements include a promise by the plaintiff to maintain confidentiality of the matter and not to make any negative statements about the defendant. This result is not available following final judgment from a court; judgment for either party becomes part of the public record of the case. Thus, attorneys can create situations that allow for results beyond what formal court procedures allows.

In legal education, despite the persistence of Bitzerian approaches to rhetorical situations, Vatz's more open, creative understanding of rhetorical situations offers an important corrective for connecting the idea of situation to the practice of law. Specifically, Vatz encourages lawyers to see lawyering as not merely about representing a client's case as given to them and defined through a specific event and issue, i.e., a predetermined rhetorical situation. Rather, Vatz invites lawyers to see their work as acts of co-authorship, as co-creating with their client the discursive space, i.e., the rhetorical situation, through which the client's issue will be addressed and resolved. Ultimately, through their choices in naming and framing the relevant issue, lawyers and their clients create the grounds upon which legal reasoning plays out by inviting in broad considerations of both legal (precedent, procedural, theoretical, etc.) and extralegal factors (historical, political, social, economic, religious, interpersonal, etc.), and in doing so, Vatz invites lawyers to see law as participating in larger processes of rhetorical circulation.

3.3. Situating rhetoric in new locations: further theoretical perspectives

Though important for its recognition of a rhetor's agency, Vatz's work also established a limited and constraining binary for evaluating rhetorical situations—an already formed situation versus a to-be-determined situation—that rhetorical scholars have been working earnestly to think beyond for nearly half a century. Across each of these extended retheorizations is an increasing appreciation for the complexity and fluidity of conditions that give rise to discourse, conditions that are both constraining and generative and that work across bounded time and space.

One way to get beyond this binary is to emphasize multiplicity or the reality of multiple audiences, exigences, and constraints that influence rhetorical situations.[15] Lawyers almost always speak to multiple audiences which requires them to be rhetorically sensitive and enact multiple roles. For instance, in drafting a Complaint, the lawyer must satisfy her client that the story is told adequately; convince the court that the complaint tells a legal story upon which relief can be based and meets applicable procedural requirements; and put the defendant on notice that this claim is serious and credible and should be treated as such. The lawyer must manage multiple constraints and communications, including demand letters she may have sent to the opposing party, the claims recognized at law, and procedural steps in the lawsuit. Constraints can also include what the client wants in the way of relief, what the court is likely to allow, and what the opposing side (or their insurer) might agree to if the resolution is to be negotiated. Every situation then requires a rhetorical sensitivity that balances multiple audiences, exigences, and constraints in order to determine what can be said in the given situation. In the case of Arbury v. Sorio, lawyers will work through expert and lay perspectives; across multiple procedural exigences; and within constraints such as the availability of client funds, attitudes of judges and juries, and past precedents.

Another approach challenges the presumptions that audiences are fully formed and unified and that rhetorical situations are identity-producing events.[16] For instance, judges may not be assigned until after the complaint is filed, as in the federal court system, or judges may rotate through cases, as in

---

15. Craig R. Smith & Scott Lybarger, *Bitzer's Model Reconstructed*, 44 COMM. Q. 197, 197 (1996).

16. Barbara A. Biesecker, *Rethinking the Rhetorical Situation from Within the Thematic of* Différance, 22 PHIL. & RHETORIC 110, 110–111 (1989).

many state court systems. A plaintiff's attorney may know that a defendant is insured but may know little about the insurer's disposition to settle or litigate claims at the outset of a matter. Finally, jurors are a very good example of an unformed audience. Until the time of trial, the attorneys have no idea who will serve on the jury. After the jury is seated, the attorneys typically only have the names and basic demographic information about the jurors. While lawyers can speculate about jurors' dispositions, they do not know enough to tailor messages closely to the jurors themselves. Each of these circumstances contributes to the uncertainty lawyers must navigate as they pursue a matter.

Other rhetorical theorists recognize that rhetorical situations are not a collection of single situations but instead are part of an ecological network of exchanges and communications that bleed between and inform each other.[17] For example, pursuing a claim against a doctor with a clean record is a different undertaking than pursuing a claim against a doctor with a long history of claims. Pursuing a claim against a doctor who has lost his medical license raises different issues still. Thus, rhetorical situation is impacted not only by factors internal to the case but also by the wider context within which the lawsuit occurs.

Finally, other writers acknowledge that discourse circulates through our everyday activities and thus does not exist in one place but instead exists as passing through and thus never located.[18] For instance, a cultural belief that doctors are untrustworthy—or, worse yet, "quacks"—can complicate (or facilitate) medical malpractice litigation in many different ways. So too can unwarranted deference to doctors' education and expertise. These perspectives, which preexist the lawsuit and circulate through all communications in it, form a foreunderstanding that shapes the ways parties and lawyers engage with issues and other stakeholders.

Together, these ideas about multiplicity, audience formation, rhetorical ecologies, and the spread of discourse push beyond a bounded idea of rhetorical situation and towards larger issues of rhetorical circulation.

17. Jenny Edbauer, *Unframing Models of Public Distribution: From Rhetorical Situation to Rhetorical Ecologies*, 35 Rhetoric Soc'y Q. 5, 19 (2005).

18. Catherine Chaput, *Rhetorical Circulation in Late Capitalism: Neoliberalism and the Overdetermination of Affective Energy*, 43 Phil. & Rhetoric 1, 20 (2010).

4. Rhetorical circulation

The theory of rhetorical circulation grows in part out of efforts to move beyond the Bitzer/Vatz debate over rhetorical situation by recognizing that situations are defined in part by rhetorical discourse that circulates throughout culture. However, the work of scholars who write about rhetorical circulation has developed to focus on the circulation process itself.

Scholars generally understand rhetorical circulation as the ways in which texts and discourse move through time and space. More specifically, rhetorical circulation attends to the movement of rhetoric, unanchored, through our everyday, situated lives.[19] An emphasis on movement within rhetorical circulation draws attention to the constitutive nature of rhetoric; rhetoric is a living environment[20] in which various rhetorical situations come together and collaborate to produce some kind of change through discourse.[21]

An outcome of the continuous change spurred by rhetorical circulation is that dialogue remains open and resists closure through new articulations that are created in communicative exchanges.[22] Of note in these exchanges is the fact that old articulations do not die off and disappear. Rather, they retain some form of discursive energy and remain available to be drawn into future circulation and participate in the accrual and evolution of meaning over time.[23]

Despite its influence on meaning making and knowledge production, rhetorical circulation operates independently of formal reasoning processes and requires no structural framework or planning for its effects to take shape.[24] That is, rhetorical circulation is always operating in the background, influencing the ways people imagine or think about how to interact. Through understanding how rhetorical circulation operates, rhetors begin to appreciate

---

19. *Id.* at 20. Chaput also notes that circulation asks rhetors to think of rhetoric as continuously moving through and connecting different instantiations within a complex world. *Id.* at 6; *see also* Jason Edward Black, *Native Authenticity, Rhetorical Circulation, and Neocolonial Decay: The Case of Chief Seattle's Controversial Speech*, 15 Rhetoric & Pub. Aff. 635, 636 (2012). Black also notes how "fragmented discourse circulates says much about a public that interprets it and the ideologies that underscore that particular public's civic imaginary." *Id.*

20. Black, *supra* note 19, at 636; Edbauer, *supra* note 17, at 13.

21. *See* Black, *supra* note 19, at 640; Chaput, *supra* note 18, at 6–7 (discussing Louis Althusser's articulation of rhetoric as an overdetermined practice).

22. *See* Black, *supra* note 19, at 637.

23. *Id.*

24. Chaput, *supra* note 18, at 11.

that discourse cannot be bound by situations.[25] By extension, rhetors also then realize that they are not bound by situations. They realize they "are never outside the network...of [circulatory] forces"[26] and will therefore create the kinds of rhetorical energy that drives rhetorical circulation through their decision making.

Lawyers who center their understanding of lawyering on rhetorical circulation strategically locate their work and their client's related interests in preexisting webs of competing claims and values about the legal issues they are pursuing. Namely, they can amplify their client's interests against competing claims and make express, explicit claims about the most salient features of an issue in a case. For instance, they can define legal issues to highlight favorable or unique aspects of a client's case. The challenge for lawyers is identifying what concepts to draw from in rhetorical circulation when attempting to frame their client's interests in a way that enlists an audience to adopt the lawyer's theory of the case.[27] Some past precedents and legal and cultural factors are helpful; others, less so.

In the Arbury v. Sorio matter, attorneys sensitive to the effects of rhetorical circulation would view every communication as an opportunity to pursue larger-scale or more ultimate goals of the representation, even as those examples evolved in the course of the ongoing discourse. A consistently reinforced message (for example, Dr. Sorio's sterling reputation and long and successful career at the hospital) may set boundaries for later settlement discussions or can prefigure the framing of the case that will later be presented to the jury if the case does not settle. Of course, it is possible that this strategy will alienate dialogue partners; connecting every conversation to the same few points can be tiresome. To combat this, attorneys may choose to devote some rhetorical energy to developing a working relationship with opposing counsel on the theory that cooperative behavior on small matters will contribute to a situation in which comprehensive settlement is possible.

---

25. *Id.* at 8.

26. Edbauer, *supra* note 17, at 10.

27. Pierre Schlag & Amy J. Griffin, How to Do Things with Legal Doctrine 29–32 (2020).

5. Rhetorical framing

As an invisible and inevitable reality of the communication process,[28] rhetorical framing is a practice that initiates conversations through the intentional selection of features of a rhetorical situation to promote a particular problem definition, causal interpretation, and approach to resolving an issue.[29] To make visible this selection, communicators use language to create interpretive storylines that signal what is at stake in a rhetorical situation.[30] In this way, framing creates invitations to dialogue that ultimately shape how interested parties interpret and discuss the framed issue.[31]

In the medical malpractice fact pattern, we can think about the influence of framing by comparing hypothetical framing choices made by Dr. Sorio and Ms. Arbury's attorneys, specifically, the former framing the case as being about following standard of care guidelines whereas the latter framing the case as one of medical negligence.[32] Both attorneys are inviting audience members (judges, jury members, mediators, insurance carriers, opposing counsels, clients, and others) to consider Dr. Sorio's actions as either meeting or failing to comport

---

28. *See* Stacey Pigg & Lindsey Ray Scheper, *When Extension and Rhetorical Engagement Meet: Framing Public Audiences for Agricultural Science Communication*, 31 TECH. COMM. Q. 385, 390 (Feb. 16, 2022) https://doi.org/10.1080/10572252.2022.2034974; Beth J. Shirley, *Post-Fact Fact Sheets: Dissociative Framing as a Strategy to Work Past Climate Change Denial*, 68 TECH. COMM., May 2021, at 41, 45; Matthew C. Nisbet, *Communicating Climate Change: Why Frames Matter for Public Engagement*, 51 ENVIRONMENT 12, 15 (March/April 2009); SCHLAG & GRIFFIN, *supra* note 27, at 32 (noting that sometimes frames are not deployed self-consciously).

29. Justin King Rademaekers & Richard Johnson-Sheehan, *Framing and Re-Framing in Environmental Science: Explaining Climate Change to the Public*, 44 J. TECH. WRITING & COMM. 3, 7 (2014) (citing Robert M. Entman, *Framing: Towards Clarification of a Fractured Paradigm*, 43 J. COMM. 51, 52 (1993)); *see also* SCHLAG & GRIFFIN, *supra* note 27 at 45.

30. Rademaekers & Johnson-Sheehan, *supra* note 29 at 7 (first citing William A. Gamson & Andre Modigliani, *The Changing Culture of Affirmative Action*, *in* RESEARCH IN POLITICAL SOCIOLOGY: VOLUME 3 137, 141 (Richard Braungart ed.,1987); and then Karen Callaghan & Frauke Schnell, *Introduction: Framing Political Issues in American Politics*, *in* FRAMING AMERICAN POLITICS 1, 2 (Karen Callaghan & Frauke Schnell eds., 2005)).

31. Rademaekers & Johnson-Sheehan, *supra* note 29 at 7; SCHLAG & GRIFFIN, *supra* note 27 at 35.

32. Alternatively, Ms. Arbury's attorney could frame the case of institutional failure, that being the hospital as having a track record of providing treatment that does not comport with standard of care guidelines which is attributable to things such as a lack of financial resources, a lack of supervisor oversight, or a lack of institutional protocols that document best practices procedures.

with standard of care guidelines established by the wider emergency physician community through research and professional practice.

To activate such interpretations and obtain an audience's adherence,[33] frames acknowledge that an audience's values and beliefs, i.e. their rhetorical commitments, are bound up in the dialogue which thus encourages their participation.[34] Importantly, such encouragement is not open-ended, as framing sets boundaries that strategically delimit audience members' participation.[35] Specifically, frames constrain an audience's focus by directing them to address what the communicator determines is most relevant to the resolution of the issue at hand.[36] In those instances where a particular frame has thickened due to repeated use over time and thus obtained more authority and influence,[37] its constraining power increases such that the communicator's framed solution speaks for itself as the obvious conclusion to be drawn.[38]

Looking to the medical malpractice fact pattern again, we can imagine Dr. Sorio's attorney appealing to audience members' sense of fairness and what it means to follow guidelines established by a community. Guidelines set expectations that physicians can plan their work around, and holding Dr. Sorio responsible if he has not acted outside the guidelines would constitute unfair surprise to him. Compounding the unfairness to Dr. Sorio is that in treating him differently, courts unwittingly may be creating conditions for Ms. Arbury to use the courts for financial gain. Alternatively, Ms. Arbury's attorney can draw from the same facts to appeal to the audience's sense of protecting the weak against the strong.[39] Why should Ms. Arbury bear the cost of a physician's error? Both defense and plaintiff's counsel in these hypothetical framing examples attempt to narrow the case and set boundaries for what ought to

---

33. J. Scott Weedon, *Representation in Engineering Practice: A Case Study of Framing in a Student Design Group*, 26 TECH. COMM. Q. 361, 373 (2017) (citing CHAÏM PERELMAN, THE REALM OF RHETORIC (1982)).

34. Shirley, *supra* note 28, at 45

35. Rademaekers & Johnson-Sheehan, *supra* note 29, at 7 (citing Callaghan & Schnell, *supra* note 30, at 2.)

36. SCHLAG & GRIFFIN, *supra* note 27, at 32.

37. Rademaekers & Johnson-Sheehan, *supra* note 29, at 7 (citing Kevin M. Carragee & Wim Roefs, *The Neglect of Power in Recent Framing Research*, 54 J. COMM. 214 (2004)).

38. SCHLAG & GRIFFIN, *supra* note 27, at 35; Rademaekers & Johnson-Sheehan, *supra* note 29, at 8. In these instances, it is difficult to "break the frame" or disrupt conceptual associations operating in a rhetorical situation. Matthew C. Nisbet, *The Ethics of Framing Science*, *in* COMMUNICATING BIOLOGICAL SCIENCES: ETHICAL AND METAPHORICAL DIMENSIONS 52 (Richard Elliott & Brigitte Nerlich eds., 2009).

39. *See generally* Linda Berger, *supra* Chapter 5.

be considered. Defense counsel's framing Ms. Arbury's suit as unfair and the underlying financial motivation as unethical is a well-worn tale in the personal injury sector, a tale that has thickened over time and become resistant through repeated use. Plaintiff's counsel's framing of Ms. Arbury's case as an example of the David versus Goliath archetype also relies on a well understood, thickened story that invites discussion about the inherent unfairness of relationships characterized by power imbalances. Ultimately, in each of these examples, we see attorneys develop frames that initiate calls for legal arguments that work at odds towards competing ends.

Additionally, frames enable rhetors to nimbly manage complex subject matter and narrow audience attention towards issue resolution. Through the rhetorical process of dissociation, communicators can unpack complexity by emphasizing certain aspects of an issue over others.[40] Communicators achieve this emphasis by partitioning[41] or splitting and disrupting well-established ties between concepts. The express aim of partitioning is to bring about changes in understanding that encourage new ways to think and talk about the issue.[42] This new dialogue creates additional opportunities to reassociate concepts and arrive at creative articulations that encourage readers to see and understand the problem differently.[43]

Working with the medical malpractice fact pattern again, it is clear that the identified fulmination is intertwined in a complex web of pre-existing health conditions, each with their own treatment protocols and each of which could have triggered the fulmination. At the same time, medical malpractice suits involve a complex web of factors or dimensions regarding treatment such as protocols, outcomes, costs, risks, patient histories, doctor histories, and hospital histories. Defense and plaintiff's counsel can unpack these webs

---

40. Nisbet, *supra* note 38, at 51; Rademaekers & Johnson-Sheehan, *supra* note 29, at 8. Notably, dissociation has been deployed effectively in law. *See generally* Roger Stahl, *Carving Up Free Exercise: Dissociation and "Religion" in Supreme Court Jurisprudence*, 5 RHETORIC & PUB. AFFAIRS 439 (2002); John Bannister, *The Dissociations of John Roberts:* National Federation of Independent Business v. Sebelius *and the Discontents of Judicial Supremacy*, 57 ARGUMENTATION & ADVOC. 123 (2021).

41. RICHARD JOHNSON-SHEEHAN, TECHNICAL COMMUNICATION TODAY 127–128 (5th ed. 2014).

42. *See* David A. Frank, *The Origins of and Possible Futures for Chaïm Perelman and Lucie Olbrechts-Tyteca's Dissociation of Concepts*, 53 PHIL. & RHETORIC 385, 385 (2020) (citing CHAÏM PERELMAN & LUCIE OLBRECHTS-TYTECA, THE NEW RHETORIC: A TREATISE ON ARGUMENTATION (1958)); Shirley, *supra* note 28, at 43.

43. *See generally* Nisbet, *supra* note 38, at 51.

by separating and partitioning out those factors or dimensions (medical care, health and well-being, financial, psychological, institutional, etc.) most relevant to their case. Dr. Sorio, for example, could focus either on the care or health dimensions—his treatment decisions and/or Ms. Arbury's pre-existing conditions—while eschewing the financial dimension that could be associated with cost-saving treatment decisions for the hospital. Defense counsel's invitation here is to focus on reasonableness, something all people value in day-to-day decision-making. Plaintiff's counsel, on the other hand, can partition and frame the financial and economic dimensions to highlight the resource disparity, namely Ms. Arbury being unable to bear the brunt of a potential loss of income and the corresponding psychological and emotional weight of an amputation and the attendant diminishment of her quality of life. Ultimately, the success of any of these frames will turn on the attorneys' ability to assess and appeal to a wide variety of audience members with competing motivations and information needs.

6. Audience

Anchoring successful issue framing across circulating rhetorical situations is a rhetor's deep knowledge of the audience(s) to whom they are communicating. As a practice, audience analysis is an essential step for discerning readers' rhetorical expectations, namely the attitudes and habits they generally work from when communicating.[44] To identify those expectations, communicators take various approaches ranging from listing audience demographics; to developing an imagined reader based on the communicator's lived experiences; or to eliciting feedback from potential audience members.[45] Across each of these approaches is a general concern with teasing out the substantive differences between audience members who are increasingly diverse in terms of languages, cultures, and life experiences.[46]

---

44. *See* Kirk St. Amant, *What do Technical Communicators Need to Know about International Environments?*, *in* SOLVING PROBLEMS IN TECHNICAL COMMUNICATION 487 (Johndan Johnson-Eilola & Stuart A. Selber eds., 2013).

45. *See* Antonio Ceraso, *How Can Technical Communicators Plan for Users, in* SOLVING PROBLEMS IN TECHNICAL COMMUNICATION 239 (Johndan Johnson-Eilola & Stuart A. Selber eds., 2013) (discussing Karen Schriver's three models of audience analysis: classification-driven, intuition-driven, and feedback-driven).

46. *See generally* Alison Cardinal, *Superdiversity: An Audience Analysis Praxis for Enacting Social Justice in Technical Communication*, 31 TECH. COMM. Q. 343 (Mar. 30 2022),

To put some nuance to the practice of audience analysis in workplace contexts, professionals often build audience profiles and draw distinctions between audience types based on their information needs and how they make decisions.[47] For example, primary audience members are action takers who rely on presented information to make decisions.[48] In legal contexts, examples of primary audience members include judges, jury members, and clients. Secondary and tertiary audience members, on the other hand, are not action oriented but instead take on advisory (secondary) or evaluator (tertiary) roles.[49] Examples of secondary audiences include experts advising on complex subject matter who have specialized knowledge that primary audience members need, whereas tertiary members range from journalists and community activists to opposing counsel who all have an interest in evaluating your work. Lastly, and perhaps most important for less experienced lawyers, are those gatekeeper audiences, e.g., partners, senior associates, or other work supervisors, who look over the lawyers' work and approve its sharing with primary audiences.

Turning again to our medical malpractice fact pattern, imagine what it might mean to construct a profile for each audience type as it relates to both defense and plaintiff's counsel. For example, at the primary audience level, what are a judge's information needs? To rule on a summary judgment motion, what would the judge need to know to either grant or deny the motion? Relatedly, does the judge have a history that reveals a general attitude and/or inclination towards summary judgment motions or medical malpractice cases? For secondary audiences like infectious disease experts, what kind of experience do they have with emergency medicine practices, ICUs, elderly patients, or pandemic treatment protocols? What are experts' understanding of and attitudes about insurance companies' influence on treatment decision-making that differs from expert advice? Do experts have experience with adverse patient outcomes that stem from insurance companies not deferring to expert advice? What do experts need to know in order to assuage their fears or concerns about commenting on emergency medical treatment? Lastly, regarding gatekeeper audiences, how might a supervisor evaluate an attorney's work? What does a supervisor need to know to allow an attorney to proceed with the theory of the case developed through a particular framing decision?

---

https://doi.org/10.1080/10572252.2022.2056637; Michael J. Albers, *Multidimensional Audience Analysis for Dynamic Information*, 33 J. Tech. Writing & Comm. 263 (2003).

47. Johnson-Sheehan, *supra* note 41, at 19–24.

48. *Id.* at 20–21

49. *Id.* at 21.

Lawyers should also remember that readers can inhabit multiple roles at once. As readers shift in and out of different audience positions, they refigure their decision-making priorities as to how to identify relevant information, how to interpret that information, and how to act on that information. Jury members, for example, operate as primary audience members when judging a case. However, one of those members also acts as a foreperson who advises other jurors during deliberations. To consider another example, an appellate tribunal functions as both a decisionmaker and guardian of the credibility of the court. When deciding a controversial matter, appellate judges typically consider the merits of the case first, but they may also be motivated by institutional concerns, such as ensuring that their decision will be accepted by the public. Ultimately, for an advocate, writing well in these circumstances involves simultaneously anticipating both the initial information needs of different reader types and the emergent needs that attend to shifting audience positionalities.

Summing It Up

- Legal persuasion presents itself in a range of personal and professional settings that require interpersonal communication skills.
- Rhetorical sensitivity presents a solid foundation for understanding interpersonal communication in your role as an attorney.
- The rhetorically sensitive attorney (1) tries to accept role-taking as part of the human condition, (2) attempts to avoid stylized verbal behavior, (3) is characteristically willing to undergo the strain of adaptation, (4) seeks to distinguish between all information and information acceptable for communication, and (5) tries to understand that an idea can be rendered in multi-form ways.
- Rhetorical situation theory provides the rhetorically sensitive attorney a framework and vocabulary for evaluating the complex array of persons, events, objects, and relations that coalesce within and/or across individual situations and create the kinds of legally cognizable issues that lawyers craft and respond to in their work.
- Rhetorical framing theory offers the rhetorically sensitive attorney useful guidelines for crafting the theory of a case and narrowing audience attention to facts and circumstances most relevant to successful representation.

- Understanding and developing tailored messages for audiences with competing information needs and goals is complex work for lawyers. Developing audience profiles that document such needs and goals positions lawyers to communicate directly to various audience types as well as anticipate how those audiences may evolve and thus require new argumentative approaches.

Suggestions for Further Reading

LINDA L. BERGER & KATHRYN M. STANCHI, LEGAL PERSUASION: A RHETORICAL APPROACH TO THE SCIENCE (2017).

CIRCULATION, WRITING, AND RHETORIC (Laurie Gries & Collin Gifford Brooke, eds., 2018).

Forum, Articles on Rhetorical Circulation, 15 RHETORIC & PUB. AFF. 609–694 (Winter 2012).

Walter J. Ong, *The writer's audience is always a fiction*, 90 PMLA 9–21 (1975).

Douglas B. Park, *The Meanings of "Audience,"* 44 COLLEGE ENGLISH 247–257 (1982).

Conclusion

DELIA B. CONTI

With this text's introduction to major rhetorical theories and theorists and their application to the field of law, we have equipped you with the fundamentals to understanding the basics of persuasion and helped prepare you for success in the study and practice of law. Socratic theory, argumentation, metaphor, narrative theory, and dramatism all illuminate distinct areas of the law. The rhetorical situation and rhetorical sensitivity yield insights into the lawyering skills of working with clients. The rhetorical foundations of the law underscore the importance of character, form, and structure to the larger questions of justice beyond individual cases and specific statutes. An understanding of the fields of law and of rhetoric are necessary to build a successful case, one premised on the fundamentals of language usage and theory.

The ancient fields studying persuasion and the more modern theories examining communication provide immeasurable contributions highlighting the role of persuasion in the field of law. Common law evolves slowly, cases are strategically chosen for relevant facts, circumstances, and plaintiffs, and this takes time. Statutory law moves at a relatively faster pace, but this is not a case of the tortoise and the hare. It is more like the tortoise and the snail. Applying rhetorical theory to the law presents an opportunity to examine the underpinnings of legal structure and thereby contributes to the understanding and thus the growth and evolution of law.

Rhetoric is concerned with persuasion in all permutations: from a limited conception focusing on a specific message aimed at a specific audience, to a broader conception focusing on the examination of ideas and the discovery of truths. Rhetoric is by its very nature an interdisciplinary subject, and it undergirds distinct fields' substance in their search for truths. In the law, truths may be found in principles of constitutional law, in higher laws focusing on more ethical precepts, and in the more mundane areas of statutory laws and legislative edicts.

The determination of truths may belong to specific fields; bringing them to efficacy belongs to rhetoric. Rhetoric is charged with supplying persuasive effectiveness to influence audiences. The subject matter of the law will determine the status of a case or the existence of a cause of action. It is rhetoric that will determine the resolution of a legal issue through the intersection of subject matter and audience.

Law is socially constructed. To study and practice law, a legal mind must extract the relevant elements from the situation. What society defines as a problem is determined by the mores of the culture and the socially constructed legal system. The social construction of the law highlights the subjective nature of the legal system and the partiality of perspective necessitated by language. To understand law you must understand its terminology and therefore you must understand language. To understand the evolution of the law you must also understand its cultural influences and its political undercurrents.

Interpretation is integral to the law through the analysis of constitutions, the application of statutes, and in the vital need to make the law a living, breathing creature that can resolve issues in society the resolution of which could not have been preordained. The law focuses on subjective truths with rhetoric advancing plausible contingencies. The effective use of rhetorical strategies is integral to success. The adversarial nature of law, the art of reconciling all sides of an issue, is fundamentally an exercise concerned with the analysis of language.

The practice of law is in essence an exercise in rhetoric. The practice of law is concerned with the operations of language. To view law rhetorically is not to dismiss the substantive component of law. Case law, statutes, legal opinions, codes, and treatises all contribute to a knowledge base that must be understood to be an effective lawyer. But in essence, an attorney is an advocate. Success at any level requires mastery of rhetoric: an understanding of the power of language and the persuasiveness of form.

Law's aim is justice. Rhetoric's aim is persuasion. Law uses rhetoric to achieve its goal. The collusion of the two fields is most aptly rooted in their grounding in the values and concerns of society. Justice cannot be defined or achieved without a conception of community, for justice rests on principles of fairness and equity derived from a distinct polity. Rhetoric's effectiveness is dependent on adapting truths to specific audiences, with appeals to values essential to the rhetorical components of ethos and pathos. The practice of law is a rhetorical one, with knowledge of community mores essential to success.

Practitioners of the law are most adept when they possess an accurate conception of the nature of the law: law as principled yet adaptive, law as grounded in precedent yet willing to overrule precedent and create new law when warranted, and law as embodied in the Constitution yet flexible enough to embrace societal change.

Interpreting the law means focusing on the audience. Legal rhetoric is constitutive of community: meaning is a joint creation of the text and the reader. In this evolving system, case law and statutory law meld into a legal rhetorical universe. Legal rhetoric is pragmatic, is attentive to audience, and allows for evolution as circumstances warrant, yet is bound within parameters consistent with principles of justice.

Dispelling the negative connotations of rhetoric is essential to understanding its fundamental importance to the law. Rhetoric does not aim at permanence as literary criticism does, and rhetoric is not empty of reason or devoid of logic as demagogues would posit. Rhetoric at its base involves critical thinking and analysis—elemental and necessary skills in the law. An examination of rhetoric not only illuminates how to argue effectively in the courtroom, how to identify issues relevant to case analysis, and how to adapt to the relevant audience, but also how to identify persuasive issues of larger import not immediately apparent. Law evolves with societal changes. Law is contextual: immersed in the situation, the attitudes of judges, the background of the jury, and the characters of the plaintiff and the defendant. There is a hierarchical system controlling the ability to speak, an important mechanism in wielding power. Law is a species of rhetoric, concerned with justice, situated and pragmatic. Rhetoric in its entirety is indispensable to law. Law is, in its essence, a rhetorical system. The practice of law is an art. An effective lawyer is an expert on persuasion, a master of language, and ultimately a rhetorician.

Index

M

T